THE SELECTED LETTERS OF

HENRY ADAMS

THE
SELECTED LETTERS OF
HENRY ADAMS

EDITED WITH AN
INTRODUCTION BY
NEWTON ARVIN

NEW YORK
FARRAR, STRAUS AND YOUNG, INC.

NOTE

The letters included in this volume, with one exception, have been reprinted, by permission of Houghton, Mifflin Co., from the following volumes: *A Cycle of Adams Letters, 1861–1865,* edited by Worthington Chauncey Ford (two vols.); *Letters of Henry Adams (1858–1891)* and *Letters of Henry Adams (1892–1918),* both edited by Worthington Chauncey Ford; *Letters to a Niece and Prayer to the Virgin of Chartres, by Henry Adams, with a Niece's Memories,* by Mabel La Farge; and *Henry Adams and His Friends,* by Harold Dean Cater. The letter of Dec. 21, 1884, to Francis Parkman, originally published in *Francis Parkman, Heroic Historian,* by Mason Wade, and reprinted in *Henry Adams and His Friends,* has been included here by permission also of the Viking Press and Mr. Wade. The original of this letter is among the Parkman papers at the Massachusetts Historical Society. The letter of August 10, 1910, to Albert Stanburrough Cook, has been reprinted from the *Yale Review* of October 1920, by permission of the *Yale Review* and the Yale University Press.

Most of these letters were originally published with some deletions by their editors; the deleted passages have not been restored, and a few further omissions have been made, to eliminate passages of little present interest or importance. Such omissions, however, are always indicated by the punctuation.

CONTENTS

INTRODUCTION

⌒

SHORTLY after Lincoln's election in the fall of 1860 Henry Adams accompanied his father to Washington, where the elder man was a member of Congress; and there they remained until the following March and the inauguration of the new President. Young Adams had gone to Washington partly to write a series of political letters for a Boston newspaper, but the work of composing them evidently failed to exhaust his literary energies, which were abounding. There were subjects, moreover, that would find no natural place in a newspaper correspondence. "I propose," Adams wrote to his brother Charles in December, "to write you this winter a series of private letters to show how things look. I fairly confess that I want to have a record of this winter on file, and though I have no ambition nor hope to become a Horace Walpole, I still would like to think that a century or two hence when everything else about it is forgotten, my letters might still be read and quoted as a memorial of manners and habits at the time of the great secession of 1860."

A series of such letters did follow, and now, nearly a century later, though "everything else" about that winter has hardly been forgotten, Adams's wish seems in a fair way to be modestly realized. More of that in a moment. Meanwhile, perhaps it is true that, as he said, he had no serious hope of becoming the Horace Walpole of his time, but certainly the example of the earlier letter-writer was much in his mind, not only then but later. Nine years afterward, again in Washington, he remarked to another correspondent that he had taken up the "ever youthful" Horace Walpole once more. "What surprises me most," he went on, "is that he is so extremely like ourselves; not so clever of course, but otherwise he might be a letter-writer of today. I perpetually catch myself thinking of it all as of something I have myself known, until I trip over a sword, or discover there were no railways then, or reflect that Lord Salisbury and not Lord Carteret lives over the way."

Without a clue like this, the parallel between the two men would probably not occur to most readers. It requires a rather forcible effort to make a connection in one's mind between the author of *The Castle of Otranto* and the author of *Mont-Saint-Michel and Chartres,* between the son of the not very austere Sir Robert Walpole and the offspring of such earnest characters as John Quincy and Charles Francis Adams, between the amiable, gossipy, pleasure-loving, assiduous dilettante of Strawberry Hill and the partly fictionalized Henry Adams with whom the *Education* has familiarized us—depressive, anxious, estranged from the life of his age, and corroded by the longing for an impossible unity. One scarcely needs to suggest the manner in which Horace Walpole would have dealt with either the Virgin of Chartres or the Second Law of Thermodynamics: it would not have been the Adams manner, one can leave it at that.

Yet it was a sagacious instinct that led Henry Adams to detect a kind of kinship with his eighteenth-century predecessor. Both men were the sons, and felt it keenly, of men who had played commanding roles in the historic drama: the status of the epigone was vital to both Walpole and Adams. They had in common the personal, the family involvement in the high politics of their respective eras; they themselves were both active, too, from time to time, and mostly behind the scenes, in political manipulation and maneuver, and the gap is no great one between Walpole's Whiggish libertarianism and the republican liberalism of Adams's early years. What is more important here, the two men took, after all, a very comparable interest in what Adams calls the "manners and habits" of their contemporaries, and aspired to very much the same sort of recognition by posterity of their achievement as observers and chroniclers. Adams may have abandoned this aspiration in the end, as he abandoned so many things; but he had begun with it.

He had begun, moreover, with a sense, inherited from the eighteenth century, of the letter as a serious literary form, a form with its own exacting demands on the feeling for structure, for movement, for tone, for narrative and picture; and this he did not abandon. He had come by it as naturally as possible, not only through his reading of letter-writers like Walpole, but through family inheritance. The writing of letters was an Adams property, almost an Adams privilege, like the mission to England or the keeping of the republican conscience. Except for Franklin, the best letter-writers of the Revolutionary period were John Adams and his wife, and John Adams himself had even theorized informally on what might pompously be called the aesthetic of the letter. The epistolary style, he remarks in a letter to Abigail, is essentially different from the oratorical and the historical. "Letters, like conversation," he observes, "should be free, easy, and familiar . . . Affectation is as disagreeable in a letter as in conversation, and therefore studied language, premeditated method, and sublime sentiments are not expected in a letter." To our own taste there are passages of rather studied diction and "sublime" sentiment in both his own letters and his wife's, but the wonder is that there is so little of either, and so much that, in the midst of great and grave events, is easy, spontaneous, unaffected, and intimate.

Henry Adams himself had a high opinion of them, or at least of Abigail's: he once observed in a letter to his friend Gaskell on the subject of American writers generally that "in the way of letters there is nothing but my old great-grandmother Abigail Adams's that are worth reading." This suggests that he rather undervalued his great-grandfather's, and that he had no special esteem, either, for the letters of his grandfather, John Quincy Adams. And in fact the epistolary style of the sixth President is far from winning; if his father ever urged "familiarity" upon him, it was in vain; his letters mostly have the air of state papers that happen to be addressed to private friends. Even in the next generation the old easiness had not quite been recaptured, and the letters that Charles Francis Adams wrote from London, during his years as Minister, are more solid than spirited. They are at any rate carefully composed, and the point is that the epistolary habit was handed on from father to son like a family heirloom. It is clear that the practice was enjoined upon Henry Adams and his brothers from an early age. In a memoir which he prefaced to his edition of John and Abigail Adams's letters, Charles Francis Adams alludes to this subject in his rather stately manner: "Perhaps there is no species of exercise, in early life, more productive of results useful to the mind, than that of writing letters. Over and above the mechanical facility of constructing sentences, which no teaching will afford so well, the interest with which the object is commonly pursued gives an extraordinary impulse to the intellect."

Doubtless there is something a little dampening here in the insistence on intellectual utility ("results useful to the mind"); and "the mechanical facility of constructing sentences" falls coldly on the heart. Another sort of man than Henry Adams might have been discouraged forever, by his father's rather arid high-mindedness, from expressing himself with any spontaneity whatever in this or any other form. Fortunately the expressive instinct was too strong in him for that, and "the interest with which the object is commonly pursued" carried the day over all mere conscientiousness. In no Adams before him had the expressive instinct been so strong: he was the first of them all who was born to be a writer and not a public servant or a wielder of political power, and it was partly because the mirage of political power thrust itself between him and his true aim so deceptively, though so inevitably, that his course as a writer was as impeded, as full of detours, as frustrated as it was. There were whole periods in his life, at any rate, when his powerful literary gift found its real outlet in correspondence; and the editor of this volume would maintain that, if one sets aside the *History,* it is in his letters that Henry Adams realized himself most completely, with the least uncertainty and unnaturalness, as a writer.

By the time, late in life, when he came to write the books on which his reputation usually rests—*Mont-Saint-Michel* and the *Education*—he had been driven, or had driven himself, into a painfully false and unwholesome relation with the audience he should normally have counted on. His publishing those books privately, with all the mystifications, the jittery precautions, the elaborate disparagements in which he enveloped the process, was a symptom of something basically unhealthy in his position as a man of letters. The consequence is that, for all their brilliance, all their weight, the two books, taken as wholes, are somehow dissatisfying to the critical sense. We dislike writing that, as Keats once said, has a palpable design upon us, and the mask of Failure in the one work, the mask of rather mawkish Mariolatry in the other, are too palpably, too insistently, too heavy-handedly thrust before our vision not to end by impressing us less as personae, in the great poetic sense, than as literary false faces. The two novels Adams wrote in his forties, *Democracy* and *Esther,* are remarkable books, more remarkable than they have usually been recognized as being; but even they were published anonymously or pseudonymously, almost clandestinely, and their publication was accompanied by a thousand facetious disclaimers of authorship. The nervous self-conscious-

[xiii]

ness of all this does something to explain what is unsatisfactory about these novels; for Adams's unwillingness to *commit himself* as a writer was obscurely associated with his failure, in both *Democracy* and *Esther,* to invent an action, a set of narrative symbols, that would bear up the pressure of his moral meanings.

For a man to whom the basic facts of the literary profession itself were as problematic as all this, the letter was an ideal medium. Here there was no reason to be tormented by the elementary problems of authorship, no reason to agonize over the question of an audience and one's right relation to it. An audience was at hand, and usually it was an understanding and responsive audience. First-rate letters depend almost as much on their recipients as on the man who writes them, and just as Byron was lucky in having Tom Moore and Hobhouse and Lady Melbourne to write to, so Adams was lucky, and must have known that he was, in having correspondents so congenial and so appreciative as Charles Gaskell and John Hay and, perhaps most of all, Elizabeth Cameron. One gets the strongest impression in reading these letters that, when Adams sat down to write them, the discomfort that so often afflicted him elsewhere quite fell away and he became simply a man with a pen —a man for whom, moreover, the pen was a predestined implement. Now he was wholly at one with himself and with his perfect audience of a single person, and all his powers as a writer—powers of sharp attention to people and things, of responsiveness to impressions, of insight and judgment, and above all of expression in language—found themselves in free and unembarrassed play.

The series of Adams's published letters covers a period of just sixty years: it begins with his letters from Germany as a young student in 1858 and ends with a letter to Gaskell a few weeks before his death in 1918. As the expression of a life so many-sided as his was, these letters are bound to exert their interest on a variety of levels. Their interest as a social chronicle— as "a memorial of manners and habits," to put it in his way—is exerted on only one of these, but on that level it is undeniable. The letters that have this value were mainly written in Adams's early years—in those months in Washington that followed Lincoln's election, in the years he spent as private secretary to his father in London, and then, again in Washington, in the disenchanting year or two that followed his return. As soon as Adams joined the Harvard faculty his attention was drawn off elsewhere; even after his resignation and the return to Washington, the writing of his *History* was his great preoccupation, and after the death of his wife he withdrew too completely from social life to think of himself as in any way a recorder of it. He emerged rather warily and briefly from this seclusion when his friend John Hay was Secretary of State, and when his friend Theodore Roosevelt was President he even ventured so far out of his retreat as to attend one or two dinners at the White House. The result was a handful of letters that have something of the old animation as chronicle. In general, however, after 1870 Adams appeals to one as a letter-writer on other grounds.

It is the letters he wrote in the sixties that chiefly show how capable he was of competing with Horace Walpole on his own terrain. He is at one disadvantage here: he was never present at any event that offered itself to the chronicler quite so gratefully or so enviably as the trial of the rebel Scotch lords or the coronation of George III. And in any case Adams's writing rarely has just the qualities of briskness, amenity, and careless precision—as of eighteenth-century music—that one comes to expect of Walpole. It is usually a little lower in pitch and more astringent in savor than his predecessor's. If it has less sprightliness and charm, however, it of course has greater density: Adams's mind, only too obviously, was a far more complex one than Walpole's, and yet his eye was no less quick and keen. It need hardly be said now that his interest in the events that passed before him was a philosophical, not a gossipy, one—but along with this he had some of the gifts of the novelist too. And what gives his letters of the sixties their special character is the union one finds in them of the general and the particular, of the broadly historical and the sharply personal, of the sense of large affairs sweeping on their way and the eye for the human actors, not always heroic actors, who are carried along with them.

How marked this is in the letters of the "great secession of 1860"! Never for more than a moment or two does one lose sight, in reading them, of the large issues that are on the verge of settlement or the failure of settlement, and of how much depends, for the future of the republic, on the outcome. The hardly bearable tensions of that winter are all here; the ebb and flow of anxiety and hopefulness; the rumors, the reassurances, the hours of optimism, the recurring shocks and setbacks. One hears much of the Congressional Committee of Thirty-Three, of the Peace Convention, of the problem of the Border States. But the potential novelist makes his voice heard also along with that of the sober young politico, and one relaxes, in the midst of these solemnities, to watch a leading figure like Seward, "with his big nose and his wire hair and grizzly eyebrows and miserable dress," smoking his eternal cigar, sprawling, snorting, belching, and doing "all sorts of outrageous things"—even patting Mrs. Charles Francis Adams on the head, like a little girl, in a manner that, instead of offending, rather flatters her. At a crush ball one sees Mrs. Stephen A. Douglas smiling and shaking hands with her guests quite as if her husband were not a drunken brute and a ruined politician; in another part of the room one observes the "ancient buffer," John Tyler, the ex-President, in the "cerements of his forgotten grave," surrounded nonetheless by a crowd of admiring devotees. How pleasurably one feels the *frisson historique* as one's eye falls on them!

There are scantier touches of this particular cinematic sort in the letters from London during the war. The unease that young Adams felt in English society may have had a bearing on this, and doubtless, too, there was a distraction in the long series of oscillations between dejection at bad news from the war front and elation over Union victories. What the London letters mostly yield up is not so much the sharply pictorial as the historically atmospheric—the intense and troubled emotional quality of a moment in British and American history, a moment of deep and potentially dangerous crisis, as a particularly proud and touchy young American would experience it. No doubt it is a partial picture that one gets, this picture of almost universal hostility toward the Union on the part of the governing groups and of hardly concealed eagerness at the prospect of its destruction; but however partial it may be, it is extraordinarily animated, personal, and infectious. The illusion of participation, of contemporaneity, is at certain moments complete. Sometimes, too, it does depend on incident and scene, as when, in the gallery of the House of Commons, the Confederate commissioner, Mason, offends against the rules of the House by crying, "Hear! hear!" to an anti-Union speech; or when, one Sunday afternoon in May, Henry Adams comes home from a walk and encounters his father, "the Chief," dancing across the entry and crying out, "We've got New Orleans!"—while the newsboys in the street outside begin shouting the news, and the whole of London is seized with excitement "as though it were an English defeat." But the letters from London are by no means exclusively obsessed with the American war, and one is reminded again of Adams's reserve powers as a reporter of the social and political scene by a letter like that in which one sees Garibaldi at a reception at the Duke of Sutherland's—the republican and revolutionary Garibaldi, in a red shirt and a blue cape lined with red, stalking through the apartments of Stafford House with the young Duchess of Sutherland, glittering with diamonds, hanging on his arm.

No reader of the *Education* needs to be told what a genius Adams had for the personal sketch, for the quick penciled drawing of the individual subject that, isolating a detail or two and giving them their full salience, has an effect of serious and truth-telling caricature. Everyone remembers the portrait of Swinburne at Monckton Milnes's country house, looking like a tropical bird, "high-crested, long-beaked, quick-moving," or the sketch of Lord Palmerston receiving his guests at a reception, with his slow, deliberate, mechanical laugh, "a laugh of 1810 and the Congress of Vienna." This gift of portraiture exhibits itself in the letters too—intermittently, to be sure; with more intermissions than one could wish; one misses any serious attempt to evoke Disraeli in the House of Commons or Grant at the White House—but at times it is in full play. The group of drawings of Seward in Washington is a case in point, and even in the London letters one comes upon glimpses like that of John Stuart Mill, dining at the Duke of Argyll's, "a curious looking man with a sharp nose, a wen on his forehead and a black cravat . . . very retiring and embarrassed in his manner." The great display-piece of Adams's achievements in this vein, however, is certainly the wonderful series of sketches of Stevenson, whom Adams encountered several times when he was in Samoa in the early nineties.

What was it—unless it was Stevenson's effortless and untroubled adoption of a vagabondage that Henry Adams could only gaze at from an envious distance—that called forth the particular vivacity, half satirical and half respectful, of this portrait? One hardly knows, and yet Adams was certainly never more inspired than when he summoned up for his correspondents the apparition of that strange, emaciated figure with the morbidly intelligent and agitated eyes, garbed in dirty striped-cotton pajamas and unmatched woolen socks, moving restlessly about "like an insane stork," and brandishing his long thin arms above his head "as though he wanted to throw them away." Every stroke of the pencil is expressive, and the cumulative effect of uncanniness is so complete that one accepts without difficulty Adams's own conclusion: Stevenson is no mere mortal but, as the Samoans would say, an *a-itu* or spirit. A not very respectable *a-itu,* either; the final word is a disparaging, and probably an unfair, one. The contrast between Stevenson's raffishness and the fineness of Adams's companion La Farge is the last note: "the oriental delicacy of La Farge seems to be doubled by the Scotch eccentricities and barbarisms of Stevenson who is as one-sided as a crab . . ."

The picture itself may be a one-sided picture, a brilliant caricature rather than a sober portrait, but of its brilliance, at all events, there can be no question. Quite by itself it would make the fortune of the letters in which it appears, yet as it happens these letters from Samoa are so rich, so spirited, even so genial, that, if the remarks about Stevenson were entirely deleted from them, they would still remain among the purest triumphs of Adams's career as a writer. In general, he was never more consistently good—never more uninterruptedly animated and vivid, or less liable to his special vices of mind and style—than in the great body of letters he wrote on his very considerable travels about the globe. If ever a man was a good traveler Henry Adams was, as he quite properly boasted in a letter to Mrs. Cameron. It is true that he went on to minimize this claim by pretending it only meant that, in any given situation, he was more comfortable than his fellow travelers. But that, as he surely knew, was a ludicrous understatement. He was a good traveler, to put it on the surface level for the moment, partly because he was extraordinarily philosophical about the discomforts and hardships of travel. There is a world of difference between Adams sitting in his study on H Street and Adams journeying on foot up a narrow river valley in Fiji or bumping along in an ox-cart through the forests of Ceylon; the same man who could be plunged into gloom by a headline seems never to have much minded a gale at sea, a snowstorm in the mountains, or the necessity of dining on squid.

That, however, was the least part of his genius as a traveler, without much more significance than his baggage. What was far more important was his real love of the various world—of the world as one sees it not in newspapers or even in historical records but literally, as it unrolls itself, in travel, before the physical senses: the landscape, the city streets, the native villages, the monuments of the past, the men and women, the very animals. Can one read these letters without discerning how strong and how genuine this loving interest was, contradictory as it may seem to the bleak repudiations that form the more familiar side of Henry Adams's mind? Clearly there was a strain of magic for him in the mere fact of movement from scene to scene, and whatever his state of mind may have been, in a Berlin boardinghouse or a Washington study, however he may have despaired and denied, he seems only to have had to board a train or embark on a steamer (despite his sufferings from seasickness) to be set free for the time from his intensest anxieties and to become the other Adams, the born poet with a poet's gust for experience. One feels it at the beginning and almost as truly at the end; one feels it in the days when, with two or three other young Americans, he sets off on a walking tour through the Thuringian Forest; it is there in the period of his grief-stricken middle life when he roams with his friend La Farge through Japan and the islands of the South Seas, and even at the time when, a solitary and embittered man in his sixties, he finds himself alone, well within the Arctic Circle, gazing upon the "terribly fascinating and fantastic" landscape of glacier-laden mountains and "silent, oily, gleaming sea" that surrounds Hammerfest in Norway.

If few letters of travel anywhere are superior to these it is because Henry Adams had so fortunate a mingling of talents for the purpose. As he moved about the world, his senses were awake and aware of everything, his feeling for the tone of places was continually at work, and at the same time his mind, with its special penetrations and its rich equipment of knowledge, was restlessly taking note of all the intangibles, the "supersensibles," the impalpable analogies and contrasts and meanings. He can give one the impression of being primarily and essentially a landscape-painter in prose, a La Farge of language. He can catch what seems to be the whole quality of a moonlight night over a Hawaiian island—as he sits on a verandah and absorbs it —with his image of two palm trees on the terrace before him, glistening in the moonlight, "their long leaves waving . . . with the human suggestion of distress which the palm alone among trees conveys to me." He likes to mythologize the features of the physical world, as he does with the volcanoes on Hawaii itself, and Mauna Loa becomes a credible deity when Adams points to its huge flat bulk stretching down an interminable slope ahead of him, "with the strange voluptuous charm peculiar to volcanic slopes, which always seem to invite you to lie down on them and caress them." Very unlike Mauna Loa, but no less mythological in their way, are the sad and silent mountains about Hammerfest, which "never knew what it was to be a volcano": "They lie, one after another, like corpses, with their toes up, and you pass by them, and look five or ten miles up the fiords between them, and see their noses, tipped by cloud or snow, high in behind, with one corpse occasionally lying on another, and a skull or a thigh-bone chucked about, and hundreds of glaciers and snow-patches hanging to them, as though it was a winter battle-field; and a weird after-glow light . . . They never can have really enjoyed themselves." It is the whole Scandinavian pantheon against the Polynesian.

Meanwhile, there is the human scene, the cities and the farms and the archaic villages, the ruined temples and the medieval churches, the human beings and the animals. The animals ought not to be forgotten; animals like the oxen that drew Adams and La Farge through the Ceylon jungle by moonlight: "our little white oxen, with their mystical straight horns, and their religious sacred humps," tripping along, "sometimes trotting and sometimes running, their bells tinkling in the quaintest way." One is unlikely to forget these charming oxen, but of course the human figures take precedence over the beasts. One recalls, for example, how in Japan "everything laughs," not only the dragonheads on the temples, but the jinrickshaw men as they run at full speed in a sizzling sun, the doll-like women, the shopkeepers when you tell them their goods are forgeries, and even the Mikado himself in cabinet council. One recalls the Mexican peasants who "have the peculiar look, though all really Indians, that the Roman empire left forever on its slave-provinces." And of course one is least likely of all to forget the "old gold" people of Polynesia; the men and women of Hawaii, Samoa, and Tahiti; the tall, strong, broad-backed, glistening young women, wreathing in near-nudity through the intricate movements of the Siva; the "splendid young men, dressed only in their waist-cloths . . . with garlands of green leaves round their heads"; the grave and ceremonious old men on whose handsome countenances one discerns "the usual rather pathetic expression of these islanders.'

They are all tremendous aristocrats, these Polynesians, especially the Samoans, and make one feel like "the son of a camel-
driver degraded to the position of stable-boy in Spokane West
Centre." Though, to be sure, they recognize other aristocrats
when they see them, and it is clear that the chief Seumano and
his people are aware that Henry Adams is not quite a plebeian.

He himself, Henry Adams, at any rate, sees at once what gentlemen they are, and in general these letters of travel owe half
their power to his ingrained habit of going beyond the mere
surface of things, the mere look of foreignness and picturesque-
ness, and making the difficult effort of social and psychological
understanding. It is what all good travel-writers do, of course;
but how many travel-writers have Henry Adams's acuteness,
his malleability, his freedom from the formulated and the preconceived? Freedom even from his own formulas—for he has no
sooner yielded himself, for example, to the romantic and archaic charm of Samoan life than his critical sense too comes into
play, and he begins to see that the reality of that life is many-
sided, and that some of its sides are not very poetic. One cannot
resist the sweet temper, the gaiety, the gentleness of the Samoans, to be sure, or their nobility of appearance and manner, but
the fact is, the more one sees of them, the more oppressively one
becomes aware that there are virtually no individuals among
them, that they are all more like one another than the inhabitants of a Yankee small town, and that they are singularly
practical, unimaginative, unromantic, without intellectual curiosity or reflectiveness. "I begin to understand," writes Adams,
"why Melville wanted to escape from Typee." At any rate, he
had begun to understand something about primitive life that no
sentimental stereotype would have prepared him for.

He may or may not have been "right" in his own reformula-
tion of it—"right" in the literal and wholly objective sense—but
he had got at something, as he almost always did, that by **no**

means leapt to the eye, and it is these repeated flights of pene-
tration into the intangibles that largely make his letters from
abroad so absorbing. That, and the imaginative use he was constantly making of his erudition as a historian. The mingling of
these elements is very striking in such a letter as the one from
Moscow in which, describing a high mass at a Greek Orthodox
cathedral, Adams remarks that it is a marvelous composite of
the Jewish tabernacle and the First Crusade, with robes like
those of Saint Louis or Godfrey of Bouillon and ceremonies like
those of Solomon's Temple. What makes the illusion more powerful, he adds, is "the wonderful tenth-century people" taking
part, with a formal devoutness such as western Europe perhaps
never knew. "In some ways," he says, "I feel sure, the Russian
of today is more primitive than the Frenchman or German ever
was, if you call this passive attitude of subjection primitive. I
never met with it in any primitive race I have struck before,
and even a monkey shows occasional scepticism." A frigid
breath from the future sweeps over these sentences, as indeed it
does over much that Adams wrote from central and eastern Europe in 1901. And in any event one knows oneself in the company of a traveler who is not only a landscape-painter but an
ideologue touched with the poetic sense.

If he had not been an ideologue, Henry Adams's letters
would have lacked one of the strands of interest which of course
they have. And this remains true even if one feels that some of
the general ideas propounded in his later books—the ideal unity
of medieval culture, the merely chaotic multiplicity of modern
culture, the application to history of the Second Law of Thermodynamics, and the like—deserve a good deal less solemn and
literal attention than has often been accorded them. The sheen
of novelty has worn off some of these "views" by this time, and
it is easier now to see the admixture in them, along with their

solid elements, of wishfulness, caprice, and intellectual dice-loading. The position Adams finally arrived at was once described by Paul Elmer More as "sentimental nihilism," and the phrase will do as well as some others to suggest its particular quality. Saying so by no means implies that Adams's mind was not one of the most interesting, in its foibles as well as in its power, in American intellectual history; one of the most complex, restless, wide-ranging, and supple. And the letters enable one to follow the *development* of his mind from phase to phase as, of course, none of his books or even all his books taken together quite do. The intellectual story they tell is, quite naturally, much less artfully shaped and organized than that in the *Education,* but it is a more complex, shifting, indecisive, and credible story.

What one gets in the letters, and fails to get in the *Education,* is the whole process by which Henry Adams moved from the great Unitarian synthesis of his fathers—from its pure, cold, arid, eighteenth-century rationality and optimism—to the mechanistic catastrophism with which he ended. This latter was, of course, his final testament to posterity, but only the reader of the letters has a full sense of the delicacy with which Adams's mind was for many years balanced between the poles of hopefulness and despair, affirmation and denial, belief and skepticism. The uncertain poise was there from the beginning, as he himself, with his peculiarly Yankee type of introspective acuteness, once observed. Still in his middle twenties, writing to his brother Charles from London, he confesses that his mind is by nature balanced in such a way "that what is evil never seems unmixed with good, and what is good always streaked with evil." Ultimately he was to reach the point where "what is evil" seemed quite unalloyed with any ingredients of goodness, and that was the state of mind in which the *Education* was written. But in writing it Henry Adams—quite properly, from the stylistic point of view—simplified, distorted, and misrepresented his own intellectual and emotional past.

No reader of the *Education* would gather that Adams had ever entertained any serious hopes for the future, even in his boyhood days in Quincy. Yet the truth is that he had oscillated between gloom and the inherited optimism to a far later period than perhaps he himself could recollect. "As I belong to the class of people who have great faith in this country," he wrote to Gaskell in 1877, "and who believe that in another century it will be saying in its turn the last word of civilisation, I enjoy the expectation of the coming day." Yet this was written nearly a decade after the period when, according to his later fable, the evil spectacle of Grantism had disabused him once for all of any dreams for the republic. Four years later still, when Garfield lay dying of an assassin's bullet, Adams was undismayed by the prospect: "Luckily," he wrote to Wayne MacVeagh, "we are a democracy and a sound one. Nothing can shake society with us, now that slavery is gone." Nor did he limit himself, in these sanguine views of his mid-forties, to the American future; at least at moments he was still capable of extending them to the human outlook generally. "There are some difficulties," he said to Gaskell, "in the path of all pessimistic reasoning which make its conclusions doubtful, and for some centuries yet may seem to confute its truth. Man is still going fast upward."

These years of the early eighties in Washington with his wife and their small circle of intimates, engrossed as he was with his great *History,* were happy years in Adams's life, and his happiness sometimes expresses itself quite directly in his correspondence. Clearly one has to see the unrelieved nihilism of his old age as the product of more than purely intellectual or historical influences: of course the social disasters of the nineties played their role in inducing it, and so, too, did the intensifying pressure upon Adams's mind of developments in the physical sciences and technology. But the strictly personal dimension cannot be left out, and the letters would tell one, if nothing else did, that the final tipping of the balance of his mind to the side of darkness was as much the consequence of personal tragedy as it was of historical decay. What his wife's suicide did to Adams was to destroy for good all the capacity he had ever had for reading the auguries cheerfully.

It did that, and at the same time it confirmed in him all the somber views he had ever taken of man's status in a soulless multiverse and especially in the multiverse of the approaching twentieth century. For it is quite true that such views had presented themselves to his mind at an early hour: in that sense the *Education* is faithful to the biographical reality. There was obviously some inner bias, very youthfully acquired, toward the darker hues of the philosophic spectrum, and one can only guess at its emotional origins—at the possibility of some obscure early injury inflicted by the necessarily exaggerated role of the father in the whole Adams order of things. A man is not with impunity the son, the grandson, and the great-grandson of a series of masterful "chiefs," and what Henry Adams may have suffered under all this is at least dimly suggested by the belatedness of his marriage, the tragedy in which it ended, and the slightly hysterical quality of his cult, in old age, of the Virgin and the Feminine Principle generally. Something of this nature was surely the emotional seedbed in which the disenchantments of Darwinism and the frustrations of Grantism could put down their roots so deep and sprout so rankly as they did.

The young Henry Adams did not need either Darwin or Grant to inspire black thoughts in his heart: Abraham Lincoln was still President, and Adams had probably not yet drunk deep of Darwinism, when, writing to Henry Lee Higginson from London, he broke out: "Meanwhile I only hope that your life won't be such an eternal swindle as most life is." And it was probably not on either scientific or political grounds that, five years later, back in Washington, he confessed in a letter to Gaskell that, even if in a few years he should have made a great reputation for himself, he would not be prepared to say what it was really worth: "The sad truth is that I want nothing and life seems to have no purpose."

The vibrations one detects in such utterances are those of an essentially personal dejection. Yet a merely private woefulness is no more characteristic of Adams's mind in his twenties than in his sixties, and already in the early letters one finds him speculating in the most impersonal terms on the nature of the world system—so evidently not a Unitarian one—that contemporary knowledge seemed more and more to be evoking. If the letters of his early and middle life reveal that he then had far higher hopes than he would later have confessed to, they also reveal how early he had arrived, tentatively anyway, at some of the grimmer conceptions that were to be characteristic of his latest thought. Something like a mechanistic theory of nature and of history had long been in his mind. "The truth is," he writes in 1863, "everything in this universe has its regular waves and tides. Electricity, sound, the wind, and I believe every part of organic nature will be brought some day within this law. But my philosophy teaches me, and I firmly believe it, that the laws which govern animated beings will be ultimately found to be at bottom the same with those which rule inanimate nature, and . . . I am quite ready to receive with pleasure any basis for a systematic conception of it all."

It was more than thirty years after he wrote these sentences that Adams got round to Willard Gibbs and Lord Kelvin, to the Law of Phase and the Second Law of Thermodynamics; but it is evident how long his mind had been wholly prepared for them. And not even at the end was he to take an essentially bitterer view of the doom to which science was hurrying mankind than he had taken in 1862: "Man has mounted science," he then wrote, "and is now run away with. I firmly believe that before many centuries more, science will be the master of man. The engines he will have invented will be beyond his strength to control. Some day science may have the existence of mankind in its power, and the human race commit suicide by blowing up the world." In 1910 he was saying not "may" but "will," and he was saying it with a gloomy eloquence of manner he had not commanded in his twenties. He was speaking, too, as one has to recognize, in the ghastly light of more evidence than there had been at hand in 1862. But he was giving voice to fears that, in one guise or another, had long tormented him.

This is not to say that there was no development whatever in Adams's intellectual life but only that the development was more continuous (as well as more contradictory) than the reader who limits himself to the late and best-known books is likely to guess. And it is certainly not to say that his intellectual interests were limited to these large historical and philosophical matters: no reader of the *Education* would suppose that they were, but only a reader of the letters will quite realize how great was the variety of ideas to which at one time or another Adams turned his mind, or with what agility and boldness his mind played over most of them. Now it is the shallow careerism of Alexander Hamilton, now the particular place of sex in Japanese life, now the vulgar mercantile quality of the architecture of the Valois and Touraine. He glances at Anglo-Saxon poetry, and his quick, offhand remarks might have come from a literary critic of genius; he animadverts on the evolution of finance capital, and seems to have given most of his life to the problem; he finds himself reflecting on the unself-consciousness of his father and that whole generation of New Englanders, and suggests in half a dozen sentences a sustained and searching essay in psychological history. Meanwhile he has been willful, petulant, illiberal, and superficial at a hundred points; he has ridden a few hobbies—and even a few phrases (his "gold bugs," for example)—to the brink of prostration and over; he has obstinately shut his eyes to every manifestation of new life that he does not wish to consider, and allowed his prophetic catastrophism to waste and weaken itself in senile hysteria. It has all mattered relatively little to the responsive reader: the foibles of a first-rate mind are always a small price to pay for its real fruits, and among the fruits of Adams's mind his letters come very close, at the least, to holding first place.

SOME IDENTIFICATIONS

BROOKS ADAMS (1848–1927). Younger brother of H. A., who wrote *The Law of Civilization and Decay* and a preface to H. A.'s posthumous essay, *The Degradation of the Democratic Dogma*.

CHARLES FRANCIS ADAMS (1807–1886). Member of the House of Representatives just before the Civil War and American Minister to England from 1861 to 1868.

CHARLES FRANCIS ADAMS, JR. (1835–1915). H. A.'s older brother, a cavalry officer in the Union Army during the Civil War, and, in the eighties, president of the Union Pacific Railroad.

JOHN QUINCY ADAMS, II (1833–1894). H. A.'s older brother.

MARIAN HOOPER ADAMS (1843–1885). Daughter of Robert William and Ellen (Sturgis) Hooper; married to H. A. in 1872.

JOHN C. BANCROFT (1835–1901). Son of the historian George Bancroft.

WILLIAM STURGIS BIGELOW (1850–1926). A cousin of Mrs. H. A.'s, who lived in Japan in the eighties, collecting works of art, studying Japanese culture, and becoming a convert to Buddhism.

ELIZABETH CAMERON (1857–1944). A niece of General Sherman and of Senator John Sherman of Ohio, who married James Donald Cameron, for twenty years Republican Senator from Pennsylvania.

MARTHA CAMERON (1887–1918). Her daughter. Married Sir Ronald Lindsay, who became British Ambassador to the United States.

MARGARET CHANLER (1862–   ). A half-sister of the popular author F. Marion Crawford. Married to Winthrop A. Chanler. Author of *Roman Spring* and *Memory Makes Music*.

ALBERT STANBURROUGH COOK (1853–1927). Professor of

English literature at Yale from 1889 to 1921. An authority on Anglo-Saxon language and literature.

BENJAMIN W. CROWNINSHIELD (1837–1892). A classmate of H. A. at Harvard.

SIR ROBERT ALFRED CUNLIFFE (1839–1905). A close English friend of H. A. from the period of the sixties. Later became an M. P. for Flint and then for Denbigh.

SIR FRANCIS HASTINGS CHARLES DOYLE (1810–1888). Minor English poet. At one time professor of poetry at Oxford. His wife and Charles Gaskell's mother were sisters.

FRANCIS GRENVILLE DOYLE (1848–1882). His son. A captain in the 2d Dragoon Guards who died from the effects of the Egyptian campaign of the early eighties.

THEODORE F. DWIGHT (1846–1917). For some time after Mrs. H. A.'s death a kind of companion and secretary to H. A.

WILLIAM MAXWELL EVARTS (1818–1901). The lawyer who acted as chief counsel for Andrew Johnson in his impeachment trial and later became Attorney General, and still later, under Hayes, Secretary of State.

ERNEST FRANCISCO FENOLLOSA (1853–1908). An American, from Salem, who became professor of philosophy at the University of Tokyo and curator of the Imperial Museum at Tokyo. A convert to Buddhism and author of *Epochs of Chinese and Japanese Art,* he made Ezra Pound his literary executor.

MORETON FREWEN (1853–1924). An eccentric English country squire who became an enthusiastic advocate of bimetallism.

CHARLES MILNES GASKELL (1842–1919). Lifelong English friend of H. A. (see *Education,* Chapter XIII). For a time, in the late eighties, Gaskell was an M. P. from Yorkshire.

E. L. GODKIN (1831–1902). Founder and editor of the *Nation* and at one period editor of the New York *Evening Post.*

JOHN RICHARD GREEN (1837–1883). English historian; author of *A Short History of the English People.*

JOHN HAY (1838–1905). Statesman and man of letters. Author of the *Pike County Ballads, The Bread-Winners* (a novel), and co-author with John Nicolay of *Abraham Lincoln: A History.* Ambassador to England in the late nineties and, under McKinley and Theodore Roosevelt, Secretary of State.

EDWARD W. HOOPER (1839–1901). Brother of Mrs. H. A.

LOUISA HOOPER. See MRS. WARD THORON.

CLARENCE KING (1842–1901). Geologist and writer. Head of the United States Geological Survey from 1878 to 1881. Author of *Mountaineering in the Sierra Nevada*. See *Education*, Chapter XX and elsewhere.

MRS. CHARLES KUHN (1831–1870). H. A.'s sister, Louisa ("Loo").

JOHN LA FARGE (1835–1910). Painter, designer of stained glass, writer. Author of *Reminiscences of the South Seas*.

MABEL HOOPER LA FARGE (1875–1944). A niece of Mrs. H. A., who married Bancel La Farge, son of the painter.

SAMUEL PIERPONT LANGLEY (1834–1906). Physicist and pioneer in the development of aviation. Secretary of the Smithsonian Institution. See *Education*, Chapters XXIV and XXV.

ANNA CABOT MILLS LODGE (1850–1915). "Sister Anne." Wife of Henry Cabot Lodge. H. A.'s brother Brooks married her sister Evelyn.

GEORGE CABOT LODGE (1873–1909). "Bay" Lodge. Son of Henry Cabot Lodge. A poet, who wrote *Cain, A Drama; Herakles,* and other volumes of ambitious but minor verse. Died suddenly and prematurely at the summer home of W. S. Bigelow on Tuckanuck Island, Nantucket.

HENRY CABOT LODGE (1850–1924). Statesman and author. A student under H. A. at Harvard in the early seventies.

EDWARD ROBERT BULWER-LYTTON, FIRST EARL OF LYTTON (1831–1891). Formerly Sir Edward Lytton. "Owen Meredith." Author of *Lucile*.

WAYNE MacVEAGH (1833–1917). Attorney General under Garfield, and Ambassador to Italy from 1893 to 1897. A brother-in-law of James Donald Cameron.

JAMES MURRAY MASON (1798–1871). Author of the Fugitive Slave Act of 1850. From 1861 to 1863 ("Mason and Slidell") one of the commissioners of the Confederate States to Great Britain.

JOHN GORHAM PALFREY (1796–1881). Unitarian clergyman and author of a standard *History of New England*. See *Education*, Chapter II.

WILLIAM W. ROCKHILL (1854–1914). Minister and consul

general to Greece, Roumania, and Servia from 1897 to 1899. A lifelong student of Oriental culture and history. Dorothy W. Rockhill ("Dolly"), his daughter (b. 1878).

AUGUSTUS SAINT-GAUDENS (1848–1907). American sculptor. In 1891 designed the Adams Memorial in Rock Creek Cemetery, Washington, as a monument to Mrs. H. A. Homer Saint-Gaudens (b. 1880), his son.

HAROLD MARSH SEWALL (1860–1924). American consul general at Samoa from 1887 to 1892.

SIR CECIL A. SPRING-RICE (1859–1918). Secretary at the British Embassy in Washington in the eighties and nineties. After a long diplomatic career, became Ambassador to the United States from 1912 on, and died suddenly in Quebec on his way to England.

HENRY OSBORN TAYLOR (1856–1941). Originally a student under H. A. at Harvard. Author of *The Mediaeval Mind, Thought and Expression in the Sixteenth Century,* etc.

MRS. WARD THORON (1874–   ). Mrs. H. A.'s niece, Louisa Hooper ("Looly"), who married Ward Thoron, a Washington lawyer and editor of the *Letters of Mrs. Henry Adams.*

ISRAEL WASHBURN (1813–1883). A founder of the Republican Party, and congressman from Maine between 1850 and 1861.

BARRETT WENDELL (1855–1921). Professor of English at Harvard from 1880 to 1917. Author of *A Literary History of America,* etc.

THE SELECTED LETTERS OF
HENRY ADAMS

I

STUDENT, PRIVATE SECRETARY, JOURNALIST

1858–1870

IN 1858, at the age of just twenty, Henry Adams graduated from Harvard, and in the fall of the year sailed for Europe to study civil law at the University of Berlin. The next two years were spent in Germany, mainly in Berlin and Dresden, and though, even at the time, Adams was far from satisfied with the purely professional results of his study, the real bases of his great erudition were certainly laid down then. Besides that, the twenty-four months in Europe were filled with a variety of experiences and impressions that, on the scene, he was far from undervaluing, and the high spirits he showed on his jaunts about Germany with Ben Crowninshield and other classmates were quite as characteristic as his dissatisfactions with the universities.

He returned to America in the fall of 1860, just before Lincoln's election to the presidency, and spent the months of the following winter in Washington with his father, Charles Francis Adams, a highly influential member of Congress on the Republican side. In March 1861, the elder Adams was appointed Minister to England, and in May set sail for Europe, taking his son Henry along with him as his private secretary. There they remained, mostly in London, until the summer of 1868. The first two or three of these years abounded in anxieties, exasperations, and at least imagined rebuffs for the private secretary, with his intense devotion to the Union

[1]

cause and his social hypersensitiveness; but after the tide began to turn in favor of the Northern armies, and the Minister's personal prestige rose to greater and greater heights, the English years proved far from disagreeable, and young Adams formed a group of friendships, with men like Charles Gaskell, Robert Cunliffe, and Frank Doyle, which he was to cherish for the rest of his life.

After his father's resignation in 1868, and their return to America, Henry Adams very soon betook himself to Washington again, eager to remain near the sources of power, and with the aim of making a reputation for himself, and perhaps of achieving office, through his work as a political journalist. He did in fact publish a series of letters and articles in journals like the *Nation* and the *North American,* but during the first year of the Grant administration he found himself losing all hope in the prospects of a serious reform movement, and in 1870, with much reluctance, he accepted a proffered appointment as assistant professor of history at Harvard.

To CHARLES FRANCIS ADAMS, JR.

Berlin, Wednesday, November 3, 1858.

With that energy of expression and originality of thought for which you are so justly celebrated, you have remarked in your last that the pleasures and pains of life are pretty equally divided. Permit me in the particular instance before us to doubt the fact. In the long run it may be so, but as between you in Boston and me in Europe I deny it in toto and without hesitation.

I humbly apologize to you for the remarks in my last letter, which were written under the supposition that you had forgotten me. Your letter was satisfaction itself. I already knew the main points, but I can ask nothing more complete than your particulars. As to the nomination [of Charles Francis Adams to Congress] I am delighted with the manner of it. The election took place yesterday and a fortnight from to-day I shall certainly know all about it, if not from you at any rate from Governor Wright at the American Legation.

Here I am, then, in Berlin. It is now night; I am writing in my room, which is about ten or twelve by eighteen or twenty feet; by the light of a lamp for which I paid yesterday two dollars; independent; unknown and unknowing; hating the language and yet grubbing into it. I have passed the day since one o'clock with Loo [his sister, Mrs. Kuhn] who is now here and remains till Friday, and with whom I go about to Galleries and Museums, and then dine at her hotel. As you say, I am not rich and am trying to institute a rigid economy in all my expenses. There is one advantage in this place; if forced to it, one can live for almost nothing. Today I was extravagant. I ordered a quantity of clothes; an inside suit and an overcoat of expensive stuffs. The overcoat is a peculiar beaver-cloth, a sort of velvety stuff; and its inside is thick fur, like sealskin, I suppose; so thick that I can't have it lined. The suit is very strong, fine cloth, as good, I fancy, as the man had. But then I had to pay dear. Altogether it cost me fifty-one American dollars. Now in Boston perhaps this is not so much, but here it is a great deal.

Then this frightful German! I have had the most amusing times with my landlady who's a jolly Dutch woman and who has a power of clack that is marvellous. If I have her called in and she once gets agoing I can no more hope to make her understand what I want than if she talked Hebrew. So I have recourse to my Dutch teacher, whom I pay very high even for America, and get him to mediate between us and look over my bills and see that I am not cheated. He comes every morning at ten and I read and talk with him and he corrects my exercises.

What shall I say of this city? Why, Lord bless my soul, I have got things enough to see and study in this city alone to take me two years even if I knew the language and only came for pleasure. The Museums, picture Galleries, Theatres, Gardens; there are enough to occupy one's time for the next six months. Then do the same with the half-million or so engravings. Lord! Such engravings!

The truth is, in the soberest earnest, I am quite as pleasantly situated as I ever expected to be. Sometimes, of course, I feel a little lonely and shall feel more so, I suppose, when Loo goes away and I have no one to think of as near me. Sometimes too I get angry at the excessive difficulty of this very repulsive language, and wearied to death at the continual and fatiguing learning by rote which is necessary for almost every pharse. But on the whole, life here is exceedingly pleasant; there is no relaxation from continual occupation; no excuse for the blues, which always with me come from ennui. Here one is surrounded by art, and I defy any one but a fool to feel ennuyéed while he can look at the works of these old masters.

Here you have my life then. It will be for the next two months a continual dig at the language varied occasionally by a moment or so of Art. The evenings at the Theatres, concerts or balls, perhaps, such as they have here, queer affairs, I imagine, and the day in hard study.

(*Saturday eve. Nov. 6.*) I resume my letter where it was broken off, and hope to send it tomorrow. I have just left Loo, who is still here but expects to go to Dresden tomorrow night. She is suffering tonight under one of her fearful headaches, or I should be with her. She has been very kind to me indeed; very kind; we have been together all the time, going from Gallery to Gallery, and I have almost been living at her expense these two days, for she would not allow me to pay for my own dinners. I sat with her till ten o'clock last night, and have passed all the afternoons with her (that is, from eleven till six) every day. In consequence I have had to sit up till twelve o'clock to write my exercises.

To CHARLES FRANCIS ADAMS, JR. [*1858*]

I have received my clothes, and on the whole they are the best I ever wore. The great coat is a miracle. I look in it like a veteran. German cloth is, if anything, even better than English. However, they ought to be good. They cost enough.

My friends here are all right. I received a letter today from Crowninshield in Hannover in answer to one of mine, in which he represents himself as pretty well except for the fleas. I was very bad that way myself on my arrival here and had a very funny scene with my landlady on the subject, which reached so involved a point at last that an interpreter was called in and as he pretended to speak English but didn't, I'm inclined to think the poor woman to this day doesn't understand. However, I instituted vigorous measures and have not been troubled lately. Anderson is settled here. I went to see him once, but he is a long way off, and I've heard nothing from him for some time. Plenty of Americans are here; one in the next house; but I have had nothing to do with them though I met half-a-dozen at the American Legation last Wednesday. They are of all kinds; some, not attractive. As soon as possible I shall make German acquaintances and in a couple of months I hope to be well enough on in the language, to join the University and make acquaintances there among the donkeys who walk around with absurd caps on their heads; rather more offensive than the soldiers.

Apropos to this, you ask me what my plans are, here and in life. I hardly know how to follow a plan here, for the way is not at all clear. When I left America my intention was first to accustom myself to the language, then to join the University and systematically attend lectures on the Civil Law, at the same time taking a Latin tutor and translating Latin into German; and to continue this course in Heidelberg or in Paris or in both. The plan was simple enough; useful enough; and comprehensive enough. But now I see difficulties. I must join the

University here in the middle of its term; I certainly can not join to any advantage before January. Shall I be likely to learn much law by breaking in on a course of lectures in this manner? To be a student of civil law I must be an absolute master of written and ordinary Latin; though I need not speak it or write it myself. Now, is it well to study law, Latin and German all at once? Can I have time enough to do all this, or ought I to resign the Law and devote myself to Latin? But supposing I were to do this, devote myself to Latin; I may as well give up the University for it would be mere waste time to attend lectures like Corny Felton's at Cambridge, and, as Carlyle says, these Germans are the worst Dryasdusts on the face of the earth.

These objections will, as I advance further and see clearer, either vanish entirely, or gain strength and finally force me into some new course. I hope it will be the former. I already see very clearly that the two years which are allotted to me here, are not nearly enough to do all that I had hoped to do, or a quarter part of it, and I tell you now fairly that if I return to America without doing more than learn German and French, I shall have done well, and these two years will be the best employed of my life. I am satisfied of this, and though I shall not work any the less hard because I believe it, still I shall feel less disappointed when I return without universal knowledge. At present I adhere to my original plan; and this plan, as you see, involves the necessity of my omitting Greek entirely. I am sorry enough to do it, but I became convinced that to attempt the study of Greek now and here, would be hopeless unless I gave up Latin. One or the other I must sacrifice. If I were to include this fourth language in my plan, I should never do anything. Two years will not teach one everything. You may think that as a scholar I should have preferred to sacrifice Latin. As a scholar I should, but as a lawyer I must have only one choice. I take it. And this brings me to the other branch of your question.

[6]

As for my plan of life, it is simple, and if health and the usual goods of life are continued to me, I see no reason why it should not be carried out in the regular course of events. Two years in Europe; two years studying law in Boston; and then I propose to emigrate and practice at Saint Louis. What I can do there, God knows; but I have a theory that an educated and reasonably able man can make his mark if he chooses, and if I fail to make mine, why, then—I fail and that's all. I should do it anywhere else as well. But if I know myself, I can't fail. I must, if only I behave like a gentleman and a man of sense, take a position to a certain degree creditable and influential, and as yet my ambition cannot see clearly enough to look further.

In a conversation I had with Mr. Dana a few days before I left home, I said all this to him, and the latter part of it he treated with a little contempt. He insisted that I was looking towards politics; and perhaps he was right. There are two things that seem to be at the bottom of our constitutions; one is a continual tendency towards politics; the other is family pride; and it is strange how these two feelings run through all of us. For my own ideas of my future, I have not admitted politics into them. It is as a lawyer that I would emigrate and I've seen altogether too much harm done in this way, to allow myself to quit law for politics without irresistible reasons.

So here you have a few of my thoughts about what I am going to do. Here in Europe, away from home, from care and ambition and the fretting of monotony, I must say that I often feel as I often used to feel in College, as if the whole thing didn't pay, and if I were my own master, it would need more inducements than the law could offer, to drag me out of Europe these ten years yet. I always had an inclination for the Epicurean philosophy, and here in Europe I might gratify it until I was gorged. Give me my thousand a year and free leave and a good conscience, and I'd pass as happy a life here as I'm afraid I never shall in St. Louis. But now I am hurried; I must work, work, work; my very pleasures are hurried, and after all, I shall get most pleasure and (I believe) advantage, from what never entered into my calculations; Art.

However, there is no use talking. The magd has just come in to prepare my room for the night, and her "Gute Nacht" tells me that it is nine o'clock, and I want still to write to John. There will be time enough to despond hereafter. Just now I am sure is the pleasantest time I shall ever see, for there is entire independence, no cares, and endless and inexhaustible pleasures. As for my expenses I cannot yet calculate them, but when I square my accounts at the end of the month I shall be able to talk with some degree of certainty how I am to come out. Incidentally you might remark in the hearing of the family circle, that an Englishman the other day said in my hearing that Berlin was an expensive place; nothing was cheap in Berlin. . . .

To CHARLES FRANCIS ADAMS, JR.

Dresden, April 22, 1859.

. . . Well, Gott sei Dank, I've seen the last of Berlin for a considerable time, and here I am in the good city of Dresden among the Saxons, and also a heap of Americans, to all of whom except two or three I've shown and shall show a very cold shoulder. On the twelfth, at seven o'clock in the morning I left Berlin in company with Crowninshield, Higginson, and Mr. Apthorp with his wife, mother-in-law and small son Willy, who went along with us so far as Wittenberg to perform a pilgrimage to the shades of Luther and partly to bid us adieu. Never mind the particulars. Wittenberg is a dirty, stupid little place, and one's elevated sensations turn into extreme weariness after a couple of hours in it. Mr. Apthorp's crowd here turned back, and we, after two hours of slightly stupid waiting at the little depot, took tickets on to Halle. To Halle we should have gone, if some restless devil hadn't inspired us with an admiration for the appearance of Dessau from the car-window, and induced us at forty seconds warning to step out of the car and sacrifice our tickets to Halle. As we had no baggage except our carpet bags, shawl-strap-contents and travelling pouches, this was easy. The inhabitants of the charmingly neat little Dessau, however, who don't see a stranger more than once in a life-time, must have been somewhat bewildered at seeing our procession march through their silent streets. For throughout our trip we insisted on carrying our own baggage and were usually accompanied to and from the hotels by from two to six large men who seemed to think we were madmen over whom it was their part to exercise a careful surveillance. We used to try all sorts of experiments on them to see what their ideas were; stopping short, to see if they also would stop too; walking fast, walking slow; but they never left us at any price. I suppose in Germany no gentleman carries his own carpet bag. Luckily there were enough of us not to care whether they did or not.

So we landed at Dessau and rambled round the town till we found a hotel. Never mind Dessau, however. I'm not going to copy Murray nor Baedeker, the German Murray, which we always carry. It's a nice, funny little Pumpernickel. Read Fitzboodle for the best idea of these one-horse principalities. We left it the next morning in the same order of march, and went on to Weimar, which is much such another, only they bore you to death there with Goethe and Schiller. Vide Murray for sights, all of which we saw, the funniest sight however being ourselves. Here unexpectedly John Bancroft joined us, as he was removing from Dresden to Düsseldorf. He was a great addition to our party. Modest, agreeable, good-natured and both able and cultivated, he is a remarkably pleasant companion, and as he talks better German than any of us, was usually our spokesman. We never put up at the best hotels if there was a cheaper one, and I can tell you, if it isn't always so comfortable, it is in the long run a great deal pleasanter. If you were as tired of great hotels as I am, you'd see why this is so, and why I, exclusive of money considerations, prefer to sacrifice a little comfort and get a little something new. We travelled cheaply sometimes, but when we chose we spent as much as we liked. It wasn't much though.

The next day we went on to Eisenach (my plans of work at Weimar were knocked in the head). Eisenach is delightful. The old Wartburg above it is covered with romance and with history until it's as rich as a wedding-cake. The walks and views are charming and I would willingly have remained two or three days, but the next morning we packed every shred of extra baggage off to Dresden; made a grand immolation of our beavers (except Higginson who clung to his with a love that was more than love, and left it with the baggage master, "to be called for") and taking an open carriage rode through a heavy rain down to Waltershausen, a little place south of Gotha, where we proposed to begin—what! Why a walk in April through the Thuringian Wood.

We carried only our great coats and Ben and I a night shirt. A tooth-brush in one pocket; some collars in another, and some handkerchiefs in a third. I strapped the coat over my shoulders with a shawl strap; the others tied theirs *à la militaire*. We never wore them while walking and though mine is very thick and heavy I never felt it disagreeably. We started from Waltershausen that afternoon and walked some three hours, stopping once only to drink a glass of bier and smoke a cigar. The scenery was very pretty and, perhaps, three centuries ago, wild. The sky reasonably clear, and the weather cool so that we were not too warm. That night we arrived at a little place called Georgenthal where we got a jolly supper and slept in two most romantically large, rickety, cold and ghostly chambers, with the wind outside blowing like fits and creaking the dismal old sign in the most pleasing manner. Up the next morning at about eight and had a delectable breakfast of which honey was the great delicacy, and I never before appreciated how good honey was. Set out under the care of a man who pretended he would guide us through the woods, but he was consummately stupid and we soon found ourselves on the high-road again. So we dismissed the guide and pegged ahead through heavy snow showers which we didn't mind in the least, stopping once at a little dorf where we had a glass of bier and smoked a cigar and Bancroft sketched a dog. Bier is a first-rate thing to walk on and we marched along for an hour up a charming valley with a clear sky and the best of spirits. Crowninshield and Higginson were geese enough to tire themselves by running up a tremendous hill on time, against bets of a bottle of wine, which they won and which like other bets we made, haven't been paid. By and by we began to get deuced tired. The road wound up and up and up and it seemed as if it would never end. We first got into mud, then into slush, then into snow two inches deep, and at last I for one was pretty much used up, and the others not much better. Oberhof appeared however after a tramp of near five hours; a little village perched on the top of the hills, where it was yet dead winter with more snow than I'd seen for a year. It snowed heavily all the afternoon, and as I declared I walked for pleasure and not to get over ground, and wouldn't stir another step that day, Higginson who urged going ahead, was forced to give in and we passed the afternoon as well as we could, finishing by a round talk and a couple of bowls of a compound known as Glühwein; claret punch, hot, with spices and things. The next morning we set off again at eight o'clock in a snow-storm, with from two to eight inches snow on the ground, over a mountainous country. You may think this wasn't much fun, and indeed I believe I was the only one who really enjoyed it, but the glow, the feeling of adventure and the novelty; above all, the freedom and some wildness after six months in Berlin, made it really delightful to me. I haven't felt so well and fresh for ever-so-long. After two hours we reached the Schmücke, a couple of houses on the other side of the hills, and here, sir, we indulged ourselves in a real American tipple. We procured the materials and under Ben Crowninshield's skilled direction, we brewed ourselves a real ten-horse-power Tom and Jerry, which had a perfectly miraculous effect on our spirits and set Ben to walking down that hill with the speed of a locomotive. Bancroft and I took it more gently and fell behind. The day cleared; the snow gradually disappeared as we descended and we got to Ilmenau to dinner at about two o'clock. Rode on in an open wagon from Ilmenau two hours to Königsee through mostly uninteresting country, and at Königsee slept. The next morning, in the most curious manner and without previous concert we all caved in and agreed nem. con. to ride the remaining day's journey. So we did ride it, whiling away the time in an intellectual and highly instructive series of free fights to keep us warm, which commonly ended in a grand state of déshabille all round. The scenery was pretty; one view quite charming, but the day was mostly cloudy and cold and for my part I was so exhausted with fighting and laughing that I hardly cared for anything. We dined at Rudolstadt, the capital of the little Principality of Schwarzenburg-Rudolstadt or something of the sort. It had as usual an enormous palace, and the Prince I believe is as poor as a rat. Hence we pressed on, hiring a lumbering old travelling-wagon, and after six hours of going up interminable hills and going down interminable hills, we jolted down by the statue of old Wieland into little Weimar and put up zum goldnen Adler as before. So our journey was over. It had been made wholly without plan. None of us knew six hours ahead what we were going to do. It was jolly as could be and the fellows were all pleasant and indifferent to everything except what was pleasant, so that we had a jovial time. Still I did not object to getting through with it. We none of us cared to lose more time. Düsseldorf and drawing were calling Bancroft. Bonn and the Pandects were yawning for Higginson. Dresden and [Georg Friedrich] Puchta shouting for me, and whatever Ben's plans are, it was time he should begin some application in earnest. So we were not sorry to find ourselves in Weimar again.

So with the exception of a few hours stay in Leipzig, here I am comfortably settled in Dresden, thanks to Higginson who got me my room. Bancroft is already in Düsseldorf. Higginson sets out in a day or two for Bonn. Ben is here seeking a family, but I doubt if he gets what he wants. Anderson is here, but unless he changes his set, he'll not see me much. Many other Americans are here, but if possible I shall not go near them. A Mr. Stockton is consul and does the hospitalities, but except under compulsion I shall not go within a mile of him. I mean to leave Arthur Dexter's letter on his brother if he's here, though I don't expect that it will do me much good. Until I get tired, there's no need of seeking this society which, I imagine is confined to the Americans and English whose name is legion.

Puchta arrives on Monday, by which time I hope all my arrears will be done up and I shall set to work to try and make something out of old Herr Justinian's Institutions, which it is quite time I was at. Dresden is a pretty place with much more attractive points than Berlin; as good a theatre and the best Gallery north of the Alps. It's shut now but reopens again soon, when I shall go and learn it by heart. Weather of course bad as usual; the worst ever known, say the Germans. But as yet I don't mind that and have got plenty to do even though in this Holy week every place of amusement is closed and not even a concert to be heard, thanks to their idiot of a King's be-ing Catholic. The change of residence has done me good and I feel better in every way than I did in that damned hole of a Berlin.

So you may count on my remaining here for two months and I imagine that they'll be pleasant ones, although after my Ber-lin experience I've become confoundedly skeptical about all places, unless there's some absorbing mental application. It's delightful to live a little while in a new city but when the fun is exhausted, it gets played out.

I've received a letter from Loo at Rome in fits about the Dy-ing Gladiator. What she means to do this summer I've no idea. I wrote to her that if she'd settle anywhere in Switzerland I'd bring my books down and walk with her husband. This blasted war which will probably break out within a week if they're not at it already, knocks the Tyrol in the head. Then there will also probably be fighting on the Rhine so that God only knows where a fellow can go, except to Norway, which indeed I would like to visit. Extras are out to-night which indicate that the Aus-trian troops are preparing to cross the Rubicon, and then all Europe's ablaze; Austria, Prussia, Bavaria, Hannover and Sax-ony, to say nothing of the various other "Bundesgenossen" who contribute ten men and a drummer apiece to the "Reichs armee."

You'll be out in the country when this reaches you, and can philosophize in peace over it there. But I recommend you if you mean to travel, to do it first in America. You speak of astonishing the relatives, I suppose by trotting off somewhere, but it don't pay to come to Europe and rush over it, and that's just what does pay at home. Go out into the wilds, boy; pass a month round among the Mormons and then come back with a clear head and a little practical knowledge. I don't know how Loo can stand her travels and be in raptures still at everything.

I get so bored by all these sights that I only want to get out of their way. A Gallery ought to be visited once a week an hour each time, to really enjoy it; otherwise one loses his power of appreciation. . . .

To CHARLES FRANCIS ADAMS, JR.

Nürnberg, July 3, 1859.

I've just come in from a walk in the dusk alone through this exquisite old city. Ben has gone to bed. . . .

This week has been a tremendously busy one and at the same time hot as tophet. Last Tuesday afternoon Ben and I visited Tharandt, a pretty little town some nine miles from Dresden. The next morning at seven we took the cars and went up the Elbe and came to Königstein, a great fortification perched on a high rock. From here we crossed the river to a place below which is pretty and commands a beautiful view. This country is called the Saxon Switzerland. I tell you what, this seeing sights on a flaming July day is tough. However, I found it very pleasant, for when at about three o'clock we came down to take the steamer, we fell in with a gentleman and two ladies, one of whom was young and quite pretty. Naturally we entered into conversation with the gentleman who was pretty well on in life. He was a Russian-Swede; spoke six languages but not English; "my daughter speaks English, however." Ja wohl! I made a note of that. We continued our conversation, steamer was late; ladies sat a little way off and were unapproachable; steamer at last came and I manœuvred so as to get a seat by the pretty girl and under the apology of bad German entered into an English conversation with her. She was clever, highly cultivated and interesting. Had just come from Italy and was strong Italian. Spoke pretty English. Was a little taller than I in figure; slim; light eyes; distingué. We talked of travelling, of poetry, of art, of Italy and of many other things. I passed a pleasant summer afternoon and liked my friend very much. We arrived at Dresden; left the boat; touched our hats; I never shall see the pretty Swede again, but that's a traveller's luck and God forbid that I ever see enough of a woman in Europe to care for her. That would make a fuss. Ten chances to one it makes a fellow unhappy. But now my pretty Swede's in Hamburg, I'm in Nürnberg; we never shall meet again, but I have a pleasant recollection and count myself richer than before by some agreeable hours.

That evening I ordered down some ice-cream and wine and treated my assembled family to an abschiedsfest. We all got tight, played Schwarzen Peter or old maid at cards and as the Frl. Camilla lost, I corked a pair of moustaches on her face. This Frl. is quite nice; we abuse each other and call each other names, but I rather like her; she's bright and not bad looking. What the family think of me I can't say. They seem to think that I'm lazy and selfish. The first I plead guilty to, but the last not. They wanted my photograph but I told them I was far too handsome to give away my likeness in that way and they must wait till all other prior claims are settled. Finally so far as this family goes I've nothing more to say than that they were aways kind, good-natured, and obliging; I have learned here twice as much German as I knew when I came here and my recollections of this place are all pleasant.

On Thursday morning began packing up in earnest. Ben left a trunk here in which I deposited ten shirts and other articles in that way and a number of books which will all go on to Boston. I visited too the Gallery for the last time and the Madonna, the most exquisite of all exquisiteness. After dinner I just managed to get my trunk packed as the time for departure came, and waited for the droschke which ought to have come at quarter past two. It knew better and nary appeared. Waited till the last instant, then rushed off with a carpet bag and

travelling pouch and great coat in a shawl strap. Since then I've
had no handkerchiefs, nor drawers nor stockings nor linen
shirts nor anything else. Rushed like a mad bull to a droschke
station; ordered the coachman to drive as fast as possible to
the depot; arrived as the door shut but bolted for a ticket "to
Nürnberg." On tearing out my purse to pay I discovered I
had only four thalers and the ticket cost eight. My money
had gone beyond all idea and I had relied on Mr. Ben, who
was already in the cars. I said that I had not enough money
and wished a ticket to Leipsic instead. No! I had ordered Nürnberg; it was stamped and I must take that or none. With a
tempest of choice English and German execrations I bolted towards the glass door to get in without a ticket. No go. Guard
forced me back. At this instant as I turned round in despair to
leave the whole concern, Ben's host who was there and had
learned my position hurried up with Ben's purse which held
just enough. I got on board the train which had probably
waited for me, and in a state of pure heat I indulged in a general curse to the whole affair, continuing steadily fifteen minutes till I got cool. Then we set to work to calculate our resources. Ben's position was the same as mine and we could raise
only four thalers between us. Both of us had however Baring's
letters in our pockets and our tickets were already paid to
Nürnberg.

So we went on to Leipzig in a heat that made us gasp for air,
and amused ourselves by reading, talking with a couple of
Cadets, and also by smoking, as I do, but Ben doesn't indulge
in the flagrant Bremen. At Leipzig we stopped an hour and at-
tempted to raise money but the fool of a banker wouldn't do it
and we had no time to enquire further. Baring has no agent
here. At seven or so we started again. In our wagon was a traveller's real set. A Russian with wonderful hair and beard
parted across his chin; three Poles who spoke their native lan-

guage, which is a mixture of French, German, Italian and Greek; one German who said Ja and Nein and no more; and ourselves. We fraternised with the hairy Russer and the Poles and had quite a jolly time and lively talk till the night came on and towards twelve o'clock at a place called Plauen, the Poles departed. We then had each a seat and it was cooler. We stretched ourselves out and slumbered as well as we could. So we went on all night, changing cars at the Bavarian frontier, till towards five o'clock I woke up feeling dirty as you please, and sticking my head out of the window got some cool morning air and watched the pretty fields of Franconia with their old road-side saints, crucifixes and Madonnas. At six or so we came to Bamberg and Ben and I here got out; we wanted to see the city and the Cathedral. Cleaned ourselves; breakfasted on milk, hard boiled eggs, bread and butter and then rambled up and saw the Cathedral which is peculiar and remarkably pretty. Here again we applied for money, but as they said we could certainly get it at Nürnberg we didn't insist on drawing here. We bought a large quantity of cherries instead and went back to our hotel, eat, drank and slept till the cars came at two and we had to go out again into the burning heat.

Two hours on to Nürnberg. A jolly Nürnberger was our only companion, and we were dead of heat. At three we arrived here and came straight to this house, the Hotel Zum Strauss. So there are our travels!

Monday, 4th. Our grand American spread eagle has been remembered by us today but not celebrated. We drank a glass of wine and water to him and let him swim.

Ben hurries me on. I would stay here a week but we go tomorrow morning. My amiable brother, what do you want me to say of this city. I hardly know how to express it at all. Think me spooney if you will, but last evening as I wandered round in the dusk smoking a cigar in these delightful old peaked, tiled, crooked, narrow, stinking lanes I thought that if ever again I enjoy as much happiness as here in Europe, and the months pass over bringing always new fascinations and no troubles, why then philosophers lie and earth's a paradise. Ben and I have passed the day in a couple of great churches, lying on the altar steps and looking at the glorious stained glass windows five hundred years old, with their magnificent colors and quaint Biblical stories. So fascinating these things are! . . . There's no use talking about it. Let it go! Nürnberg is Nürnberg. If I go on I shall be silly, even if I've not been already.

So tomorrow we bid good-bye to Dürer and old Peter Vischer, the churches and the streets; the glorious old windows and the charming fountains and all the other fascinations of this city, and march on to Munich. The weather bids fair to last forever; we roast and broil in this absolutely cloudless sky, but sleep well and enjoy life. How long München will take us is a problem, but not more than a week. Ben wants to get through. As I'm determined at any price not to return to Berlin before the November semester begins, and hate the very idea of seeing that city, I'm in no hurry.

I've not got your letter by me. As to the lecture you administer in regard to writing and money, I'm obliged but just now can't undertake to discuss it. As for my studying, although I still assert the principle that it is well to work I must confess that any slight efforts I've made in that direction have ludicrously failed. Since I left Berlin I've not done a thing except pretend to read a page of law a day, an effort which unhappily never succeeded. In fact I've acted precisely as you recommended, and am quite well satisfied that so far as real work goes I shall do little in Europe. At the same time I do not think that the time could be better employed and believe that what I'm picking up now is of more use than my two years of Blackstone and Carry Bigelow, etc., would have been at home. Nevertheless you need not scare the Governor by this reflection. Next winter in self-defense I must peg away and probably hard. But as for the law I learn in that way making me a jurist, I doubt it. That it may help to make me a strong man is more possible; that it may be a mere extra accomplishment kept for show is most likely of all. . . .

To CHARLES FRANCIS ADAMS, JR.

Dresden, 23 November, 1859.

Your letter arrived this morning and I will try to answer it at once though I can't make my answer as long as yours. I've too many letters to write for that. But I do what I can.

To condense then. As you seem to begin by wishing to force me to eat my own words I will grant you that pleasure without an argument. I'm not the first nor likely to be the last whose ideas on subjects of which he is ignorant have turned out to be silly. I acknowledge therefore as broadly as you wish, that so far as my plan went, I have failed and done little or nothing. At the same time I feel for myself convinced that this last year has been no failure, but on the contrary is worth to me a great deal; how much depends on the use I make of it; but the worth is there. You say you think I'm a humbug. That implies that you once believed I was something. I don't pretend to know how far you're right or wrong, but I protest against your judging about the advantages of a few years in Europe from my case. The problem is in fact just this. I have acquired here great advantages; if I am a humbug, they wont help me; but I shouldn't have done any better if I'd remained in Boston; if I am not a humbug, we shall see; but in either case the advantages are there, and the failure, if failure it is, will be in me and not in the European experiment which may be of immense use to a capable man.

As to my occupation for the next year, I am now going on in a general course of German reading mostly in the constitutional history of various countries and desultory light reading, but the German is still the main object. This means you see in point of fact that I'm doing nothing. So far as learning a trade goes, idle I'm likely to remain until I return home. So far as education goes, I consider these two years as the most valuable of my life. Indefinite, you will say. But so far as I can see, it is what you yourself recommend.

You recommend me to write. My dear boy, if I write, I must write as I think. Amusing, witty, and clever I am not, and to affect the style would disgust me and bore you. If I write at all in my life out of the professional line, it will probably be when I have something to say, and when I feel that my subject has got me as well as I the subject. Just now this is anything but true, for I can't seem to master any of the matters that interest me. So don't ask me to be sprightly and amusing for that is what I never was, am not, never shall be. . . .

Your suggestion about rouge et noir is therefore a mistake, though not uningenious. The money I won paid my hotel bills several days and I have never seen a gambling table since. As the Governor has been kind enough to leave me here without money I've had to write to London to ask an extension of credit which I got and the Governor may send when he chooses.

This contest of purpose; this argument about aims, you began against, or if you will, for me. You blame me very fairly no doubt, and try to protect yourself from retaliation by pleading guilty; a sort of Yankee Sullivan tactics, hitting a lick and going down. Face the music yourself. I acknowledge I've failed but I believe I've discovered a treasure if I can but use it. But you; why do you plead guilty to the "tu quoque" before I'd said it. Why do you recommend writing to me who has been hurrying around Europe like a steam engine and am so busy with learning that I can't spare a second for teaching; why recommend this to me when you yourself are smouldering worse than I, when you have never published a word so far as I know. Busy you are, no doubt, and have worked and studied hard; I believe it; but physician, heal thyself. Nearly three years older than I, plead guilty to a "tu quoque" and pass the 5+xth winter dancing with little girls just out of the nursery. The Governor's last letter warned me against writing magazine articles on the ground that they are ephemeral. Is that your objection too? Or why have you, who urge it so on me when I'm busy with another language and haven't properly any right to talk, think or write English, why have you in those three years of law not broken the path yourself? You haven't even used the chances you have. Of the society of Boston outside of Beacon Street, I don't believe you know a soul. Of the distinguished men there who could aid you a little and change your course of thought, I doubt whether it ever occurred to you to make the acquaintance of one. There is a very good literary society whom it would be well worth while to know, beginning with Waldo Emerson and going down, and it's from able men that one learns; not from talking old woman's nonsense with girls, however good fun that may be. You talk about being stifled in Boston and I don't believe you know anything of Boston except half a dozen drawing rooms and bar ditto. You haven't or hadn't a friend in it, worth having. You try to be a society man and yet want to do work that would necessarily cut you off from that society.

Do as Frank Palfrey does, according to Mr. Hillard. "Oh, he's very well; getting along quite encouragingly. Works hard. Only he is *such* a favorite in society that he has to go out more than he ought. It distracts him, but among the young ladies he is *so* liked that the temptation is too much."

You mention the position I shall have to take when I come back as if you expected me to return a complete lawyer or a Professor or something. Of course I shall stand to all appearances as you stood on entering an office. I don't see how *you* can expect anything else, though I am fully prepared to hear the Governor lay the fault of every failure and every error in my life to Europe. God Almighty could not get an idea out of his head that had once got in. I shall return and study law; when that's done I shall call my preparations finished, and shall toss up for luck. What I have learned here is a part of my capital and will probably show itself slowly and radically.

I have dived into your letter and hauled out these few points to answer. If it pleases you to criticise the answers, do so. No doubt it's good practice, this fencing with each other, and I certainly, as it concerns me, am the very last to find fault. If I had more time and could dilate more, I should like to do it, but home letters come round so fast that I have to hurry them off as fast as I can.

You mention politics. It's my own opinion, believing as I do in an "irrepressible conflict," that I shall come home just in time to find America in a considerable pickle. The day that I hear that Seward is quietly elected President of the United States, will be a great relief to me, for I honestly believe that that and only that can carry us through, even if that can. We've set our hands to the plough and wouldn't look back if we could, but I would thank God heartily to know that comparatively conservative men were to conduct this movement and could control it. If the Governor weathers this storm he has a good chance of living in the White House some day. All depends on the ability he shows as a leader now.

But if things go wrong as they easily may; if a few more Sumner affairs and Harper's Ferry undertakings come up, then adieu my country. I wouldn't give a bad grosschen for the

United States debt. We shall have made a brilliant failure with our glorious Republic and the prophet can't say what'll turn up. If our constitution stands this strain, she's a stunner, that's all.

What effect all this may have on our lives, we can't calculate in any way. I mean to come home prepared as well as I know how for luck or unluck, and not be frightened if I can help it. In America the man that can't guide had better sit still and look on. I recommend to you to look on, and if things don't change within a year then I'll eat my head. If all goes right, the house of Adams may get its lease of life renewed—if, as I've various times remarked, it has the requisite ability still. Till then we needn't compromise ourselves and will watch what comes. . . .

To CHARLES FRANCIS ADAMS, JR.

[Washington] December 9, 1860.

I propose to write you this winter a series of private letters to show how things look. I fairly confess that I want to have a record of this winter on file, and though I have no ambition nor hope to become a Horace Walpole, I still would like to think that a century or two hence when everything else about it is forgotten, my letters might still be read and quoted as a memorial of manners and habits at the time of the great secession of 1860. At the same time you will be glad to hear all the gossip and to me it will supply the place of a Journal.

The first week is now over and I feel more at home, though I've not made many acquaintances. It's a great life; just what I wanted; and as I always feel that I am of real use here and can take an active part in it all, it never tires. Politically there is a terrible panic. The weak brethren weep and tear their hair and imagine that life is to become a burden and the Capitol an owl-nest and fox-hole. The Massachusetts men and the Wisconsin men and scatterers in other states are the only ones who are really firm. Seward is great; a perfect giant in all this howling. Our father is firmer than Mt. Ararat. I never saw a more precious old flint. As yet there has been no open defection, but the pressure is immense and you need not swear too much if something gives at last.

Of course your first question would be about Seward. He came up here last Tuesday evening and I heard him talk for the first time. Wednesday he came up to dinner and was absolutely grand. No one was there but the family, and he had all the talking to himself. I sat and watched the old fellow with his big nose and his wire hair and grizzly eyebrows and miserable dress, and listened to him rolling out his grand, broad ideas that would inspire a cow with statesmanship if she understood our language. There's no shake in him. He talks square up to the mark and something beyond it.

He invited us down to dine with him on Friday. His wife hasn't come here this winter, so he has persuaded Mr. and Mrs. Israel Washburn to put up with him till they go off. We six had a dinner, at which the Governor caused a superior champagne to be brought out; not his usual tap. Israel was as usual; ugly as the very devil, but good-humored and nervous and kindhearted as ever. The Governor was chipper as a lark and swore by yea and by nay that everything was going on admirably. The state of society here worries mamma very much and she was sorrowing over the bitterness of feeling and change of bearing in her acquaintances, but the Governor was implacable. He swore he was glad of it and delighted to see 'em down. He'd been through all that and come out on the other side. They had been all graciousness to him as a Whig while they tabooed Hale and Sumner and Giddings. They had tried to taboo him too, later, but then it was too late, and now he was glad they did feel cut up and meant they should.

He is the very most glorious original. It delights me out of my skin to see the wiry old scare-crow insinuate advice. He talks so slowly and watches one so hard under those grey eye-brows of his. After our dinner we went into the parlor and played whist. Gradually a whole crowd of visitors came in, mostly staunch men such as Potter and Cad. Washburne, Sedgwick and Alley and Eliot, etc. Among others who should turn up but the two Rhode Island Senators, Anthony and Simmons, both very fishy and weak-kneed. Anthony is the man whom mamma gave a tremendous hiding to last spring, for a remark he made more than usually treacherous, but he called on us the other evening notwithstanding. The whole company knew all about it, however, and Seward knew they did. I was sitting somewhat back, just behind Anthony and Seward and watched them both carefully. Anthony remarked deprecatingly: Well, things look pretty bad, Governor, don't you think so? No, growled Seward, I don't see why they look bad. Well, said Anthony still more timidly, these financial troubles coming so with the political ones. Why, answered Seward, you can't run a financial and a political panic together, the first will regulate itself. Poor Anthony fairly broke down and acquiesced. The manner in which Seward spoke fairly bluffed him. But Seward was unmerciful. The first thing we knew he dragged mamma out; wanted to put her against some of these Carolinians; she was the person to take care of them; put 'em in a dark room and let 'em fight it out, etc., etc.; to all which mamma of course answered laughingly while everyone in the room was on the broad grin. I thought he'd never leave off this talk. He wouldn't stop, but rubbed it in and in till Anthony looked blue. At the very first pause and change of topic he got up and took leave. Of course it did not please mamma too well to be used as a sort of a false target in this way, but the Governor only smiled grimly and neither apologised nor confessed his intentions. . . .

To CHARLES FRANCIS ADAMS, JR.

Washington, February 13, 1861.

The family have gone up to the Capitol to see the counting of the votes. As I don't anticipate any show, and am no longer a reporter and wanted a little leisure to write to you, I've remained at home.

Charles Hale has come on and means to stay over the 4th. I have of course stopped writing for the *Advertiser,* and left it to him. He evidently had no objection, though complimentary in his remarks generally. On looking back over my letters this winter, I am on the whole tolerably well satisfied with them and their effect. They have had some good influence in shaping the course of opinion in Boston, and the *Advertiser* and the *New York Times* have both profited by them. Now that I'm out of the traces I'm not sorry for it on some accounts. I'm no longer at home, and living out of the house destroys my evenings. Then our house is so full, and there are so many people here and so much society that it's next to impossible to do anything And finally, the [Peace] Convention has assumed the whole affair and I should have to take a world of trouble to find out what was going on, and probably couldn't do it at all. At any rate Charles Hale can do it better than I, and wants to, so I am willing.

I don't think much of the Convention. I don't see much ability in it, nor much life. I don't believe any great good can come from it, except to gain time. I think the battle is won. I'm beginning to lose my interest in it since the Tennessee election. In my belief everything is going to simmer down, and wise men will keep quiet. The next administration will give us trouble enough, and I for one am going upon the business or the pleas ure that shall suit me, for every man hath business or desire such as it is, and for my own poor part—look you—I will go write an article for the *Atlantic Monthly,* intituled "The Great Secession Winter of 1860–61."

Mrs. [Stephen A.] Douglas gave a crush ball last night. Her little beast of a husband was there as usual; God pardon me for abusing my host, whose bread and salt it is true I had no chance to touch, but a very little of whose champagne I drank, diluted with water, the common property of the human race. Mamma and Fanny went first to the President's reception and afterwards to the ball, and I assure you, the young Crowninshield was some astonished with the sights she saw. It was without any exception the wildest collection of people I ever saw. Next to the President's receptions, the company was beyond all description promiscuous. Mrs. Douglas, who is said to be much depressed by the general condition of things, received and looked as usual, handsome—"Splendidly null." Poor girl! what the deuce does she look forward to! Her husband is a brute—not to her that I know of—but gross, vulgar, demagogic; a drunkard, ruined as a politician; ruined as a private man; over head and ears, indeed drowned lower than soundings reaching in debt; with no mental or literary resources; without a future; with a past worse than none at all; on the whole I'd rather not be Mrs. Douglas. Still, there she stood and shook hands with all her guests, and smiled—and smiled.

A crowd of admiring devotees surrounded the ancient buffer [John] Tyler; another crowd surrounded that other ancient buffer Crittenden. Ye Gods, what are we, when mortals no bigger—no, not so big as—ourselves, are looked up to as though their thunder spoke from the real original Olympus. Here is an old Virginia politician, of whom by good rights, no one ought ever to have heard, re-appearing in the ancient cerements of his forgotten grave—political and social—and men look up at him as they would at Solomon, if he could be made the subject of a resurrection. I nearly got into several fights with various men and women, in the attempt to get through the crowd. . . .

I have little to tell you in politics. I am so taken up with work and play that I've no time to hunt secrets. Sumner still holds out and has not been near us, though he is very cordial when we meet. The trouble there was greater than I supposed. Our irascible papa got into a passion with him for attempting to cal' Alley to account in his (C.F.A.'s) presence. Perhaps Summer might have forgiven this, but then Massachusetts has preferred C.F.A.'s lead, and that finished him. However, all quarrels and secessions must be healed soon. It's the order of the day.

I've not seen Seward very lately and don't know much about him. He is hard at work I suppose, and I don't like to go down and interrupt him. I can't get over my modesty about those things. The last time he was here he was very jolly indeed and sanguine as could be. Between Lincoln and the secessionists he must have a hard time. . . . Dana's step is a great thing. It raps those confounded Rump Whigs who are doing their worst to hurt us. As its ground is more than usually distinct and independent it will support us the more.

To CHARLES FRANCIS ADAMS, JR.

London, February 14, 1862.

Good morrow, 't is St. Valentine's day
All in the morning betime.
And I a maid at your window
To be your Valentine.

Hail, noble lieutenant! I have received your letter written on board ship, and I am with you. Now that you are at work, if you see or do anything or hear something that will make a good letter to be published, send it to me and I think I can promise that it shall see the light. Thus you can do double work, and if you write well, perhaps you can get double pay. I shall exercise my discretion as to omissions. . . .

You find fault with my desponding tone of mind. So do I. But the evil is one that probably lies where I can't get at it. I've disappointed myself, and experience the curious sensation of discovering myself to be a humbug. How is this possible? Do you understand how, without a double personality, *I* can feel that *I* am a failure? One would think that the *I* which could feel that, must be a different *ego* from the *I* of which it is felt.

You are so fortunate as to be able to forget self-contemplation in action, I suppose; but with me, my most efficient channels of action are now cut off, and I am busy in creating new ones, which is a matter that demands much time and even then may not meet with success.

Politically there is no news here. We shall be allowed to fight our battle out, I think; at least for some time yet. Parliament has met and the speeches have been very favorable to neutrality. I think our work here is past its crisis. The insurgents will receive no aid from Europe, and so far are beaten. Our victory is won on this side the water. On your side I hope it will soon be so too. . . . John Bright is my favorite Englishman. He is very pleasant, cheerful and courageous and much more sanguine than I have usually been. . . .

To CHARLES FRANCIS ADAMS, JR.

London, March 15, 1862.

Times have so decidedly changed since my last letter to you, which was, as I conceive, about three weeks or a month ago, that I hardly know what to write about. My main doubt is about your prospects. I see no reason why Davis and his whole army should n't be shut up and forced to capitulate in Virginia. If so, you will be spared a summer campaign. But if he is allowed to escape, I shall be disgusted, and God only knows what work may be before you.

Meanwhile it worries me all the time to be leading this thoroughly useless life abroad while you are acting such grand parts at home. You would be astonished at the change of opinion which has taken place here already. Even the *Times* only this morning says: "The very idea of such a war is American, multitudinous, vast, and as much an appeal to the imagination as the actual brunt of arms." And again in speaking of the tone of the Southern papers it says in a striking way: "Some of their expressions recall those in which the Roman historians of the later Empire spoke of the Northern tribes." The truth is, as our swarm of armies strike deeper and deeper into the South, the contest is beginning to take to Europeans proportions of grandeur and perfection like nothing of which they ever heard or read. They call us insane to attempt what, when achieved, they are almost afraid to appreciate. A few brilliant victories, a short campaign of ten days or a fortnight, rivalling in its vigor and results those of Napoleon, has positively startled this country into utter confusion. It reminds me of my old host in Dresden, who, when he heard of the battle of Magenta, rushed into my room, newspaper in hand, and began measuring on the map the distance from the Ticino to Vienna. The English on hearing of Fort Donnelson and the fall of Nashville, seem to think our dozen armies are already over the St. Lawrence and at the gates of Quebec. They don't conceal their apprehensions and if we go on in this way, they will be as humiliated as the South itself. The talk of intervention, only two months ago so loud as to take a semi-official tone, is now out of the minds of everyone. I heard Gregory make his long-expected speech in the House of Commons, and it was listened to as you would listen to a funeral eulogy. His attacks on us, on Seward and on our blockade were

cheered with just enough energy to show the animus that ex
isted in a large proportion of the members, but his motion, a
simple and harmless request for papers, was tossed aside without a division. I saw our friend Mason [the Southern Commis-
sioner] on the opposite side of the House to where I was sitting
with Thurlow Weed. He is unlucky. One of the Bishops who
happened to have come in and was seated near the door, heard
a "Hear! hear!" behind him, and looking round saw Mason.
For a stranger to cheer is a breach of privilege, and the story
went all over town creating quite a row. Mr. Mason now denies
it, I am told, and says it was someone else who cheered. He
maintains now that the South always expected to lose the border States and that now they are retiring to the cotton region
the war has just begun. He coolly talks this stuff to the English
people as if they had n't always asserted that the border States
were a vital point with them. We on the other hand, no longer
descend to argue such stories, or to answer the new class of lies;
but smile blandly and compassionately on those who swallow
them and remark that so far as advised, the nation whom we
have the honor to represent is satisfied with the progress thus
far made, and sees no reason to doubt that the Union will be
maintained in its fullest and most comprehensive meaning.

The blockade is now universally acknowledged to be unob-
jectionable. Recognition, intervention, is an old song. No one
whispers it. But the navy that captured Port Royal, Roanoke
and Fort Henry, and that is flying about with its big guns up all
the rivers and creeks of the South, is talked of with respect.
And the legion of armies that are winning victory after victory
on every side, until we have begun to complain if a steamer arrives without announcing the defeat of some enemy, or the occupation of some city, or the capture of some stronghold, are a
cause of study to the English such as they've not had since
Napoleon entered Milan some seventy years ago. I feel like a

King now. I assert my nationality with a quiet pugnacity that tells. No one treads on our coattails any longer, and I do not expect ever to see again the old days of anxiety and humiliation. . . .

To CHARLES FRANCIS ADAMS, JR.

London, May 16, 1862.

. . . Before this reaches you I suppose you will be in motion, and I hope that the war will be at an end. It would be a mere piece of unjustifiable wantonness for the Southern generals to defend Charleston, if they are defeated in Virginia. So, although I would like to see you covered with glory, I would be extremely well satisfied to hear that you had ended the campaign and ridden into Charleston without firing a shot or drawing a sabre.

Last Sunday afternoon, the day after my letter to you had gone, telling how hard it was to sustain one's own convictions against the scepticism of a nation, I returned from taking a walk on Rotten Row with my very estimable friend Baron Brinken, and on reaching home, I was considerably astounded at perceiving the Chief in an excited manner dance across the entry and ejaculate, "We've got New Orleans." Philosopher as I am and constant in a just and tenacious virtue, I confess that even I was considerably interested for the moment. So leaving Sir Charles Lyell regarding my abrupt departure through one eye-glass with some apparent astonishment, I took a cab and drove down to Mr. Weed. Meeting him in the street near his hotel, I leaped out of the cab, and each of us simultaneously drew out a telegram which we exchanged. His was Mr. Peabody's private business telegram; mine was an official one from Seward. We then proceeded together to the telegraph office and sent a dispatch to Mr. Dayton at Paris, and finally I went round to the Diplomatic Club and had the pleasure of enunciating my sentiments. Here my own agency ended, but Mr. Weed drank his cup of victory to the dregs. He spread the news in every direction, and finally sat down to dinner at the Reform Club with two sceptical old English friends of our side and had the pleasure of hearing the news-boys outside shout "Rumored capture of New Orleans" in an evening extra, while the news was posted at Brookes's, and the whole town was in immense excitement as though it were an English defeat.

Indeed the effect of the news here has been greater than anything yet. It has acted like a violent blow in the face on a drunken man. The next morning the *Times* came out and gave fairly in that it had been mistaken; it had believed Southern accounts and was deceived by them. This morning it has an article still more remarkable and intimates for the first time that it sees little more chance for the South. There is, we think, a preparation for withdrawing their belligerent declaration and acknowledging again the authority of the Federal Government over all the national territory, to be absolute and undisputed. One more victory will bring us up to this, I am confident. That done, I shall consider, not only that the nation has come through a struggle such as no other nation ever heard of, but in a smaller and personal point of view I shall feel much relieved and pleased at the successful career of the Chief.

You can judge of the probable effect of this last victory at New Orleans from the fact that friend Russell of the *Times* (who has not yet called) gravely warned the English nation yesterday of the magnificent army that had better be carefully watched by the English people, since it hated them like the devil and would want to have something to do. And last night I met Mr. John Bright at an evening reception, who seemed to feel somewhat in the same way. "Now," said he, "if you Americans succeed in getting over this affair, you must n't go and get

stuffy to England. Because if you do, I don't know what's to become of us who stood up for you here." I did n't say we
would n't, but I did tell him that *he* need n't be alarmed, for
all he would have to do would be to come over to America and
we would send him to Congress at once. He laughed and said
he thought he had had about enough of that sort of thing in
England. By the way, there is a story that he thinks of leaving
Parliament. . . .

To CHARLES FRANCIS ADAMS, JR.

London, June 6, 1862.

. . . The evening before the Derby, the Chief [his father]
and I were down at the House of Commons from five o'clock
P.M. till one A.M., listening to the great debate of the season.
This is one of the sights that I enjoy most. With us debate has
gone out, and set speeches and personalities have taken its
place. But here, though they no longer speak as they used in the
old days of Pitt and Fox, with rhetorical effort and energy,
there is still admirable debating. That night we heard Palmerston, Disraeli, Horsman and Cobden. Palmerston is a poor
speaker, wants fluency and power, and talks the most miserable
sophistry, but he does it so amusingly and plausibly and has
such prestige that even Disraeli's keenness puts no quencher on
him. Gladstone is the best speaker in the house, but next to him
I should place Disraeli. He looks precisely like the pictures in
Punch, and speaks with a power of making hits that is infinitely
amusing. He kept me in a roar three quarters of an hour, and
the House cheered him steadily. Cobden was very good too. He
damaged Horsman dreadfully. But the most striking part of the
debate was that not a word as to America or interference was
said in it. This was peculiar because the debate was on the subject of retrenchment, and retrenchment was necessary because

of the American war. Six months ago such a debate would not have taken place, but in its place we should have had war speeches with no end.

Our position here now, putting aside a few diplomatic questions, is much as it might be at home. The Speaker calls the Chief "The Conqueror," and it is only now and then, when our armies stop a moment to take breath, and they think here that we are in trouble, that the opposition raises its head a little and barks. Indeed the position we have here is one of a great deal of weight, and of course so long as our armies march forward, so long our hands are elevated higher and higher until we bump the stars. I hear very little about our friend Mason. He is said to be very anxious and to fear a rebellion within the rebellion. He has little or no attention paid him except as a matter of curiosity, though occasionally we are told of his being at dinner somewhere or other. A Southern newspaper called the Index lately started here, contains numbers of southern letters, all of which are so excruciatingly "never conquer" in their tone, that one is forced to the belief that they think themselves very near that last ditch. . . .

To CHARLES FRANCIS ADAMS, JR.

London, November 21, 1862.

. . . My work is now limited to a careful observation of events here and assistance in the manual labor of the place, and to a study of history and politics which seem to me most necessary to our country for the next century. The future is a blank to me as I suppose it is also to you. I have no plans nor can have any, so long as my course is tied to that of the Chief. Should you at the end of the war, wish to take my place, in case the services of one of us were still required, I should return to Boston and Horace Gray, and I really do not know whether I should regret the change. The truth is, the experience of four years has done little towards giving me confidence in myself. The more I see, the more I am convinced that a man whose mind is balanced like mine, in such a way that what is evil never seems unmixed with good, and what is good always streaked with evil; an object seems never important enough to call out strong energies till they are exhausted, nor necessary enough not to allow of its failure being possible to retrieve; in short, a mind which is not strongly positive and absolute, cannot be steadily successful in action, which requires quietness and perseverance. I have steadily lost faith in myself ever since I left college, and my aim is now so indefinite that all my time may prove to have been wasted, and then nothing left but a truncated life.

I should care the less for all this if I could see your path any clearer, but while my time *may* prove to have been wasted, I don't see but what yours *must* prove so. At least God forbid that you should remain an officer longer than is necessary. And what then? The West is possible; indeed, I have thought of that myself. But what we want is a *school*. We want a national set of young men like ourselves or better, to start new influences not only in politics, but in literature, in law, in society, and throughout the whole social organism of the country—a national school of our own generation. And that is what America has no power to create. In England the Universities centralize ability and London gives a field. So in France, Paris encourages and combines these influences. But with us, we should need at least six perfect geniuses placed, or rather, spotted over the country and all working together; whereas our generation as yet has not produced one nor the promise of one. It's all random, insulated work, for special and temporary and personal purposes, and we have no means, power or hope of combined action for any unselfish end.

One man who has real ability may do a great deal, but we ought to have a more concentrated power of influence than any that now exists.

For the present war I have nothing to say. We received cheerful letters from you and John today, and now we have the news of McClellan's removal. As I do not believe in Burnside's genius, I do not feel encouraged by this, especially as it shakes our whole structure to its centre. I have given up the war and only pray for its end. The South has vindicated its position and we cannot help it, so, as we can find no one to lead us and no one to hold us together, I don't see the use of our shedding more blood. Still all this makes able men a necessity for the future and if you're an able man, there's your career. I have projects enough and not unpromising ones for some day, but like most of my combinations, I suppose they 'll all end in dust and ashes.

We are very comfortable here in London fog. Some sharp diplomatic practice, but, I hope, not very serious. People don't overwhelm us with attentions, but that is excusable.

To CHARLES FRANCIS ADAMS, JR.

London, January 27, 1863.

. . . Spring has come again and the leaves are appearing for the third time and we are still here, nor does there seem any immediate probability of our moving. In fact we are now one of the known and acknowledged units of the London and English world, and though politics still place more or less barriers in our path, the majority of people receive us much as they would Englishmen, and seem to consider us as such. I have been much struck by the way in which they affect to distinguish here between us and "foreigners"; that is, persons who don't speak English. The great difficulty is in the making acquaintances, for London acquaintances are nothing.

To CHARLES FRANCIS ADAMS, JR. [*1863*]

After a fortnight's violent pulling, pushing, threatening, shaking, cursing and coaxing, almost entirely done through private channels, we have at least succeeded in screwing the Government up to what promises to be a respectable position. How steady it will be, I don't know, nor how far they will declare themselves, do I know. But between our Government at home and our active and energetic allies here, we seem to have made progress. I went last night to a meeting of which I shall send you a report; a democratic and socialist meeting, most threatening and dangerous to the established state of things; and assuming a tone and proportions that are quite novel and alarming in this capital. And they met to notify Government that "they would not tolerate" interference against us. I can assure you this sort of movement is as alarming here as a slave insurrection would be in the South, and we have our hands on the springs that can raise or pacify such agitators, at least as regards our own affairs, they making common cause with us. I never quite appreciated the "moral influence" of American democracy, nor the cause that the privileged classes in Europe have to fear us, until I saw how directly it works. At this moment the American question is organizing a vast mass of the lower orders in direct contact with the wealthy. They go our whole platform and are full of the "rights of man." The old revolutionary leaven is working steadily in England. You can find millions of people who look up to our institutions as their model and who talk with utter contempt of their own system of Government. Within three months this movement has taken a development that has placed all our enemies on the defensive; has driven Palmerston to sue for peace and Lord Russell to proclaim a limited sympathy. I will not undertake to say where it will stop, but were I an Englishman I should feel nervous. We have strength enough already to shake the very crown on the Queen's head if we are compelled to employ it all. You are not to suppose that we are intriguing to create trouble. I do not believe that all the intrigue in the world could create one of these great demonstrations of sympathy. But where we have friends, there we shall have support, and those who help us will do it of their own free will. There are few of the thickly populated districts of England where we have not the germs of an organisation that may easily become democratic as it is already antislavery. With such a curb on the upper classes, I think they will do little more harm to us.

The conduct of the affairs of that great republic which though wounded itself almost desperately, can yet threaten to tear down the rulers of the civilised world, by merely assuming her place at the head of the march of democracy, is something to look upon. I wonder whether we shall be forced to call upon the brothers of the great fraternity to come in all lands to the assistance and protection of its head. These are lively times, oh, Hannibal.

To CHARLES FRANCIS ADAMS, JR.

London, May 14, 1863.

The telegraph assures us that Hooker is over the Rappahannock and your division regally indistinct "in the enemy's rear." I suppose the campaign is begun, then. Honestly, I'd rather be with you than here, for our state of mind during the next few weeks is not likely to be very easy. . . .

It was a party of only eleven, and of these Sir Edward [Lytton] was one, Robert Browning another, and a Mr. [E. M.] Ward, a well known artist and member of the Royal Academy, was a third. All were people of a stamp, you know; as different from the sky-blue, skim-milk of the ball-rooms, as good old burgundy is from syrup-lemonade. I had a royal evening; a feast of remarkable choiceness, for the meats were very excellent good, the wines were rare and plentiful, and the company was of earth's choicest.

Sir Edward is one of the ugliest men it has been my good luck to meet. He is tall and slouchy, careless in his habits, deaf as a ci-devant, mild in manner, and quiet and philosophic in talk. Browning is neat, lively, impetuous, full of animation, and very un-English in all his opinions and appearance. Here, in London Society, famous as he is, half his entertainers actually take him to be an American. He told us some amusing stories about this, one evening when he dined here.

Just to amuse you, I will try to give you an idea of the conversation after dinner; the first time I have ever heard anything of the sort in England. Sir Edward is a great smoker, and although no crime can be greater in this country, our host produced cigars after the ladies had left, and we filled our claret-glasses and drew up together.

Sir Edward seemed to be continuing a conversation with Mr. Ward, his neighbor. He went on, in his thoughtful, deliberative way, addressing Browning.

"Do you think your success would be very much more valuable to you for knowing that centuries hence, you would still be remembered? Do you look to the future connection by a portion of mankind, of certain ideas with your name, as the great reward of all your labor?"

"Not in the least! I am perfectly indifferent whether my name is remembered or not. The reward would be that the ideas which were mine, should live and benefit the race!"

"I am glad to hear you say so," continued Sir Edward, thoughtfully, "because it has always seemed so to me, and your opinion supports mine. Life, I take to be a period of preparation. I should compare it to a preparatory school. Though it is true that in one respect the comparison is not just, since the time we pass at a preparatory school bears an infinitely greater proportion to a life, than a life does to eternity. Yet I think it may be compared to a boy's school; such a one as I used to go to, as a child, at old Mrs. S's at Fulham. Now if one of my old school-mates there were to meet me some day and seem delighted to see me, and asked me whether I recollected going to old mother S's at Fulham, I should say, 'Well, yes. I did have some faint remembrance of it! Yes. I could recollect about it.' And then supposing he were to tell me how I was still remembered there! How much they talked of what a fine fellow I'd been at that school."

"How Jones Minimus," broke in Browning, "said you were the most awfully good fellow he ever saw."

"Precisely," Sir Edward went on, beginning to warm to his idea. "Should I be very much delighted to hear that? Would it make me forget what I am doing now? For five minutes perhaps I should feel gratified and pleased that I was still remembered, but that would be all. I should go back to my work without a second thought about it.

"Well now, Browning, suppose you, sometime or other, were to meet Shakespeare, as perhaps some of us may. You would rush to him and seize his hand, and cry out, 'My dear Shakespeare, how delighted I am to see you. You can't imagine how much they think and talk about you on the earth!' Do you suppose Shakespeare would be more carried away by such an announcement than I should be at hearing that I was still remembered by the boys at mother S's at Fulham? What possible advantage can it be to him to know that what he did on the earth is still remembered there?"

The same idea is in LXIII of Tennyson's In Memoriam, but not pointed the same way. It was curious to see two men who, of all others, write for fame, or have done so, ridicule the idea of its real value to them. But Browning went on to get into a very unorthodox humor, and developed a spiritual election that would shock the Pope, I fear. According to him, the minds or souls that really did develope themselves and educate themselves in life, could alone expect to enter a future career for which this life was a preparatory course. The rest were rejected, turned back, God knows what becomes of them, these myriads of savages and brutalized and degraded Christians. Only those that could pass the examination were allowed to commence the new career. This is Calvin's theory, modified; and really it seems not unlikely to me. Thus this earth may serve as a sort of feeder to the next world, as the lower and middle classes here do to the aristocracy, here and there furnishing a member to fill the gaps. The corollaries of this proposition are amusing to work out.

To CHARLES FRANCIS ADAMS, JR.

London, October 2, 1863.

The Scotia's telegram has just arrived, and for an hour or two past, I have been reflecting on the news it brings of what I conceive to be a very severe defeat of Rosecrans. At this distance and with our mere scraps of doubtful intelligence, I am painfully impressed with the conviction that our Government has been again proved incompetent, and has neglected to take those measures of security which it ought to have done, expecting as we all did, just this movement, or the corresponding one on Washington. I imagine that this mischance insures us another year of war, unless the army of the Potomac shows more energy than usual and more success than ever yet. The truth is, everything in this universe has its regular waves and tides. Electricity, sound, the wind, and I believe every part of organic nature will be brought some day within this law. But my philosophy teaches me, and I firmly believe it, that the laws which govern animated beings will be ultimately found to be at bottom the same with those which rule inanimate nature, and, as I entertain a profound conviction of the littleness of our kind, and of the curious enormity of creation, I am quite ready to receive with pleasure any basis for a systematic conception of it all. Thus (to explain this rather alarming digression) as sort of experimentalist, I look for regular tides in the affairs of man, and of course, in our own affairs. In every progression, somehow or other, the nations move by the same process which has never been explained but is evident in the ocean and the air. On this theory I should expect at about this time, a turn which would carry us backward. The devil of it is, supposing there comes a time when the rebs suddenly cave in, how am I to explain that!

This little example of my unpractical experimento-philosophico-historico-progressiveness will be enough. It suffices to say that I am seeking to console my trouble by chewing the dry husks of that philosophy which, whether it calls itself submission to the will of God, or to the laws of nature, rests in bottom simply and solely upon an acknowledgment of our own impotence and ignorance. In this amusement I find, if not consolation at least some sort of mental titillation. Besides, I am becoming superstitious. I believe Nick Anderson's killed. Write me that he's not yet gone under, and I will say defiance to the vague breath of similar chimaeras. . . .

To JOHN GORHAM PALFREY

London, 15th April, 1864.

. . . Time rattles along so fast that this letter will scarcely reach you before the third anniversary of our departure. We are settled here now nearly as much at home as though we were in Boston, so far as familiarity with our surroundings go, and yet London never seems to me to allow any homelike feelings. I never quit it even for an afternoon at Richmond or a Sunday at Walton, without feeling a sort of shudder at returning, to be struck as freshly as ever with the solemnity, the gloom, the squalor and the horrible misery and degradation that seem to me to brood over the place. The magnificence I know and can appreciate. It has done its best to make me a socialist and has nearly succeeded. The society I think dull, and the art and literature poor. So that you see I am well suited to return to Boston unspoiled by my travels, a sadder and a wiser man.

Our great event just now is the arrival of Garibaldi, and his reception. Of all curious events, this is the most extraordinary. You know what Garibaldi is; the companion of Mazzini; the representative of the "cosmopolitan revolution"; a regular "child of Nature," unintellectual, uncultivated; but enthusiastic and a genius. Every Government in Europe dreads him, or rather his party, and he is the enemy of them all and of none more, whether he will or no, than of England. Suddenly he drops down here, and the people, the real "dangerous classes" go out to meet him with such a reception as never was known before. It was a regular uprising of democracy. But then to our delight, the young Duke and Duchess of Sutherland get hold of him, and at once compromise the whole English aristocracy, and give a hoist to the *rouges* and the democracy throughout Europe, by bringing him to Stafford House and making themselves co-conspirators with every refugee in England, to murder Napoleon, destroy Victor Emmanuel, and proclaim equality and division of property. I don't think I exaggerate the moral effect of this affair on the minds of the democrats. I am a real Garibaldian, and ready to accept, if necessary, his views, at the same time that I think hero-worship, as such, is a precious dangerous thing to meddle with. But here is the whole Clan Sutherland, with the young Duke dancing about at its head, forcing Garibaldi down the throats of the English nobility, who daren't openly say no, and who make the worst faces at the process, you can conceive. A few nights since, Stafford House was thrown open for a reception in honor of the General. By the way, what a glorious palace it is. I would like to have such a one at Quincy. We went; the only diplomats there except the Turk. Garibaldi was there; quantum mutatus ab illo Garibaldio that I saw four years ago, surrounded by a yelling mob in Palermo, with a few hundred guerilla troops, and not a nobleman among them. The beautiful young Duchess had him by the arm; she glittering with *the* diamonds; he in a military, loose poncho, or cape. The Duke pirouetted before, behind, and on either side. The Duchess Dowager sailed majestically alongside, battling fiercely for the honor of being chief-keeper, but kept silent by her splendid daughter-in-law. In a tangled and promiscuous medley followed the Argylls, Tauntons, Howards, Blantyres, and every Leveson-Gower that draws breath. They paraded through the apartments, as well as Garibaldi could limp along, and we poor lookers-on drew aside and formed a passage for the procession triumphant to pass through. It was superb! And yet almost the last great occasion that Stafford House was open, was to allow this perfect nobility to do honor to Mrs. Beecher Stowe, and both then and now the whole thing too strongly resembles a desperate humbug for me to be much impressed by it. Sentimental liberalism is pretty, but it won't hold. Garibaldi is pretty safe to suffer the fate of Mrs. Stowe, and American anti-slavery, whenever he stands in need of aristocratic aid. Meanwhile he sits at the feet of the beautiful Duchess (and there he is indeed to be envied) and smokes his cigars in her boudoir, and goes to bed immediately after dinner, and smokes in bed; and has two shirts (the famous red flannel) and a light blue cape lined with red (*rouge,* you see, always), which constitute his entire wardrobe. And in short, I rather doubt whether the good hero yet quite knows where he is, or has any clear idea of how it happens that he who has de-

clared war to the knife against aristocracy and privilege everywhere, has become himself an aristocrat so suddenly. Meanwhile the non-Sutherland aristocracy growl fiercely, but are regularly over-sloughed by the popular wave, and we outsiders
think it all as good a practical joke as ever was got up.

When shall we come home? After this season is over, we shall
become very restless and if the war is over, as we strongly hope,
we must leave here. I wonder whether Sumner wouldn't take
the place. I suppose he might get it if he wanted it, on our departure. Then Gov. Andrew could replace him in the Senate,
which would be an improvement. I hope to find you and yours,
including Frank, well and prosperous at my return; and for
my own part am ready to leave the Society of Courts to those
that are courtiers, and rest awhile at the law-school in Cambridge or elsewhere. . . .

To CHARLES FRANCIS ADAMS, JR.

London, November 25, 1864.

. . . The election is over then, and after all that excitement,
worry and danger, behold, all goes on as before. It was one of
those cases in which life and death seemed to hang on the issue,
and the result is so decisive as to answer all our wishes and
hopes. It is a curious commentary upon theoretical reasoning as
to forms of Government, that this election which ought by all
rights to be a defect in the system, and which is universally considered by the admirers of "strong Governments" to be a proof
of the advantage of their own model, should yet turn out in
practice a great and positive gain and a fruitful source of national strength. After all, systems of Government are secondary
matters, if you've only got your people behind them. I never yet
have felt so proud as now of the great qualities of our race, or so
confident of the capacity of men to develop their faculties in the
mass. I believe that a new era of the movement of the world

will date from that day, which will drag nations up still another step, and carry us out of a quantity of old fogs. Europe has a long way to go yet to catch us up.

Anything that produces a great effect in our favor on this side, usually produces a sort of general silence as the first proof of its force. So this election has been met on this side by a species of blindness. People remark the fact with wonder and anger, but they have only just such a vague idea of what are to be its consequences, as shuts their mouths without changing their opinions. Only the most clear-headed see indistinctly what bearing it is likely to have on English politics, and I expect that it will be years yet before its full action gets into play. Meanwhile the Government is now stronger than ever and our only weak point is the financial one. May our name not have to stand guard on that! . . .

To CHARLES FRANCIS ADAMS, JR.

Florence, 10 May, 1865.

I can't help a feeling of amusement at looking back on my letters and thinking how curiously inapt they must have been to the state of things about you. Victories and assassinations, joys, triumphs, sorrows and gloom; all at fever point, with you; while I prate about art and draw out letters from the sunniest and most placid of subjects. I have already buried Mr. Lincoln under the ruins of the Capitol, along with Cæsar, and this I don't mean merely as a phrase. We must have our wars, it appears, and our crimes, as well as other countries. I think Abraham Lincoln is rather to be envied in his death, as in his life somewhat; and if he wasn't as great as Cæsar, he shows the same sort of tomb. History repeats itself, and if we are to imitate the atrocities of Rome, I find a certain amusement in conducting my private funeral service over the victims, on the ground that is most suitable for such associations, of any in the world.

But the King being dead, what then? Are we to cry "Live the King" again? To me this great change looks like a step downward to our generation. New men have come. Will the old set hold their ground, or is Seward and the long-lived race about him, to make way for a young America which we do not know? You may guess how I have smiled sweetly on the chains that held me here at such a time, and swore polyglot oaths at Italy and everything else that keeps me here. I have looked towards London as earnestly as What's-her-name looked from Bluebeard's tower, for the signs of the coming era, but no sign is given. The Minister is waiting also apparently. I have written to him that *of course* now he must remain where he is, but whether he agrees to the of course or not, I can't say. It is clear to me that if Seward lives, he must stay; and if Seward retires, he should leave upon the new Secretary the responsibility of making a change. To throw up his office would be unpatriotic; it would be a blunder. Do you assent to my doctrine? To be away from my place at such a time is enough to enrage a tadpole. And I can't be back before the end of June. . . .

To CHARLES MILNES GASKELL

158 G Street, Washington, D.C.,
5 November, 1868.

Eccolà! If you can master the idea of streets named after letters of the alphabet, know that the above is my address. Moreover, "D.C." stands for District of Columbia, though you mightn't guess it. The great step is taken, and here I am, settled for years, and perhaps for life. Your last letter was sent on to me a few days ago.

My experiences so far have not been disagreeable, and yet I

think and hope they have been the least agreeable part of my experiences past or to come. I left Boston on the 12th of October and stopped several days in New York, intending to come on here and stay at a hotel until I could move into rooms. But one day I met Mr. Evarts on the street. You recollect his visit to Cambridge with me in 1863, since which he has become a great man, saving the President in the Impeachment by his skill as Counsel, and in consequence of his services then, appointed a member of the Cabinet as Attorney General not long afterwards. He stopped me to urge that I should stay at his house in Washington until I settled myself. Naturally I assented and we came on together. His family was all away, and he and I kept house for ten days. He took me to call on the President, who was grave and cordial, and gave me a little lecture on constitutional law. The Secretary of State, as we call the Foreign Secretary, Mr. Seward, was also cordial, and his major-domo selected rooms for me. With the Secretary of the Treasury [Hugh McCulloch], I am on the best of terms and he pats me on the back, not figuratively but in the flesh. Finally the Secretary of War [J. McA. Schofield] and I are companions. The account so far is a good one, is it not? Unfortunately this whole Cabinet goes out on the fourth of March, and in the next one I shall probably be without a friend. Politics make a bad trade.

I staid ten days with the Attorney General and then I moved to the house of an aunt I have here, where I still remain while my rooms get into shape. If you come over, I can give you a bed and you can stay as long as you will. You will find all my old books in my cases, my drawings (and memorials of Cannes) on the walls, and my lion and ostrich magnificent and beautiful for ever. My establishment is modest, for my means are exiguous, but it has more civilisation in it than the rest of Washington all together. Come and see.

In fact this is the drollest place in Christian lands. Such a thin veil of varnish over so very rough a material, one can see nowhere else. But for all that, there are strong points about it. From the window of my room I can as I sit see for miles down the Potomac, and I know of no other capital in the world which stands on so wide and splendid a river. But the people and the mode of life are enough to take your hair off. I think I see you trying to live here. You couldn't stand it four-and-twenty hours. Alas! I fear I never shall eat another good dinner.

My geological article was published a month ago, after I left Boston and I have heard nothing of it (the best news I could hear), except that it has paid me £20. I am now beginning Finance again, and you will probably read as much as the title of my next production. In about five years I expect to have conquered a reputation. But what it may be worth when got, is more than I can tell. The sad truth is that I want nothing and life seems to have no purpose.

Our elections as you see, have passed off as everyone expected and we are approaching a new reign. Personally we have nothing to expect from it. My father is not in sympathy with the party in power, and my brother [John] is a prominent opponent of it. I am too insignificant a cuss to have my opinion asked, but my eyes and ears are wide open, and we mean to be seen and be heard as well as see and hear. I wait now with great interest for your election. Write soon about it. Give my best love to everyone. I shall write again soon.

To CHARLES FRANCIS ADAMS, JR.

Friday, 21 May, 1869.

. . . I see you are getting back to your old dispute with me on the purpose of life, by means of an attack on my self-esteem. You are quite right in the point you make. I do think too much about my own productions and myself generally. Stick to that and you may kick me all day long. I will not go down into the rough-and-tumble, nor mix with the crowd, nor write anonymously, except for mere literary practice. My path is a different one; and was never chosen in order to suit other people's tastes, but my own. Of course a man can't do this without appearing to think a great deal about himself, and perhaps doing so in fact. The very line he draws requires care to observe, and is invidious to everyone else. In America there is so such class, and the tendency is incessant to draw everyone into the main current. I have told you before that I mean to be unpopular, and do it because I must do it, or do as other people do and give up the path I chose for myself years ago. Your ideas and mine don't agree, but they never have agreed. You like the strife of the world. I detest it and despise it. You work for power. I work for my own satisfaction. You like roughness and strength; I like taste and dexterity. For God's sake, let us go our ways and not try to be like each other.

To CHARLES MILNES GASKELL

Quincy, Massachusetts, 5 October, 1869.

Yours of 12th September having reached me, I disinterred your last three letters to discover what it was I had failed to answer, but am still left in the dark. My disquisition on American literature was, I think, exhaustive, to use a newspaper expression. I called your attention to all that was worth it. You asked about Jefferson and I recommended his famous Declaration of Independence as the best specimen of his style. You can quote a few paragraphs with effect. There is nothing in Everett. Webster's best things were legal arguments and you don't care for got-up eloquence. By all means quote the whole of Lincoln's little speech at Gettysburg and a sentence or two from his second Inaugural to show the biblical influence on American minds. In poetry you might extract from Bryant the last few lines of Thanatopsis, or the lines to a water-fowl, or the "melancholy days have come;" from Longfellow a stanza or two of the Wreck of the Hesperus or the Skeleton in Armor, both pretty ballads well adapted to a popular audience; from Lowell a stanza or two from the first series of Biglow Papers, the one signed "Bird o' Freedom Sawin" would be best for your purpose and would make your audience laugh, or in another poem the "Vision of Sir Launfal" there is a pretty description of June and winter as an example of Lowell's other style; from Whittier a ballad, say Maud Muller, or two or three verses about scenery, "nowhere fairer, sweeter, rarer," in the Ranger. If you want a specimen of style from Hawthorne, take the description of old Pynchon sitting dead in his chair, in the *Seven Gables,* or the discovery of Zenobia's body, in the *Blithedale Romance.* Your audience will listen hard to either. Mrs. Stowe's scenes with Topsy in *Uncle Tom* are about as good as anything she has done—always excepting her *Byron.* It is a pity you can't quote some choice lines from Walt Whitman. In the way of letters there is nothing but my old great-grandmother Abigail Adams's that are worth reading, and I don't remember anything to your purpose in them. You don't want to be didactic and you do want to amuse your audience, so I advise you not to dwell long on historians, essayists or critics, except in the case of Washington Irving whose account of Bracebridge Hall might amuse, and is a good specimen of his style. A few sentences or half a page of it would do for you to point the customary allusion to Addison upon. Cooper's novels are no great.

But if you want really to run over the old ground there is a sort of *Cyclopædia of American literature,* full of biographical notices and elegant extracts, like the English one of Chambers. If you are in London you will find it at some of the libraries. There is nothing very new. We have no writers now.

Since my last, we have been invaded by Englishmen. Old Sir

H. Holland has been with us, as much of a bore as ever. Your friend Robarts too has turned up and passed a night here. We were agreeably disappointed in him. He is perhaps a bore, but not very radical, and decidedly a gentleman in manners and talk. In fact, my boy, if you could see the Britishers we do groan under in this country, you would think Robarts a model of everything attractive. He returns to England tomorrow with Sir H. H. Another individual named Lawrence has also been here from Wimbledon way. I know no more of him.

A letter from Robert [Cunliffe] at Cologne reached me with yours, bringing me the pleasant suggestion of honeymoons, the Rhine, Venice and Sorrento. I suppose the youth is lost to us, but don't, for the Lord's sake, allow yourself to be lost too. The only condition on which existence is tolerable for solitary fowl like you and me, is that of living in the thickest of the world. Once fall and let it go over us, and we had better die. . . .

I have no special news for you. I believe I told you that I am just *accouché* of another article in the *N. A. R.* which will appear in a fortnight. It is rather bitter, rather slashing, very personal, and the editor and my brother speak highly of it. No one else has seen it. I expect to get into hot water, and shall be disappointed if no one retaliates on me. Three weeks hence I return to Washington to start again, and expect to have work to do. Meanwhile I am reading Gibbon and wasting time. . . .

To CHARLES MILNES GASKELL

Washington, 23 November, 1869.

I sit down to begin you a letter, not because I have received one since my last, but because it is one of the dankest, foggiest, and dismalest of November nights, and, as usual when the sun does not shine, I am as out of sorts as a man may haply be, and yet live through it. Do you remember how, on such evenings we

have taken our melancholy tea together in your room in Strat-
ford Place? My heart would rejoice to do it now, but solitude
is my lot. This season of the year grinds the very soul out of me.
My nerves lose their tone; my teeth ache, and my courage falls
to the bottomless bottom of infinitude. Death stalks about me,
and the whole of Gray's grisly train, and I am afraid of them,
not because life is an object, but because my nerves are upset.
I would give up all my pleasures willingly if I could only be a
mouse, and sleep three months at a time. Well! one can't have
life as one would, but if ever I take too much laudanum, the
coroner's jury may bring in a verdict of wilful murder against
the month of November. Bah! I never felt it half so keenly
when I was in England where there is never any sun.

Now then, where may we sometimes meet and by the fire
help waste a sullen day, what time we can from the sad season
gaining? And to think that the brute Robert is happy and gay
in the sunshine of Rome! I am as lonely as a cat here. Acquaintances without number I have, but no companion. And what
avails it to be intimate with all men if one comes home at five
o'clock and abhors life! Send a decent Britisher here, do!

Do you know I have taken up the ever youthful Horace Walpole again, and make him my dinner companion. What surprises me most is that he is so extremely like ourselves; not so
clever of course, but otherwise he might be a letter-writer of today. I perpetually catch myself thinking of it all as of something
I have myself known, until I trip over a sword, or discover there
were no railways then, or reflect that Lord Salisbury and not
Lord Carteret lives over the way. But all seems astonishingly
natural to me; strangely in contrast to what it once seemed. If
we didn't know those people—Primo-ministerio Palmerstonis—
then we knew some one for all the world like them. Florence
too! *Peste!* how little the world has changed in a century.

Hanbury-Williams and Watkin-Wynn, Hervey; Arlington Street; I know I shall find Lady Sebright further on, and Lady Salisbury will come in for a wipe.

What! shall I imitate H. W. and tell you about this Court; a pack of boobies and scoundrels who have all the vices of H. W.'s time, with none of its wit or refinement? Or force either, for the matter of that! For where to find a Walpole or a Pitt here, I am at a loss to know. We are all Pelhams, and our President is as narrow, as ignorant, and as prejudiced as ever a George among you. Your friend—*que voici*—alone, and a few others, have any brain. But what of that! The world goes on, and I send you herewith my last political pamphlet which, I have reason to know, represents the opinions of a minority, and, I think, of a majority of the Cabinet. The violent attack on the Treasury has done me no harm.

I am writing, writing, writing. You must take the *New York Nation* if you want to read me. I have written that animal Reeve a letter, offering him an article—such an article!—and he does not even answer it! I have written to Palgrave to make advances to the *Quarterly,* and I will make my article *SUPERB* to disgust Reeve. I enclose you a puff—from my own paper. But it is written by a Britisher.

To CHARLES MILNES GASKELL

Washington [Dec. 13], 1869.

. . . At length I expect to conclude this species of autobiography which is becoming a volume. I have no news to give you of my family except that all were well last week, and actively employed in beginning their fashionable season. They seem to be very happy and contented as usual. My father is hard at work arranging family papers for publication, and is likely to do nothing else for years to come. My mother is doing nothing but fuss over her household, which is now quite a small one, as my younger brother [Brooks] is at College and I am away.

You talk of "celebrating" my arrival next year. Ah, my child, hold thyself far from it! Let us be quiet and sober lest the Gods should again be wrathful! We will silently eat our chop (with sauce Soubise; my weakness when well made) and drink a very little really dry champagne (which, alas, does not exist in this hemisphere) and when we talk just an old hour afterwards, we will talk soberly, allowing ourselves to sink out of our weary minds, and drawing mild hope and consolation from literature, art, society, if you will, but not from that society where our calmness is ruffled by obnoxious people. I go to England for a moral bath. I want to wash out the dirty creases which life is making in the corners of my soul's eyes. I want to forget myself if I can, and enjoy what is outside of me. Let us get rid, therefore, so far as may be, of the vanities of life and of its social trials, and become serene Epicureans for a month, at least. Find me a place in London where we can be contented with a little, but let that little be so good that it will reconcile us with the fatigue of living, and strengthen our faith in Providence!

Don't show this at Pantyochin! The old ladies might not quite see that my influence is good in the main.

What is your uncle's [Sir F. Doyle] address? I want to send him a copy of my pamphlet in acknowledgment of his lectures last year. I would send one to Lady Salisbury if they weren't such bitter America-phobists in that house. As my production would flatter their pride and encourage their contempt, I prefer to wash my dirty linen quietly at home. I would like to show you some of the attacks I have met in the press here. They are usually based on my great-grandfather, but occasionally on my extreme youth, and I expect to catch it hotter than ever in the course of the winter when the subject comes up in Congress. Before long I expect to be quite crushed, and then, please God, I will retaliate with a Dunciad.

Last evening I went with General Badeau to call for the first time on the President and his wife. We were admitted to the room where General Grant and half a dozen of his intimates sat in a circle, the General smoking as usual. There was some round conversation, rather dull. At last Mrs. Grant strolled in. She squints like an isosceles triangle, but is not much more vulgar than some Duchesses. Her sense of dignity did not allow her to talk to me, but occasionally she condescended to throw me a constrained remark. I chattered, however, with that blandness for which I am so justly distinguished, and I flatter myself it was I who showed them how they ought to behave. One feels such an irresistible desire, as you know, to tell this kind of individual to put themselves at their ease and talk just as though they were at home. I restrained it, however, and performed the part of guest, though you can imagine with what an effort.

Won't you be glad to find this letter has an end! And nothing to talk about either! Well! addio! sleep well after it.

II

THE HARVARD YEARS AND WASHINGTON

1870–1885

ADAMS's career as a college professor lasted just seven years—the period beyond which, as he later remarked, a man ceases to be good for anything else. He had proved to be a distinguished teacher, nevertheless, and some of the fruits of his teaching appeared in 1876 when, in company with some of his best students, he published a volume of studies entitled *Essays in Anglo-Saxon Law*. Meanwhile, in 1871, with his brother Charles, he had reprinted some of his political and financial essays in a collaborative volume called *Chapters of Erie*. From 1870 to 1876 Adams also found the time and energy to edit the *North American Review*, but finally resigned from his editorship owing to a political disagreement with the publisher.

In 1872 he had married Marian Hooper, of Boston, and the following year was spent in Europe and Egypt on a wedding tour. After Adams resigned from his professorship, in 1877, he and his wife moved to Washington, where he wrote his *Life of Albert Gallatin* (1879) and began work on his great *History of the United States during the Administrations of Jefferson and Madison*. Much of the research for his history was done in London, Paris, and Madrid during a European stay in 1879. In 1880 Adams published anonymously a political novel, *Democracy*, and in 1884 a second novel, *Esther*, under the pseudonym Frances Snow Compton. These years, in short, were extremely productive ones, and the friendship of people like Clarence King, the John Hays, and the Camerons made them, at least for Adams himself, happy years. Such happiness as they brought him, however, was abruptly and terribly destroyed when, on Dec. 6, 1885, after some months of severe depression, Marian Adams committed suicide.

To CHARLES MILNES GASKELL

Harvard College, Cambridge, Mass.
19 November, 1870.

Besides a letter from Frank Doyle, with his photographs, I have lately received a letter from Robert, yours of October 28, and this morning one from Palgrave, so that I am now deep in debt. As it happens that I am fearfully hard worked, my chances for letter-writing are fewer than I could wish, but then you will no doubt be recompensed by your appreciation of my great importance, which lends so much more value to my remarks. My reputation for deep historical research is awful. I have, however, unearthed only one important fact on which I propose to dwell at great length to my classes, which is that your Norman ancestors were principally distinguished as a class for one peculiar vice which modern prejudice has absurdly condemned as unnatural, and thus that Messrs. B——, P—— and Lord A—— C—— are evidently descended from William the Conqueror and proudly justify their claim to be considered among your best and oldest families. Unfortunately I have to devote so much time to the mere work of my lectures that I cannot go so deeply into this interesting subject as I should.

Between my history and my *Review* I have all I can manage. The retirement from Washington has by no means thrown me out of politics. On the contrary, as editor I am deeper in them than ever, and my party is growing so rapidly that I look forward to the day when we shall be in power again as not far distant. Two or three years ought to do it. Meanwhile I am smashing things here, and have declared war against the old system of teaching, in a manner which is not respectful to the University though my students like it. All this is very grand of course. Equally of course it is probably unmitigated rot. But who cares? So long as I am amused, I mean to go on with it, and to be very busy is a sort of amusement. At any rate I have no time to think of disagreeable subjects, and if our climate were less of a nuisance I should feel fairly satisfied.

I see that the last *Westminster* contains my article, about which I had so much difficulty while with you. I sent it to the editor just as I was coming away, as a last experiment, and heard no more of it till I saw it in print. The editor has not written to me on the subject, and I have not written to him.

Your English gossip interests me in my western banishment. I am sorry for the Motleys, especially as he has now received his *coup de grâce* in peremptory dismissal. For skill in insulting people commend me to our excellent President [Grant]. I suspect he will get us into trouble with you before long, and if you go to war with Russia as you seem bent on doing, you will certainly have us on your backs. It is not very creditable to us to pursue a policy of this sort, but I have no doubt we shall do it, as we have made no secret of our intentions. In case of a war, I shall wait till it is over before I next visit England, for I don't mean to fight and I shall not be found in the ranks of the army that sacks Wenlock. I presume you will not cross the ocean to attack Quincy, but if you are the destined man to plunder my ancestral halls, I prefer your doing it to another. You'll find little to loot. Save the spoons. They will serve for Wenlock when I next come. . . .

My people seem to be tolerably well. They are now in Boston

and I go in occasionally and dine with them. As yet I have seen no society. I am too busy and have to read every evening as my young men are disgustingly clever at upsetting me with questions. Luckily I have a little general knowledge which comes in. I gave them the other day a poetical account of Wenlock in relation to Gregory VII and Cluny. You see how everything can be made to answer a purpose.

Next week I go on to New York to a political gathering of members of the press on my side; quite a demonstration, which will make a noise in the newspapers. I go to press the interests of my *Review*. Meanwhile my flock must wait for their historical fodder till I return.

Frank's photographs are very pleasant little reminders of our summer. I shall stick them in a book with—F. Doyle, Maj. Gen. fecit—under them. Give my love to Robert. I shall write to him soon. Also to his wife. I suppose things look lively in politics now, and I hope your turn is coming.

To CHARLES MILNES GASKELL

Harvard College, 19 December, 1870.

It's an age since I wrote, but if you will credit the alarming fact, I am now driven to use the official time of the College to give to you. Here I sit, at the regular meeting of the College Faculty, while some thirty twaddlers are discussing questions of discipline around me, and I have to hear what they say, while I indulge you in the charms and fascinations of my style. This is what it is to be a Professor, not to say an editor. I have not had a clear hour of time for a month. I have read more heavy German books and passed more time in the printing-office; I have written more letters on business, and read more manuscripts of authors; I have delivered more lectures about matters I knew nothing of, to men who cared nothing about them; and I have

had my nose ground down more closely to my double grind-
stone, than ever a cruel Providence can have considered possible. My happy carelessness of life for the last ten years has departed, and I am a regular old carthorse of the heaviest sort.
As for society, I have not seen the hem of a female garment
since I came out here. Life has resolved itself into editing and
professing. I always swore I never would descend to work, but
it is done. Lo! the poor fallen one!

The curious part of it all is that I don't dislike it so much as
I expected. I am so busy that I have not had the time to think
whether I enjoyed myself or not, and now the Christmas holidays are nearly here, and I am so nearly half through the year,
at least in labor, that it quite bewilders me to think how time
goes. I wish you would try a few months of good hard work,
when you have to count your minutes to keep abreast of the
team, and then tell me how you like it. I believe it would do
you good. But how these old buffers do bore me! They talk!
talk! talk! Ugh!! I wish I could scalp 'em.

Have I sent you my circular? No? I will!! It is grand, and involves the deepest interests of literature. I am sending it to all
mankind, and of course mankind rushes to see it. Apropos! I
have never sent you the reply which Senator Howe of Wisconsin
made to my "Session." He blackguards me and all my family
to the remotest generation. He calls me a begonia! a plant, I
am told. To be abused by a Senator is my highest ambition,
and I am now quite happy. My only regret is that I cannot afford to hire a Senator to abuse me permanently. That, however, might pall in time, like plum-pudding or——.

At the end of this week, just as soon as I have got my January *Review* off my shoulders I shall go on to Washington for
the holidays. This is the only recess I get for six months, and I
want to make the most of it. What do I do after getting there? I

go to my dentist's, oh, my friend! Yes! I pass a fortnight with my dentist. At any rate he will stop my talking for a time.

Will Everett is here in the room. Shall I ask him whether he has any message to send you? I will——

He says he is going to write to you himself and send you some of his publications.

By the way, I am told that his children's books are not at all bad. Perhaps your mind, after Siluria, will be ready to unbend to them. I see poor old Murchison has gone up. He ought to, after such a work. Will is now making a speech—Heaven bless him! Lord, how dull they all are!

What a droll idea it is that you should be running about England, visiting people, and I shut up in this Botany Bay, working like a scavenger. Lord bless me! Do those people really exist, or did I dream it all, after reading Horace Walpole and eating a heavy dinner? I doubt your existence at times, and am not altogether certain about my own. Give my tender love to Gretchen—I mean Lady Margaret. What dress does she wear now? How are the Marguerites?

By the bye! Do you know that I hope to appear soon at the bar of the Old Bailey, or whichever of your Courts has the jurisdiction? James McHenry wants to sue me for a libel. I have written over that this is precisely what would suit me, and that he may try it if he likes. You will, I doubt not, hear of it, if the *Westminster Review* is brought into Court. Perhaps it would bring me over to England again, as I mean to hurt him if he gives me a chance.

I went to New York a month ago to a political meeting, and we laid vast and ambitious projects for the future.

But the Meeting is breaking up, and I must break up too! Thank the Lord! The clack is passed for one week, and a week hence I shall be in Washington.

To CHARLES MILNES GASKELL

Cambridge, 20 June, 1871.

Your letter and manuscript arrived some time ago, but I have been so busy finishing up the year's work, that I have not had a minute to spare. I was glad to hear that you had got into harness, not that I think your enjoyment of the work will be intense, but that, such as it is, it will drive you to new fields and make you think of new subjects. If you are half as bored as I am by thinking of the old ones, you will find the change agreeable.

I write now from among a dozen of my boys who are indulging in the excitement of an "Annual," an institution not unlike your Cambridge "Little go," except that ours come every year. The poor wretches have to pass a week in the examination rooms and I am sorry to say that I am the object of unlimited cursing, owing to the fact that I intentionally gave them papers so difficult that half the youths could do very little with them. I very nearly had a rebellion, but I think they will find out that no one is hurt who doesn't deserve it. Mine is an "elective" department, and I have been obliged to drive the lazy men out of it, which can only be done by putting gentle pressure on them, the "gentleness" consisting in telling them that I will take away their degrees if they ever put themselves in my clutches again. It would be fun to send you some of my examination papers. My rule in making them up is to ask questions which I can't myself answer. It astounds me to see how some of my students answer questions which would play the deuce with me.

After this week I am, I hope, free again, and unless some unexpected difficulty arises I shall at once start on an expedition which will lead me for the next six weeks into paths unknown to European blokes. My friend [Samuel Franklin Emmons] who is engaged on a government survey in the West has asked me to go with his party on an expedition down the cañon of the Green river, an upper branch of the Colorado. If you have a modern atlas you may find the district not far from Salt Lake and the Mormons, a hundred or two miles to the Southeast. Of course it is an absolute wilderness. We carry our camp with us and geologise, shoot, fish, or march, as occasion requires. I shall not be back within reach of mankind before the 1st September, and my next letter to you may perhaps be written from a country wilder than anything in Siberia.

At the same time I shall not feel sure of getting away until I am fairly a day's march from Fort Bridger. As luck will have it my sister has just been taken down with one of her terrible colds, and I may have to remain about here in order to travel with her, as she needs a change. Then, too, I have so many irons in the fire, so much printing going on, and correspondence to look to, that I never feel sure of my own time. My July *Review*, a very dull number, is just going through the press (you will appear in it in due course, not, I hope, to the increase of its dulness,) and my October number has got to be seen to. Meanwhile my lectures are all in arrears, and literally I have no time for reading or study. The last few weeks of the year are mere drudgery. Luckily the weather has been cool and we have had rain, not before it was needed. Within three months of the time when I wrote you that the thermometer was at 10° below zero, the same thermometer at my window stood at 93° in the shade. I call that a fair range.

Now that my first year is fairly over I am racking my brains to decide whether I ought to consider it successful or not. As things go, and as professors run, I suppose I have done fairly, but from any absolute point of view I am still nowhere. Fortunately I came here with few illusions, and have had all the advantage I counted on. Whether Will Everett is equally self-satisfied I don't know. He has had more difficulties to meet, and

two hundred very unruly boys to control. I am told that his eccentricities are growing on him; he is more than ever given to
hysterics; but he has held his own better than I expected. As
I have managed to get into the "inside ring," as Americans say,
the small set of men who control the University, I have things
my own way. Will is less lucky. He can't get things to suit him.

So you are fairly in Norfolk Street. I hope you find it swell. I
hear nothing of the London season. Are there any new beauties? Are any of our friends going into the Tuileries when re-
built? And are any Britishers coming over here? I have seen
none for an age. . . .

To CHARLES MILNES GASKELL

Harvard College, 26 March, 1872.

Your Roman epistle of the 5th inst. has just reached me. As
you are on your wanderings, I rather doubt whether my letter
written in a great hurry some four weeks since, with announcement of my engagement, has yet reached you. As the event became public here about the tenth, and created quite a lively
sensation in this rural community, I suppose some one will have
posted you up about it before you reach England.

Having now had a month to quiet down, I start on another
letter to tell you all I did not tell you before. Imprimis and to
begin with, the young woman calls herself Marian Hooper and
belongs to a sort of clan, as all Bostonians do. Through her
mother, who is not living, she is half Sturgis, and Russell
Sturgis of the Barings is a fourth cousin or thereabouts. Socially
the match is supposed to be unexceptionable. One of my con-
gratulatory letters further describes my "fiancée" to me as "a
charming blue." She is certainly not handsome; nor would she
be quite called plain, I think. She is twenty-eight years old. She
knows her own mind uncommon well. She does not talk *very*
American. Her manners are quiet. She reads German—also

Latin—also, I fear, a little Greek, but very little. She talks garrulously, but on the whole pretty sensibly. She is very open to instruction. *We* shall improve her. She dresses badly. She decidedly has humor and will appreciate *our* wit. She has enough money to be quite independent. She rules me as only American women rule men, and I cower before her. Lord! how she would lash me if she read the above description of her!

We sail for Liverpool on the 9th July, and are to be married a week or so before sailing. I expect to pass a fortnight or three weeks in England, before going to the continent. And we shall probably pass the season in London next year. I have work to do there and people to meet. We shall probably take a house, and a cook. Will you dine with us? cold roast mutton at seven.

Further information may be deferred till we meet, which will, I suppose, be soon. Of course I shall go to Geneva, if my people are there, but just now, no one knows what is to happen. I expect to see as much of you as you can reconcile yourself to, and if life will only run smooth, I trust to enjoy it still.

Of course all this new complication has thrown a deal more in the way of business onto me than I had before, and what with teaching, editing and marrying, I am a pretty well-occupied man. I have however found time to write to Robert and Palgrave, so that as you are still perambulating the continent, you will hardly have the satisfaction of giving them the first information of this news. Meanwhile, to stop my intended's mouth, who was worrying me to know if I had ever met a very attractive Englishwoman, I have given her your aunt's letters to read, with which she expresses herself greatly delighted and has insisted on making half her friends read the volume.

My father has taken passage for the 24th April and in case the Geneva business is not stopped, he and my mother and sister will be in England early in May. I shall be married very quietly, without any company outside our immediate families, about the 1st July in the country.

I am sorry that Italy seems so dull as your letter suggests. But things change awfully fast, and one is always in danger of being the last at the party. I don't want *you* to marry though. One of us surely should remain single for the good of all.

I must stop to make love.

To HENRY CABOT LODGE

Beverly Farms, Mass., Thursday, 25 June [*1874*].

I return the [Herbert] Spencer ["The Philosophy of Style"]. It has disappointed me. If his other works are not better thought out, they must have very little sound method to recommend them.

I cannot conceive how any rule of prose can be made that shall not require the subject to stand first. This is a general law, and is equivalent to saying that one ought to begin at the beginning. "Jack loves Joan" is right. "Joan loves Jack" is not the forcible way of saying that Jack loves Joan. "Diana is great" is the ordinary, correct and regular mode of stating the fact. "Great is Diana" requires an interjection mark after it. You may test this rule in practice to any extent. I am satisfied that the first canon of good narrative or argumentative prose requires the subject to precede the predicate.

But as an equally important rule I should insist on the law of variety. The two canons go together and ought to be studied together. The thought should not flow in monotonous forms. And why? The law of economy does not explain this. Poetic rhythm would seem to contradict it. I believe the reason to be that in poetry or prose, monotony ultimately wearies the nerves, just as lying in one position does.

When we come to applying this second canon, the difficulties begin. And these difficulties are essentially the same in verse and prose. To vary your regular construction you may put the predicate first. But clearly this must be done with discretion. Hence we get Canon III: where accentuation is wanted, begin with the word or idea to be accented, whether subject or predicate.

> "*I* only lived; *I* only drew
> The accursed air of dungeon dew."

Would Byron have made this more forcible if he had put the predicate first?

"The Senator walks off under the States-rights banner; let him go; *I* remain."

"Then Seymour arose," says Macaulay. "Then arose Seymour" is feeble in comparison, as one reads it in the story.

Or as an example in regard to the position of the adjective, which is part and parcel of the same question, take Shelley's famous touch in his Dream of the Unknown:

> "And in the warm hedge grew lush eglantine,
> Green cow-bind and the moonlight colored May,
> *And wild roses,* and ivy serpentine."

There is a delicious flavor in those *wild roses,* and why? Simply because the rhythm requires *roses wild.* It is the variety which pleases, not the mere relative position of the words.

So my Canon III would absolutely disregard every rule except one's ear. Canon III requires that in narrative, where the rule is to construct sentences according to Canon I, accentuation is to be gained by putting the accentuated word or idea first. The ear alone can decide what that word or idea had best be.

Another rule, however, which seems to me essential to good prose, is that the reader ought to be as little conscious of the style as may be. It should fit the matter so closely that one should never be quite able to say that the style is above the matter—nor below it. But great effects are best produced by lowering the general tone. Follow Canon I as a rule, and it becomes easy to make a sensation with Canon III. The higher you pitch the key, the harder it is to sing up to it, and the effect no greater.

This is not Spencer's way of putting it. He starts from the idea of variety. To me the simple idea precedent is uniformity. He thinks Ossian's is "the theoretically best arrangement." I think the very absurdity refutes itself. Ossian's uniformity is worse than ordinary uniformity because it applies a wrong rule badly. In short Spencer's essay seems to me to be neither philosophical nor accurate. I am not encouraged to read his larger works.

If you ever feel like it, and want a talk, bring your carpet-bag over here and pass the night.

To JOHN G. PALFREY

Beverly Farms, Mass., 1 July, 1874.

I want to keep them [proof-sheets] only long enough to read them; not above a week. Whenever you are ready, if you will direct them to me, as above, *"By Smith's Manchester Express,"* and will give them to Laurin, *charged to me,* I shall be infinitely obliged.

I shall look up your Report. I believe I understand the shortcomings of my uncle Sam as an administrator and constitution-maker, and lawyer generally. I think however that even here they have been exaggerated. Perhaps you can correct me if I question whether there is any evidence to prove that he favored a single legislative assembly, except such *ex post facto* evidence as in the face of the general tone of his writing, is unsatisfactory. As for his anti-federalism, in these days I think I am rapidly coming to the conclusion that he was right, and J. Q. Adams certainly went over to his party.

However, I grant all you may claim, if you like, and still adhere to my uncle Sam who was a wonderful man, without whom I rather doubt whether we should have had any John, or any union at all.

To HENRY CABOT LODGE

Beverly Farms, 15 May, 1876.

I have read your MS. [on "Alexander Hamilton"] and think it will do you credit. Of course I have made many alterations, not in the sense, but in the words. I have cut out all the "we's" I could get at, and tried to make it less objectionably patronising toward Morse. . . . Probably much further labor may be profitably expended on it in proof.

You do not of course expect me to acquiesce entirely in your view of A. H. I can hardly explain the reasons of my own *kind* of aversion to him. That it is inherited is no explanation, for I inherit feelings of a very different sort towards Jefferson, Pickering, Jackson, and the legion of other life-long enemies whom my contentious precursors made. I dislike Hamilton because I always feel the adventurer in him. The very cause of your admiration is the cause of my distrust; he was equally ready to support a system he utterly disbelieved in as one that he liked. From the first to the last words he wrote, I read always the same Napoleonic kind of adventuredom, nor do I know any more curious and startling illustration of this than the conclusion of that strange paper explaining his motives for accepting Burr's challenge. I *abhor,* says he, the practice of duelling, but "the ability to be in future useful in those crises of our public affairs which seem likely to happen, would probably be inseparable from a conformity with prejudice in this particular." What should you or I say if our great-grandfathers had left us those words as a deathbed legacy? I think we should not have so high a moral standard as I thank those gentlemen for leaving us. And I confess I think those words alone justify all John Adams's distrust of Hamilton. Future political crises all through Hamilton's life were always in his mind about to make him commander-in-chief, and his first and last written words show the same innate theory of life.

But you will not be able to assent to this.

To CHARLES MILNES GASKELL

Beverly Farms, 14 June, 1876.

I was rejoiced to see your hand again the other day, and to hear a little of your news. Our correspondence, for the first time has flagged of late, and indeed it is a wonder to me that it does not expire, for I have literally nothing to write that can possibly be of more than a very vague interest to you. If the world in London grows old and wanes towards its dotage, the world here stands still. Boston is a curious place. Its business in life is to breed and to educate. The parent lives for his children; the child, when educated himself, becomes a parent, or becomes an educator, or is both. But no further result is ever reached. Just as at twenty the parent reproduces himself in a child, so the teacher reproduces himself in his scholar. But neither as child nor as scholar does the new generation do more than devote itself to become in its turn parent and teacher. Nothing ever comes of it all. There is no society worth the name, no wit, no intellectual energy or competition, no clash of minds or of schools, no interests, no masculine self-assertion or ambition. Everything is respectable, and nothing amusing. There are no outlaws. There are not only no convictions but no strong wants. Dr. Holmes, who does the wit for the city of three hundred thousand people, is allowed to talk as he will—wild atheism commonly—and no one objects. I am allowed to sit in my chair at Harvard College and rail at everything which the College respects, and no one cares. Apparently the view of life fairly adopted here is that the business of each generation shall be to generate and educate a succeeding generation. English women would open their eyes to see the elaboration of our nurseries. Englishmen would be utterly bewildered at the slavery of the parents to their children. As an educator and not as a parent, I am exasperated by the practical working of the system at college, where the teacher assumes that teaching is his end in life, and that he has no time to work for original results. But when a society has reached this point, it acquires a self-complacency which is wildly exasperating. My fingers itch to puncture it; to do something which will sting it into impropriety.

The year's work draws to its end. My lectures are over and my classes dispersed. My book will be out, I hope, in about a month. . . . The book is fearfully learned. You cannot read it, and I advise you not to open it. But I shall send you a copy. It will cost me about four hundred pounds, very little of which I expect to get back except in my three students, whose work fills three-fourths of the volume. Their success is mine, and I make the investment for them, expecting to draw my profit from their success. My own postion will only bring your friend Freeman about my ears. I have contradicted every English author, high and low. . . .

I recollect that my last letters have dealt largely with politics. We organized our party, and as usual have been beaten. After our utmost efforts we have only succeeded in barring the road to our opponents and forcing them to nominate as candidate for the Presidency one Hayes of Ohio, a third rate nonentity, whose only recommendation is that he is obnoxious to no one. I hope to enjoy the satisfaction of voting against him. The only good result of all the past eighteen months of work has been the savage hunting-down of powerful scoundrels and the display of the awful corruption of our system in root and branch. But our people as yet seem quite callous. If any storm of popular disgust is impending, no sign of it as yet darkens the air. We shall keep at it, and good will come in time. I hope only mildly, but croaking is little better than confessing to be a bore. . . .

To CHARLES MILNES GASKELL

1501 H Street, Washington, 25 November, 1877.

. . . We have made a great leap in the world; cut loose at once from all that has occupied us since our return from Europe, and caught new ties and occupations here. The fact is I gravitate to a capital by a primary law of nature. This is the only place in America where society amuses me, or where life offers variety. Here, too, I can fancy that we are of use in the world, for we distinctly occupy niches which ought to be filled. We have taken a large house in which we seem lost. Our watercolors and drawings go with us wherever we go, and here are our great evidence of individuality, and our title to authority. As I am intimate with many of the people in power and out of power, I am readily allowed or aided to do all the historical work I please; and as I am avowedly out of politics, there will, it is to be hoped, be no animosities to meet. Literary and nonpartisan people are rare here, and highly appreciated. And yet society in its way is fairly complete, almost as choice, if not as large, as in London or Rome.

One of these days this will be a very great city if nothing happens to it. Even now it is a beautiful one, and its situation is superb. As I belong to the class of people who have great faith in this country and who believe that in another century it will be saying in its turn the last word of civilisation, I enjoy the expectation of the coming day, and try to imagine that I am myself, with my fellow *gelehrte* here, the first faint rays of that great light which is to dazzle and set the world on fire here-after. Our duties are perhaps only those of twinkling, and many people here, like little Alice, wonder what we're at. But twinkle for twinkle, I prefer our kind to that of the small politician. . . .

To CHARLES MILNES GASKELL

Gibraltar, 21 November, 1879.

Perhaps a letter from you is waiting our arrival at Seville. If so I will answer it in advance, for I have just now a little leisure, and my science is not extensive enough to tell me when I shall have any more. My last letter to you was from Madrid, written when Spain was new to me, and when I was still wondering what to expect. Nearly a month has passed, and I feel as though I were a pure Spaniard—or perhaps a Jew, for of late I have been a bit more Jewish than anything else. Chequered is the ocean of life, my dear friend, and I think the part of that ocean in which Spain lies is decidedly more chequered than most. When I wrote to you I was exulting in my first experience of Spanish sun. Hardly three days passed when the skies clouded over, rain began, and for the next ten days we had what the Madrileños were pleased to call their rainy season. At best Madrid is a hole, but in rainy weather it is a place fit only to drown rats in. At the same time the Duke of Tetuan, who is the Foreign Secretary, let me know that there were very few papers to be found, of the class I wanted to see, and the few that existed were too delicate to be shown. Finally, poor Mrs. [J. R.] Lowell, my Minister's wife, seemed to be rapidly sinking, and I was very unwilling to go off and leave Lowell in the utter solitude which weighed on him almost as much as the illness itself. For a whole week we groaned and suffered. Our only bright spot was Lady Bonham who enlivened us now and then. At length we became desperate, and as Mrs. Lowell was rather better than otherwise, we bolted on Monday, the 3d, and, seizing the first express train, we fled southward. Andalusia received us with open arms. The sun came out. Cordova was fascinating. The great mosque was glorious. The little houses, and especially their hammered iron gates, were adorable. We reached Granada Tuesday evening and stayed there a week with more amusement than I ever supposed my effete existence was now capable of feeling. Everyone has his own standards of taste, and many travellers are bored by Granada. So they are by Rome, Venice and the Nile. To my mind Granada ranks with the *first*-class places, and for beauty stands only second to Naples. While there I made acquaintance with one of the best of the Granadans, Don Leopoldo Equilaz, the local antiquarian, a charming fellow, who took us about, told us stories and showed us curiosities, had us at his house, and led us into temptation, for he inflamed our minds with a wild fancy for following up the Granada fugitives to their final refuge at Tetuan. You would have been delighted if you had seen us at an evening tea in Don Leopoldo's renaissance palace, talking fluid Spanish with the Señora, two padres of the holy inquisition, and two pure Moors of the race of Boabdil; it was life of the fifteenth century with full local color. Among them they persuaded us to visit Tetuan, and so we came down to Gibraltar, crossed to Ceuta, and rode nine hours on donkeys last Sunday to Tetuan, returning on Wednesday, and reaching here yesterday, whence we start on Sunday for Cadiz. The Tetuan journey was hard. Ceuta was awful. The dirt of these eastern cities, like Tetuan, is indescribable. The Hebrew is pervasive and irrepressible. Nevertheless I enjoyed the trip, or parts of it, immensely; the scenery was charming; Tetuan is more eastern than the east, and filthily picturesque beyond anything I ever saw. We brought back a mule-load of rugs and embroideries, and had glorious June weather. But whether my name is now

Abd-el-adem, or Ben-shadams, or Don Enrique Adamo, I couldn't take oath, for I have been utterly bewildered to know what has become of my identity, and the Spaniards have been so kind to us that I feel as though I owed them a name. . . .

To HENRY CABOT LODGE

22, Queen Anne's Gate [London], S. W., 13 May, 1880.

Yours of March 21st has been lying a month in my drawer and, grateful as I am for all the news you are the only person to send me, I have so little to say in reply that a letter is hardly writeable. The *Boston Sunday Herald* and the *New York Herald* keep me tolerably well posted about home affairs, and Harry Sturgis tells me much more. You will be amused to hear that your friend Portal is soon to be married to a Miss Glyn, a girl rather in the style of Mrs. Harry Sturgis at eighteen. I have seen so little of the Portals that I hardly know how the match is liked, but on the face of it I should suppose that it was meant for wear rather than for show. The English are very sensible about these things. Portal is to live in the country and will make an excellent country gentleman, shaming us poor cockneys by his devotion to fox-hounds and cold roast beef.

The American colony is rather large here just now, and decidedly respectable. Besides the Sturgises, Morgans, Walter Burns, Harcourts, Playfairs, Smalleys, and Mistress Alice Mason with her callow brood, there is a swarm of swells whom I don't know and who bask in the smiles of royalty. We are very quiet ourselves, go out little, and as the fashionable people come to town our little tallow-dip disappears in the glare. There is nothing very much worth seeing. No new books have come out to create even a ripple, so far as I know. There is not even a new man of any prominence. Yet society lumbers ahead and one manages to get a good deal of amusement out of it without getting any excitement to speak of. We were more startled by George Eliot's marriage to John Cross than by the elections themselves. As Cross is semi-American by his business connection, she is half-way to emigration. I suppose her American admirers will howl over the fall of their idol, but I can't say I care much for the idol business, and I am clear that if she found her isolation intolerable, she was quite right to marry Cross if she could get him. It is not quite so easy to explain why Cross should have been willing to marry her, for most men of thirty or forty prefer youth, beauty, children and such things, to intellect in gray hairs. Some people say it was a pure marriage of convenience on both sides, but I know that the Cross family have a sort of superstitious adoration of her.

My odds and ends are gradually getting into shape. I have finished with the Record Office, completed my search through the newspapers, collected the greater part of my pamphlets, and sounded all the wells of private collections I could find. In Paris and Madrid copyists are at work for me and ought soon to send their copy. I foresee a good history if I have health and leisure the next five years, and if nothing happens to my collections of material. My belief is that I can make something permanent of it, but, as time passes, I get into a habit of working only for the work's sake and disliking the idea of completing and publishing. One should have some stronger motive than now exists for authorship. I don't think I care much even to be read, and any writer in this frame of mind must be dull reading. On the other hand I enjoy immensely the investigation, and making little memoranda of passages here and there. Aridity grows on me. I always felt myself like Casaubon in *Middlemarch,* and now I see the tendency steadily creeping over me.

This makes me all the gladder to see you plunged into active life. I envy you your experience at Chicago, though I cannot for my life see how you can manage to worry through it without getting squeezed. I still stick to [John] Sherman. Edmunds is totally unfit to be President and I should prefer Blaine. Massachusetts ought to throw her whole weight energetically for Sherman in convention; it is the only way to be dignified and consistent. If Sherman is withdrawn, then let the State give its vote to the most respectable candidate on the list, but I confess I think it ought in that case, as a mere matter of respect to a most successful administration, to throw one complimentary vote for Hayes.

Many thanks for your Pinkney minutes which I shall be glad to have. He and Monroe made an awful blunder in signing that treaty; they were fairly scared to death. Now that I see the English side, they appear utterly ridiculous, and poor dear old Jefferson too, but our beloved Federalists most of all. Ye Gods, what a rum lot they were! . . .

Lowell is expected here on the 17th. I fear his wife is still very poorly, but he has not written me the details. He takes a house near Sarah Darwin's in Southampton, and I suppose will come up at intervals. Harry James is expected from Italy at about the same time. He gave us his newspaper criticisms to read, but as I've not read his books I couldn't judge of their justice. These little fits of temper soon blow over, however, and if he is good-natured about it he will get straight again soon.

I am much touched by your loyalty to your venerable Professor, and I feel like two Casaubons, rather than one, at the idea of standing in the attitude of a gray-haired Nestor surrounded by you and Young and poor Laughlin. By the way, did you see how elaborately Stubbs refers to us in his new edition? John Green is one of my intimate friends here, but how he objurgates you fellows for your German style. He says my Essay is bad enough, but you others are clean mad. We chaff each other thereupon.

To CHARLES MILNES GASKELL

Washington, 29 January, 1882.

I did not see the *XIX Century* article and was in hopes to get it from you, for here I am so absorbed in my own pursuits that I see nothing else. Palgrave did not send me his volume of historico-poetic verses, and therefore I have not seen it. I have not seen Green's new volume, but Woolner sent us "Pygmalion." As I write for five hours every day, and ride two, and do society for the remainder, the opportunity for literature is not a vast one.

Henry James has been in Washington for a month, very homesick for London and for all the soft embraces of the old world. He returns to your hemisphere in May next. I frankly own that I broke down on *The Portrait of a Lady*, but some of my friends, of whose judgment I think highly, admire it warmly, and find it deeply interesting. I hope you may be of their opinion.

I have not read the Life of Cobden or that of Lyell, and it strikes me with a little wonder to think that I should have known both of these men well. It is only not the *fugaces annos*, but the *fugaces continentes* that bewilder me with a sense of leading several lives. Just at present, however, life seems as real and enjoyable as ever. Indeed, if I felt a perfect confidence that my history would be what I would like to make it, this part of life—from forty to fifty—would be all I want. There is a summer-like repose about it: a self-contained, irresponsible, devil-may-care indifference to the future as it looks to younger eyes; a feeling that one's bed is made, and one can rest on it till it becomes necessary to go to bed for ever; in short, an *editio princeps* quality to it, with a first class French binding, which only a Duke, or a very rich Earl of ancient foundation, could feel at twenty-five.

You know my life here, for I have described it to you many

times. Poor Henry James thinks it revolting in respect to the
politics and the intrigues that surround it. To me its only objection is its over-excitement. Socially speaking, we are very
near most of the powerful people, either as enemies or as
friends. Among others our pet enmity is Mr. Blaine, whose
conduct towards your government has perhaps not endeared
him to you. His overthrow has been a matter of deep concern
to us, both politically and personally, for we have always re-
fused him even social recognition on account of his previous
scandals, and I assure you that to stand alone in a small society like this, and to cut the Secretary of State for Foreign Affairs, without doing it offensively or with ill-breeding, requires
not only some courage but some skill. We have gone through
this ordeal for many months until at length there has come relief, and I trust that Mr. Blaine is blown up for ever, although
it is costing us the worst scandal we ever had in our foreign
politics. Today there are plenty of people who would like very
well to have made as strong a protest. At the same time I am
curiously without political friends, and know not a single man
in public life who agrees with me. All my friends have been
swept away in the changes of the past year, and I am more
despondent about this new administration than about any other
of late years. It is wretchedly feeble and characterless. We shall
however, I think, make no more outrageous foreign indecen-
cies. . . .

The other day we went out to dine, and to my horror I came
face to face with your ursine and ursa-maximine countryman,
Edward A. Freeman. I say "to my horror" because I had re-
viewed very sharply two of his books when I edited the *North
American,* and he knew it. He made himself as offensive as
usual at the dinner. At the end he attacked me as I knew he
would, and told me he had replied to my charges, as I would
see in the Preface to the first volume of his third edition of

the *Norman Conquest*. I feel not the slightest curiosity to see the reply, and should not know what to think of it, but if you wish to see the *disjecta membra* of your old friend scattered among the other bones in this "Zummerzetshire" bear cave, you can some day glance at the Preface in question and shed a tear over my untimely fate. . . .

To WILLIAM JAMES

Beverly Farms, Mass., 27 July, 1882.

I have read your two papers with that attention which, etc., etc., etc., and am partially prepared to discuss them with you. As I understand your Faith, your X, your reaction of the individual on the cosmos, it is the old question of Free Will over again. You *choose* to assume that the will is free. Good! Reason proves that the Will cannot be free. Equally good! Free or not, the mere fact that a doubt can exist, proves that X must be a very microscopic quantity. If the orthodox are grateful to you for such gifts, the world has indeed changed, and we have much to thank God for, if there is a God, that he should have left us unable to decide whether our thoughts, if we have thoughts, are our own or his'n.

Although your gift to the church seems to me a pretty darned mean one, I admire very much your manner of giving it, which magnifies the crumb into at least forty loaves and fishes. My wife is quite converted by it. She enjoyed the paper extremely. Since she read it she has talked of giving five dollars to Russell Sturgis's church for napkins. As the impression fades, she talks less of the napkins.

With hero-worship like Carlyle's, I have little patience. In history heroes have neutralysed each other, and the result is no more than would have been reached without them. Indeed in military heroes I suspect that the ultimate result has been retardation. Nevertheless you could doubtless at any time stop the entire progress of human thought by killing a few score of men. So far I am with you. A few hundred men represent the entire intellectual activity of the whole thirteen hundred millions. What then? They drag us up the cork-screw stair of thought, but they can no more get their brains to run out of their especial convolutions than a railway train (with a free will of half an inch on three thousand miles) can run free up Mount Shasta. Not one of them has ever got so far as to tell us a single vital fact worth knowing. We can't prove even that we are.

Meanwhile I enclose your letter to Monod.

Pleasant voyage and happy return. Our love to Harry.

To JOHN HAY
Washington, 23 January, 1883.

. . . Would that you were now here. Things are getting mixed. The pot boils. If you have a candidate for the Presidency, set him up! I've none, but your friend Miss Beale has got my promise for Logan of Peoria.

Please tell me of something to read. At this season my wife and I stay at home every evening, and our literature is low. Trollope has amused me for two evenings. I am clear that you should write autobiography. I mean to do mine. After seeing how coolly and neatly a man like Trollope can destroy the last vestige of heroism in his own life, I object to allowing mine to be murdered by any one except myself. Every church mouse will write autobiography in another generation in order to prove that it never believed in religion.

To JOHN HAY
Beverly Farms, 24 September, 1883.

While waiting anxiously to hear of your welfare in those wild regions which you inhabit, I write a line of interest in the present literary problem of our day.

I am glad you did not write the "Bread-winners" [Hay's novel]. It is a real joy to me to feel that there are two men west of the Alleghanies who are capable of doing first rate literary work, and who join humor with style. Should I ever come to Cleveland, I hope you will introduce me to the author. Meanwhile I would like to read his other books, for, of course, all of us, who try to write, know only too well that such skill is only acquired by long and painful effort. As a work of art, I should not hesitate to put the "Bread-winners" so far as the story has gone, quite at the head of our Howells'-and-James' epoch for certain technical qualities, such as skill in construction, vivacity in narration, and breadth of *motif*. It has also one curious and surprising quality, least to be expected from an unknown western writer. Howells cannot deal with gentlemen or ladies; he always slips up. James knows almost nothing of women but the mere outside; he never had a wife. This new writer not only knows women, but knows *ladies;* the rarest of literary gifts. I suppose he has an eastern wife? Under ordinary circumstances, there might be a doubt as to the sex of the author, but here none is possible, for he also knows men and even gentlemen. His sense of humor, too, is so markedly masculine as to take away all doubt on the matter.

If I had a criticism to make it would be that he is a little hard on reformers; he shows prejudice against his own characters. George Eliot used to do this. For my part, I always thought that if I tried to write a novel, I would make it overflow with kindness and see nothing but virtues in the human race.

If the author wrote *Democracy* as is said, he has made a great stride in every way, especially in humor, which is rather conspicuously wanting in that over-ambitious and hard-featured book. . . .

To FRANCIS PARKMAN

1607 H Street [Washington], 21 December, 1884.

Your two volumes on Montcalm and Wolfe, which you were so kind as to send me, deserve much more careful study than I am competent to give them; for my work lies in different times, and throws no light on the colonial period. To say nothing at all when I can say nothing which I think worth saying has been the rule I have tried to follow in literature; and so far as I can see, you have so thoroughly exhausted your sources as to leave little or nothing new to be said. The book puts you in the front rank of living English historians, and I regret only that the field is self-limited so that you can cultivate it no further. The most curious fact connected with the French colonization seems to me to be its sterility. I do not know that the French Canadians have been more barren in influence than the Pennsylvania Germans; but the overpowering energy of the English stock has absorbed what was useful in both.

Your book is a model of thorough and impartial study and clear statement. Of its style and narrative the highest praise is that they are on a level with its thoroughness of study. Taken as a whole, your works are now dignified by proportions and completeness which can hardly be paralleled by the "literary baggage" of any other historical writer in the language known to me today. George Bancroft has the proportions but not the completeness; for, as I often tell him, he has written the History of the United States in a dozen volumes without reaching his subject. The English are just now poorly off. Except Gardiner and Lecky I know of no considerable English historians besides the old war-horses Freeman and Froude. My favorite John Green was the flower of my generation; and in losing him, I lost the only English writer of history whom I loved personally and historically.

Now that your niche is filled, I hope you will go over all the work. File and burnish. Fill in with all that you can profitably add, and cut out whatever is superfluous. Give us your ripe best, and then swing the whole at the head of the public as a single work. Nothing but mass tells.

My own labor is just half done. Two heavy volumes have been put into type, partly for safety, partly to secure the advantages of a first edition without the publicity. The more I write, the more confident I feel that before long a new school of history will rise which will leave us antiquated. Democracy is the only subject for history. I am satisfied that the purely mechanical development of the human mind in society must appear in a great democracy so clearly, for want of disturbing elements, that in another generation psychology, physiology, and history will join in proving man to have as fixed and necessary development as that of a tree; and almost as unconscious.

To OLIVER WENDELL HOLMES

1607 H Street, Washington, 4 Jan. 1885.

Will you forgive me for writing a few words to say with how much pleasure I have read your volume on Emerson? I fear that Emerson, with all his immortal longings and oneness with nature, could not have returned such a compliment in kind. He had neither the lightness of touch nor the breadth of sympathy that make your work so much superior to anything that we other men, who call ourselves younger, succeed in doing.

As a mere student I could have wished one chapter more, to be reserved for the dissecting-room alone. After studying the scope of any mind, I want as well to study its limitations. The limitations of Napoleon's, or Shakespeare's minds would tell me more than their extensions, so far as relative values are concerned. Emerson's limitations seemed to me very curious and interesting. At one time I had a list of five dicta of his, some of which belonged probably to the narrowed perceptions of his decline. I have forgotten some of them, but they began: No. 1, "There is no music in Shelley." No. 2, "There is no humor in Aristophanes." No. 3, "Photographs give more pleasure than paintings": (i. e. the photograph of a painting gave him more pleasure than the painting itself). No. 4, "Egypt is uninteresting."

In obtaining extreme sublimation or tenuity of intelligence, I infer that sensuousness must be omitted. If Mr. Emerson was in some respects more than human, he paid for it by being in other respects proportionately less.

Will you pardon my asking a favor? When you print another edition, will you not insert more specimens of the poetry? As a rule you cannot underrate the knowledge of your readers. Crass ignorance is the natural condition of the wisest and most learned of men. Even admirers of Emerson may not carry all his poetry in their heads, or have a copy of his works at their elbow. If I were daring enough to hint it, I would even go so far as to say that however much respect the public may feel for Judge Hoar, Mr. Freeman Clarke and Mr. Alcott, they feel a strong and decided preference for yourself, in the matter of literature; and would be willing to spare no small part of Chapter XV, if by doing so they could correspondingly enlarge Chapter XIV.

This is an Art-criticism which I ought not to venture; but we unillumined, although pleased and proud to admire and study Mr. Emerson, must always indulge in a little kick or snort of protest at having Mr. Emerson's echoes make themselves heard. Human nature is but a reed shaken by a breeze. The Concord breeze shakes it sometimes like an east wind.

Old Mr. Bancroft is quite delighted with your book, and cries for his eighty years again to do it justice. I am, for my own account, sadly struck by the vast superiority you literary gentlemen maintain over us politicians. I cannot but think the poorest volume of the "Men of Letters" better than the best volume of the "Statesmen." . . .

To EDWIN LAWRENCE GODKIN

Washington, 16 Decr. 1885.

Thanks for your sympathy.* For the present I try to think of nothing but how to make the days pass till my nerves get steady again; so I will say nothing that would tend to prolong the strain.

I am glad to think of you as in the sunshine again. Never fear for me. I have had happiness enough to carry me over some years of misery; and even in my worst prostration I have found myself strengthened by two thoughts. One was that life could have no other experience so crushing. The other was that at least I had got out of life all the pleasure it had to give. I admit that fate at last has smashed the life out of me; but for twelve years I had everything I most wanted on earth. I own that the torture has made me groan; but, as long as any will is left, I shall try not to complain.

* Mrs. Henry Adams died December 6, 1885.

III

JAPAN, CUBA, THE SOUTH SEAS, CEYLON

1886–1891

AFTER the all but mortal blow of his wife's death in 1885, Adams found the courage to continue work on his *History,* which he at length finished in 1888 and which was published in nine volumes during the years 1889–1891. The emotional and intellectual strain of those years, however, had induced in him a compulsive restlessness, and in 1886 he began his long series of wanderings with a visit to Japan in the company of the painter John La Farge. In 1889 came a short trip to Cuba with his secretary and companion, Theodore Dwight, and then in 1890 Adams and La Farge set out again together on what was to prove a much more ambitious expedition than any hitherto. For twelve months the two men, so dissimilar yet so companionable, traveled about the island groups of the South Seas, remaining for weeks and even months at such places as Hawaii, Samoa, and Tahiti, and saturating themselves thoroughly in the engrossing world of Polynesia. In June 1891 they moved on to Fiji, which pleased them less, and then, after touching at Batavia and Singapore, traveled to Ceylon and visited the ruins of the Buddhist temples at Anuradhpura in the forested interior. Sitting under a sacred bo tree there, Adams had the disappointment of failing to attain Nirvana. The two men parted after reaching Europe in the autumn, La Farge to return to America, and Adams to spend the winter partly in Paris, partly in London.

To JOHN HAY

Yokohama, 9 July, 1886.

We have been here a week. Between the wish that you were here with us, and the conviction that you would probably by this time be broken up if you had come, I am distraught. Amusing it certainly is—beyond an idea—but comfortable or easy it is not by any means; and I can honestly say that one works for what one gets.

We have devoted the week to Tokio, and you can judge what sort of a place it is from the fact that there is neither hotel nor house in it where we can be so nearly comfortable as we are in a third-rate hotel at Yokohama, twenty miles away. Here we have rooms directly on the bay, with air as fresh as the Japs make it; and here we return every evening to sleep. Sturgis Bigelow acts as our courier and master of ceremonies, but La Farge has mastered Mandarin Chinese, and hopes soon to be a fluent talker of Daimio Japanese. As for me, I admire.

Fenollosa and Bigelow are stern with us. Fenollosa is a tyrant who says we shall not like any work done under the Tokugawa Shoguns. As these gentlemen lived two hundred and fifty years or thereabouts, to 1860, and as there is nothing at Tokio except their work, La Farge and I are at a loss to understand why we came; but it seems we are to be taken to Nikko shortly and permitted to admire some temples there. On secret search in Murray, I ascertain that the temples at Nikko are the work of Tokugawa Shoguns. I have not yet dared to ask about this apparent inconsistency for fear of rousing a fresh anathema.

The temples and Tokugawas are, I admit, a trifle baroque. For sticking a decisive bit of infamous taste into the middle of a seriously planned, and minutely elaborated mass of refined magnificence, I have seen no people—except perhaps our own—to compare with the Japs. We have the future before us to prove our capacity, but they now stand far

[91]

ahead. Some of the temples are worse than others, but I am inclined to let Fenollosa have his way with them, if he will only let me be amused by the humor. Positively everything in Japan laughs. The jinrickshaw men laugh while running at full speed five miles with a sun that visibly sizzles their drenched clothes. The women all laugh, but they are obviously wooden dolls, badly made, and can only cackle, clatter in pattens over asphalt pavements in railway stations, and hop or slide in heelless straw sandals across floors. I have not yet seen a woman with any better mechanism than that of a five-dollar wax doll; but the amount of oil used in fixing and oiling and arranging their hair is worth the money alone. They can all laugh, so far. The shop-keepers laugh to excess when you say that their goods are forgeries and worthless. I believe the Mikado laughs when his ministers have a cabinet council. The gilt dragon-heads on the temples are in a broad grin. Everything laughs, until I expect to see even the severe bronze doors of the tombs, the finest serious work I know, open themselves with the same eternal and meaningless laughter, as though death were the pleasantest jest of all.

In one respect Japan has caused me a sensation of deep relief. In America I had troubled myself much because my sense of smell was gone. I thought I never should again be conscious that the rose or the new-mown hay had odor. How it may be about the rose or the hay I know not; but since my arrival here I perceive that I am not wholly without a nose. La Farge agrees with me that Japan possesses one pervasive, universal, substantive smell—an oily, sickish, slightly fetid odor—which underlies all things, and though infinitely varied, is always the same. The smell has a corresponding taste. The bread, the fruit, the tea, the women, and the water, the air and the gods, all smell or taste alike. This is monotonous but reassuring. I have reasoned much and tried many experiments to ascertain the cause of this phenomenon, but it seems to be a condition of existence, and the accompaniment of Japanese civilisation. Without the smell, Japan would fall into dissolution.

I am trying to spend your money. It is hard work, but I will do it, or succumb. Kaki-monos are not to be got. Porcelain worth buying is rare. Lacquer is the best and cheapest article. Bronzes are good and cheap. I want to bring back a dozen big bronze vases to put on the grass before our houses in summer, for palms or big plants, so as to give our houses the look of a cross between curio shops and florists. Tokio contains hardly anything worth getting except bronzes. A man at Osaka has sent up some two hundred and fifty dollars worth of lacquers, sword-hilts, inlaid work, and such stuff. As he has the best shop in Japan we took the whole lot, and have sent for more. Inros are from ten to fifteen dollars. I shall get a dozen for presents. Good cloisonné, either Chinese or Japanese, is most rare. Fine old porcelain is rare and dear. Embroideries are absolutely introuvable. Even books seem scarce. Japan has been cleaned out. My big bronze vases will cost from fifty to two hundred dollars apiece, but these will be good. . . .

I have not presented my Japanese letters of introduction, as I found it would imply a course of entertainments which I would rather avoid. Tokio is an impossible sort of place for seeing anyone. It is a bunch of towns, and the Europeans live all over it, so that one goes five miles or so to make a call or to see one's dearest friend for five minutes. The thermometer today is anywhere between 90° and 200° in the streets, and calling on formal ministers of state under such conditions is not amusing. . . .

I shall go to Osaka and Kioto in September, unless the country is absolutely closed by cholera. Indeed I should do many other things if I were not anxious to spare La Farge the risk of illness. He continues to be the most agreeable of companions, always cheerful, equable, sweet-tempered, and quite insensible to ideas of time, space, money or railway trains. To see him flying through the streets of Tokio on a jinrickshaw is a most genial vision. He peers out through his spectacles as though he felt the absurdity as well as the necessity of looking at the show as though it were real, but he enjoys it enormously, especially the smell, which quite fascinates him. He keeps me in perpetual good humor. . . . I am lost in wonder how he ever does work; but he can be energetic, and his charm is that whether energetic or lazy he has the neatest humor, the nicest observation, and the evenest temper you can imagine. When he loses the trains, I rather enjoy it. After all, who cares?

Of startling or wonderful experience we have had none. The only moral of Japan is that the children's story-books were good history. This is a child's country. Men, women and children are taken out of the fairy books. The whole show is of the nursery. Nothing is serious; nothing is taken seriously. All is toy; sometimes, as with the women, badly made and repulsive; sometimes laughable, as with the houses, gardens and children; but always taken from what La Farge declares to have been the papboats of his babyhood. I have wandered, so to express it, in all the soup-plates of forty-eight years' experience, during the last week, and have found them as natural as Alice found the Mock Turtle. Life is a dream, and in Japan one dreams of the nursery.

To ELIZABETH CAMERON

Nikko, 13 August, 1886.

Thanks for your kind little note which gave me real pleasure in my Japanese retreat. In return I can only tell you that Japan is a long way from America, but that it is not far enough to prevent my thinking too much about home matters. I have heard but once from there, since I sailed, and luckily all my news was pleasant. In six weeks more I shall be starting for home. . . .

La Farge and I have found shelter in the mountains from the heat and hotels of Japan. We have a little box of a Japanese house, where we look out on a Japanese temple-garden, and on Japanese mountains, all like the pictures that one sees on plates. We are princely in our style. The dealers in *curios* send us, from far and wide, whatever they can find that we like, and our rooms are full of such rubbish. La Farge sketches. I waste time as I can, sometimes walking, or going over the hills on rats of pack-horses; sometimes photographing in the temple grounds; sometimes sitting cross-legged, and looking at bales of stuffs or lacquers; sometimes at tea-houses, watching the sun when it kindly sets behind the big mountain Nan-tai-zan, and leaves us in a less perspiring condition than we are by day. The scenery is very pretty; not unlike that of the Virginia Springs; and the temperature much the same though very moist. Of interesting people I see nothing. I doubt whether there are any such. The Japanese women seem to me impossible. After careful inquiry I can hear of no specimen of your sex, in any class of society, whom I ought to look upon as other than a *curio*. They are all badly made, awkward in movement, and suggestive of monkeys. The children are rather pretty and quite amusing, but the mammas are the reverse; and one is well able to judge at least the types of popular beauty, seeing that there is little clothing to hide it, and that little is apt to be forgotten.

This branch of my historical inquiries has not proved rich; but, though the people are not a success in regard to personal attractions, they are very amusing indeed, and have given us infinite varieties of laughter ever since we saw our first fishing-boat. I do not advise you to allow yourself three months' leisure in order to get used to various pervasive smells, and to forget all your previous education in the matter of food, houses, drains, and vehicles. If you can live on boiled rice or stewed eels, or bad, oily, fresh tea; or in houses without partitions or walls except of paper; or in cities absolutely undrained, and with only surface wells for drinking water; or if you can sit on your heels all through five hours at the theatre, and can touch the floor with your forehead when I call upon you; and say *Hei* and *Ha* at stated intervals, you will do very well in Japan. I do all these things with less success than is to be desired, for I cannot sit on my heels at all, and I suffer to the extent of anguish even in sitting cross-legged; Japanese food makes me sea-sick, and the smell of Tokio seems to get into food, drink, and dreams; but I have not yet had my three months' education, and have even evaded it by flying to the mountains and by getting myself fed and protected after the American manner. After ten days of modified Japanese experiments I was content with what I had learned. Nothing but necessity would induce me to try another Japanese article of food or to pass another night in a Japanese inn, for the first experiment proved nearly fatal; and although I did not fear death, I shrank from dying of Japanese soup in a Japanese inn, with Japanese women to look at as my last association with earth. This weakness on my part shows the sad effects of too long life. One ought to enjoy poisonous mushrooms fried in bad oil, and to delight in looking at wooden women without any figures, waddling on wooden pattens.

Our faculty for laughing has been greatly increased, but we try in vain to acquire the courteous language of the country. No European can learn to track out the intricate holes and burrows in which Japanese courtesy hides itself. I wish I could master, in order to teach you, the ceremony of the *Ocha-no-yu,* or honorable five-o'clock tea. I declined to buy a book which contained paintings showing fifty arrangements of the charcoal to boil the kettle on this occasion; and as many more of the ways in which a single flower might be set in a porcelain stand. My friend Bigelow bought the pictures and is professor of the art. Simpler tasks satisfy me. Seeing the woman who has charge of our horses eating hard green plums, I requested Bigelow to tell her with my compliments that she would suffer from stomach-ache. Her reply, profoundly serious, was to the effect that my remark had truth; her stomach did respectfully ache. I learned much from this attitude of respect which even the digestive apparatus of a Japanese peasant woman assumes towards a stranger.

I have bought *curios* enough to fill a house, but nothing that I like, or want for myself. The stuffs are cheap and beautiful, but I have found no really fine embroidery. The lacquer is relatively cheap, but I do not care for it. I can find no good porcelain or bronze, and very few wall-pictures. Metal work is easy to get, and very choice, but what can one do with sword-guards and knife handles? I am puzzled to know what to bring home to please myself. If I knew what would please you, I would load the steamer with it. . . .

To JOHN HAY

Nikko, 22 August, 1886.

I have still to report that purchases for you are going on, but more and more slowly, for I believe we have burst up all the pawn-brokers' shops in Japan. Even the cholera has shaken out the little that is worth getting. Bigelow and Fenollosa cling like misers to their miserable hoards. Not a kakimono is to be found, though plenty are brought. Every day new bales of rubbish come up from Tokio or elsewhere; mounds of books; tons of bad bronze; holocausts of lacquer; I buy literally everything that is merely possible; and yet I have got not a hundred dollars' worth of things I want for myself. You shall have some good small bits of lacquer, and any quantity of *duds* to encumber your tables and mantles, but nothing creditable to our joint genius. As for myself, I have only one *Yokomono*— or kakimono broader than it is long—and one small bronze, that I care to keep as the fruit of my summer's perspiration.

For Japan is the place to perspire. No one knows an ideal dogday who has not tried Japan in August. From noon to five o'clock I wilt. As for travelling, I would see the rice-fields dry first. I have often wondered what King would have done, had he come with us. I've no doubt he would have seen wonderful sights, but I should have paid his return passage on a corpse. For days together I make no attempt at an effort, while poor La Farge sketches madly and aimlessly.

By the bye, a curious coincidence happened. Bigelow announced one morning that King and Hay were coming from Tokio with loads of curios for us. La Farge and I stared and inquired. Then it appeared that Bigelow and Fenollosa employ two men—Kin, pronounced King, and Hei, pronounced Hay—to hunt curios for them, and had sent them word to bring up whatever they could find. I thought this one of the happiest accidents I ever heard, and I only wish that Messrs. King and Hay had brought better things, as their American namesakes expected. They meant well, but they lacked means. Nevertheless they brought a few nice bits, to sustain the credit of their names.

Fairly bored by sweltering in this moistness, I stirred up Mrs. Fenollosa to a little expedition last Tuesday. Fenollosa is unwell; La Farge is hard at work; but Mrs. Fenollosa, Bigelow and I, started to visit Yumoto, the Saratoga, or White Sulphur, of Japan. Yumoto lies just fourteen miles above us among the mountains, and with one of my saddle horses I could easily go there and return on the same day; but such a journey in Japan is serious. Only pedestrians, coolies, or Englishmen work hard. Mrs. Fenollosa summoned five pack-horses. All

Japanese horses known to me are rats, and resemble their pictures, which I had supposed to be bad drawing; but these pack-horses are rats led by a man, or more often by a woman, at a very slow walk. Mrs. Fenollosa mounted one; Bigelow another; I ascended a third; a servant and baggage followed on a fourth; the fifth carried beds, blankets, linen, silver, eatables, and drinks. At half past eight the caravan started, and at half past ten it arrived at the foot of Chiu-zen-ji pass, where one climbs a more or less perpendicular mountain side for an hour. I preferred my own legs to the rat's, and walked up. So we arrived at Lake Chiu-zen-ji, a pretty sheet of water about seven miles long, at the foot of the sacred mountain Nan-tai-zan. On the shore of this lake is a temple, where pilgrims begin the ascent of the mountain, sacred to Sho-do Sho-nin, who devoted fifteen years of his valuable existence, in the eighth century, to the astounding feat of climbing it. As it is very accessible, and only eight thousand feet above the sea, Sho-do Sho-nin is a very popular and greatly admired saint, and some five thousand pilgrims come every August to follow his sainted steps. Next the temple are some inns, but not a farm or a human dwelling exists on the lake or among the mountains; for if the Japanese like one thing more than another it is filthy rice-fields, and if they care less for one thing than another, it is mountains. All this lovely country, from here to the sea of Japan, is practically a dense wildernes of monkeys, as naked as itself; but the monkeys never seem out of place as a variety, though I have not met them in society, and speak only from association. We stopped at an inn, and while lunch was making ready, Bigelow and I went out in a kind of frigate for a swim in the lake. After lunch, sending our beasts ahead, we sailed to the next starting-point, just the length of a cigar. Another two miles of rise brought us to a moor for all the world like Estes Park and the Rocky Mountains. Crossing this, we climbed another ascent, and came out on an exquisite little green lake with woody mountains reflected on its waters. Nothing could be prettier than the path along this shore, but it was not half so amusing to me as our entrance into the village of Yumoto, with its dozen inns and no villagers; for, by the roadside, at the very entrance, I saw at last the true Japan of my dreams, and broke out into carols of joy. In a wooden hut, open to all the winds, and public as the road, men, women and children, naked as the mother that bore them, were sitting, standing, soaking and drying themselves, as their ancestors had done a thousand years ago.

I had begun to fear that Japan was spoiled by Europe. At Tokio even the coolies wear something resembling a garment, and the sexes are obliged to bathe apart. As I came into the country I noticed first that the children were naked; that the men wore only a breech-clout; and that the women were apt to be stripped to the waist; but I had begun to disbelieve that this disregard of appearances went further. I was wrong. No sooner had we dismounted than we hurried off to visit the baths; and Mrs. Fenollosa will bear me witness that for ten minutes we stood at the entrance of the largest bath-house, and looked on at a dozen people of all ages, sexes and varieties of ugliness, who paid not the smallest regard to our presence. I should except one pretty girl of sixteen, with quite a round figure and white skin. I did notice that for the most part, while drying herself, she stood with her back to us.

When this exceptionally pleasing virgin walked away, I took no further interest in the proceedings, though I still regard them as primitive. Of the habits and manners of the Japanese in regard to the sexes, I see little, for I cannot conquer a feeling that Japs are monkeys, and the women very badly made monkeys; but from others I hear much on the subject, and what I hear is very far from appetising. In such an atmosphere one talks freely. I was a bit aghast when one young woman called my attention to a temple as a remains of phallic worship; but what can one do? Phallic worship is as universal here as that of trees, stones and the sun. I come across shrines of phallic symbols in my walks, as though I were an ancient Greek. One cannot quite ignore the foundations of society.

23 August. My poor boy, how very strong you do draw your vintage for my melancholy little *Esther.* Your letter of July 18 has just reached me, and I hardly knew what I was reading about. Perhaps I made a mistake even to tell King about it; but having told him, I could not leave you out. Now, let it die! To admit the public to it would be almost unendurable to me. I will not pretend that the book is not precious to me, but its value has nothing to do with the public who could never understand that such a book might be written in one's heart's blood. Do not even imagine that I scorn the public, as you say. Twenty years ago, I would have been glad to please it. Today, and for more than a year past, I have been and am living with not a thought but from minute to minute; and the public is as far away from me as the celebrated Kung-fu-tse, who once said something on the subject which I forget, but which had probably a meaning to him, as my observation has to me. Yet I do feel pleased that the book has found one friend.

25 August. I can't say, "let's return to our sheep," for there are no sheep in Japan, and I have eaten nothing but bad beef since landing. As for returning to my remarks on Yumoto as connected with the sexes, I decline to do it. In spite of King, I affirm that sex does not exist in Japan, except as a scientific classification. I would not affirm that there are no exceptions to my law; but the law itself I affirm as the foundation of archaic society. Sex begins with the Aryan race. I have seen a Japanese beauty, which has a husband, *Nabeshame,* if

I hear right—a live Japanese Marquis, late Daimio of Hizo, or some other place; but though he owns potteries, he has, I am sure, no more successful bit of bric-à-brac than his wife is; but as for being a woman, she is hardly the best Satsuma. . . .

To CHARLES MILNES GASKELL

Los Baños de S. Diego, 8 March, 1888.

In the course of aimless wandering I have drifted for a day to this Spanish hole in the middle of Cuba, and bethink myself that I owe you a letter. An evening with nothing to do at a Cuban sulphur-bath tends to recall one's friends to one's mind. While the chattering Cubans are playing loto at the next table, I will try to write a few pages to bore you.

I forget where or when my last letter was written. I can only remember that I had a more than usually unsatisfactory winter at Washington. I have got into a bad way of never leaving my house except to see one or two intimates, like John Hay. Society scares and bores me, and I have wholly dropped it. During the cold weather I pass an hour every afternoon at my greenhouse and watch my roses. If it were not that friends are very good natured, and come in unasked to breakfast and dinner, I should be a hermit. One of my most valuable allies is a young fellow of your Legation, whose name I have already mentioned to you—Spring Rice—who not only comes two or three times a week to dinner, and keeps me posted about the world's doings, whether I care for them or not, but also brings Englishmen with him, if he thinks them worth knowing. Among others he brought Mr. [Joseph] Chamberlain, who took kindly to my habits, and asked himself several times to dinner without other company than ourselves. Chamberlain amused and interested me. He talked much and well, very openly, and with a certain naïveté that I hardly expected. He was a success in society, and was received with an amount of attention that seemed to puzzle him, considering how little favor he got from newspapers and politicians. . . . On the whole he made a decided mark, and held more than his own against all comers. His opinion of America is not a high one, and he took little trouble to disguise it; but as he studied it only on the political side, he did not disturb our complacency. His chief objection was that we cared little for statesmen and orators. . . .

I have been particularly well all winter, but the disease of restlessness is quite as trying as most fevers. Clarence King was ordered by his physicians to take these absurd baths for rheumatism. I made every arrangement to come with him. John Hay, who has some chronic inflammation of the vocal cords, agreed to be of the party. At the last moment King's physicians would not let him go; but I was bound to go somewhere, so I took my companion, Theodore Dwight, and started with him and Hay for Florida three weeks ago. Hay left us after a fortnight, to return home, but Dwight and I rambled on, crossed from Florida to Havana, and have been a week in Cuba. I like summer, and palms, Spain and garlic; I do not much object to dirt or smells; and this time I thought my stomach so strong that I went even to a bull-fight, which was declared to be the most splendid ever seen in Havana. Splendid it certainly was, but one bull settled my stomach so effectually that I left the other five to the mercies of the rest of their admirers. Havana is a gay ruin, but after being kept awake five nights by the noise and smell, I thought that country air would do us good, so we came about a hundred miles into the western end of the island. Next Wednesday I expect to start back in order to reach Washington on the 18th.

Meanwhile history has made little progress. I want to go to the Fiji Islands next summer, a five months affair; but am in doubt whether I can fairly get away. The object of such long expeditions about the Pacific is to tire myself out till home becomes rest. If I can do this within two years, things will be sim-plified. Otherwise, there is no help but to start then for good, and go till I drop. You can have no idea of the insanity of restlessness. Reason is helpless to control it. . . .

To ELIZABETH CAMERON

Steamer "W. G. Hall." 13 Sept., 1890.

At sea again, or rather in port, for just now, at seven o'clock in the morning, we are leaving the little village of Kailua, and running along the south coast of the island of Hawaii. We tore ourselves yesterday morning from our comforts at Honolulu, and after a day and night of seasick discomfort on a local steamer, filled with natives, we are now in sight of Mauna Loa, and at evening shall land at Punaluu on the ex-treme south-eastern end of the island. As I detest mountains, abominate volcanoes, and execrate the sea, the effort is a tremendous one; but I make it from a sense of duty to the savages who killed Captain Cook just about here a century ago. One good turn deserves another. Perhaps they will kill me. I never saw a place where killing was less like murder. The ocean is calm and blue; the air so warm that I turned out of my sleepless berth at the first light of dawn. The huge flat bulk of Mauna Loa stretches down an interminable slope ahead of us, with the strange voluptuous charm peculiar to volcanic slopes, which always seem to invite you to lie down on them and caress them; the shores are rocky and lined with palms; the mountain-sides are green, and packed with dark tufts of forest; the place is—an island paradise, made of lava; and the native boats—queer long coffins with an outrigger on one side resting in the water—are now coming out at some new landing-place, bringing mangoes, pine-apples, melons and alligator-pears, all which I am somewhat too nauseated to eat. Our steamer is filled with plaintive-looking native women—

the old-gold variety—who vary in expression between the ferocious look of the warriors who worshipped Captain Cook and then killed him, and the melancholy of a generation obliged to be educated by missionaries. They have a charm in this extraordinary scope of expressions which run from tenderness to ferocity in a single play of feature, but I prefer the children, who are plaintive and sea-sick in stacks about the decks, and lie perfectly still, with their pathetic dark eyes expressing all sorts of vague sensations evidently more or less out of gear with the cosmos. The least sympathetic character is the occasional white man. Third-rate places seldom attract even third-rate men, but rather ninth-rate samples, and these are commonly the white men of tropical islands. I prefer the savages who were—at least the high chiefs—great swells and very much gentlemen and killed Captain Cook. . . . We have been ashore to see where Captain Cook was killed, a hot little lava oven where the cliffs rise sharp over deep water—some old crater-hole—of all sorts of intense blue. Only a hut was there, donkeys and mules, a few natives and a swarm of crabs jumping over the red rocks by the black-blue water. Mauna Loa slopes back for forty miles. . . .

Kilauea Volcano House, Monday, Sept. 15. 7 a.m. Our pilgrimage is effected at last. I am looking, from the porch of the inn, down on the black floor of the crater, and its steaming and smoking lake, now chilled over, some two or three miles away, at the crater's further end. More impressive to my fancy is the broad sloping mass of Mauna Loa which rises beyond, ten thousand feet above us, a mass of rugged red lava, scored by deeper red or black streaks down its side, but looking softer than babies' flesh in this lovely morning sunlight, and tinged above its red with the faintest violet vapor. I adore mountains—from below. Like other deities, they should not be trodden upon. As La Farge remarked yesterday when I said that the ocean *looked* quiet enough: "It *is* quiet if you don't fool with it. How would *you* like to be sailed upon?" The natives still come up here and sit on the water's edge to look down at the residence of their great Goddess, but they never go down into it. They say they're not rich enough. The presents cost too much. Mrs. Dominus, the king's sister, and queen-expectant, came up here in the year 1885, and brought a black pig, two roosters, champagne, red handker-chiefs, and a whole basket of presents, which were all thrown on the lava lake. The pig, having his legs tied, squealed half an hour before he was thoroughly roasted, and one of the roosters escaped to an adjoining rock, but was recaught and immersed. Only princesses are rich enough to do the thing suitably, and as Mrs. Dominus is a Sunday-school Christian, she knows how to treat true deities. As for me, I prefer the bigger and handsomer Mauna Loa, and I routed La Farge out at six o'clock—or was it five—to sketch it with its top red with the first rays of the sun. . . . We had a lovely day's drive yes-terday up here, over grassy mountain-sides, and through lava beds sprinkled with hot-house shrubs and ferns. The air is delicious, and the temperature, when the clouds veil the sun, is perfect either for driving or walking. If we can only escape the steamer on the windward side! but that implies sixty miles of horseback, partly in deluges of rain.

Hilo, Sept. 18. If you do not know where Hilo is don't look for it on the map. One's imagination is the best map for travellers. You may remember Hilo best because it is the place where Clarence King's waterfall of old-gold girls was situated. The waterfall is still here, just behind the Severance house where we are staying. Mrs. Severance took us down there half an hour ago. She said nothing about the girls, but she did say that the boys used habitually to go over the fall as their after-school amusement; but of late they have given it up, and must be paid for doing it. The last man who jumped off the neighboring high rock required fifteen dollars. Mrs. Severance told this sadly, mourning over the decline of the arts and of surf-bathing. A Bostonian named Brigham took a clever photograph of a boy, just half way down, the fall being perhaps twelve or fifteen feet. So passes the glory of Hawaii, and of the old-gold girl—woe is me!

As La Farge aptly quoted yesterday from some wise traveller's advice to another, à propos of volcanoes: "You will be sorry if you go there, and you will be sorry if you don't go there, so I advise you to go." We went. The evening before last we tramped for two hours across rough blocks and layers of black glass; then tumbled down more broken blocks sixty or eighty feet into another hole; then scrambled half way down another crater—three in succession, one inside the other —and sat down to look at a steaming black floor below us, which ought to have been red-hot and liquid, spouting fountains of fire, but was more like an engine house at night with two or three engines letting off steam and showing head-lights. The scene had a certain vague grandeur as night came on, and the spots of fire glowed below while the new moon looked over the cliff above; but I do not care to go there again, nor did I care even to go down the odd thirty or forty feet to the surface of the famous lake of liquid fire. It was more effective, I am sure, the less hard one hit one's nose on it. We tramped back in the dark; our lanterns went out, and we were more than three hours to the hotel. . . .

Tomorrow we start, through mud and gulches of torrents, on a five days' ride to Kawaihae, eighty miles to the westward, where we take steamer again. If you will believe it, I do this to avoid a day's seasickness.

Steamer "Kinau," Tuesday, 23 Sept. I take it all back. Hawaii is fascinating, and I could dream away months here.

Yet dreaming has not been my standard amusement of late. Never have I done such hard and continuous travelling as during the last ten days, since leaving Honolulu. I have told you how we reached Hilo. Friday morning early we left Hilo, according to our plan, with a circus of horses, to ride eighty miles, divided into four days. Rain was falling as we drove out the first eight miles to take horse at the end of the road, but we started off like Pantagruel, and in an hour arrived at a lovely cove or ravine called Onomea, where La Farge sketched till noon; one of the sweetest spots on earth where the land and ocean meet like lovers, and the natives still look almost natural. That afternoon we rode eight miles further. The sky cleared; the sun shone; the breeze blew; the road was awful, in deep holes of mud, with rocky cañons to climb down and up at every half mile; but I never enjoyed anything in travel more thoroughly than I did this. Every ravine was more beautiful than the last, and each was a true Paul and Virginia idyll, wildly lovely in ways that made one forget life. The intensely blue ocean foamed into the mouths of still inlets, saturated with the tropical green of ferns and dense woods, and a waterfall always made a background, with its sound of running water above the surf. The afternoon repaid all my five thousand miles of weariness, even though we had to pass the night at one of Spreckles' sugar plantations where saturnine Scotchmen and a gentle-spoken Gloucestershire housekeeper entertained us till seven o'clock Saturday morning; when we started off again over the same mud-holes and through more cañons, which disturbed La Farge because the horses were not noble animals and warranted little confidence; but to me the enjoyment was perfect. At noon we lunched at another plantation where a rather pretty little German-American woman, of the bride class, entertained us very sweetly, and closed our enjoyment by playing to us

Weber's last waltz, while we looked out under vines to the deep blue ocean as one does from the Newport cottages. That was at Laupahoehoe plantation, and that afternoon we passed Laupahoehoe and rode hard till half-past five, when I dismounted before a country-house, and, before I realised it, tumbled up steps into an open hall where three ladies in white dresses were seated. I had to explain that we had invited ourselves to pass the night, and they had to acquiesce. The family was named Horner, and were Americans running several plantations and ranches on the island. We passed the night of Sunday at the plantation of another son, or brother, of the same family, at Kukuihaele, and strolled down to see the Waipio valley, which is one of the Hawaiian sights. Yesterday we rode twelve miles up the hills, stopping to lunch at the house of one Jarrett who manages a great cattle ranch. Jarrett was not there, but two young women were, and though they were in language and manners as much like other young women as might be, they had enough of the old-gold quality and blood to make them very amusing to me. They made me eat raw fish and squid, as well as of course the eternal *poi* to which I am now accustomed, then after lunch, while La Farge and I smoked or dozed and looked across the grass plains to the wonderful slopes of Mauna Loa and Mauna Kea, the two girls sat on mats under the trees and made garlands of roses and geranium which they fastened round our necks— or rather round my neck and La Farge's hat. I was tremendously pleased by this, my first *lei*—I believe they spell the word so, pronouncing it *lay*—and wore it down the long, dusty ride to Kawaihae where we were to meet the steamer, and where we arrived just at dark in an afterglow like Egypt. The girls also drove down, one of them returning to Honolulu by the same steamer. Kawaihae seemed a terrible spot, baked by the southern sun against a mountain of brown lava without a drop of fresh water for miles. When I dismounted and entered the dirty little restaurant, I found our two young ladies eating supper at a dusky table. They had ordered for me a perfectly raw fresh fish, and the old-goldest of the two showed me how to eat it, looking delightfully savage as she held the dripping fish in her hands and tore its flesh with her teeth. Jarrett was there, and took us under his care, so that an evening which threatened to be so awful in heat and dirt, turned out delightful. They took us to a native house near by, where a large platform thatched with palm-leaves looked under scrubby trees across the moonlit ocean which just lapped and purred on the beach a few yards away. Then they made the mistress of the house—an old schoolmate, but a native and speaking little English—bring her guitar and sing the Hawaiian songs. They were curiously plaintive, perhaps owing to the way of singing, but only one—Kamehameha's war-dance—was really interesting and sounded as though it were real. A large mat was brought out, and those of us who liked lay down and listened or slept. The moon was half full, and shone exquisitely and Venus sank with a trail like the sun's.

From this queer little episode, the only touch of half-native life we have felt, we were roused by the appearance of the steamer at ten o'clock, and in due time were taken into the boat and set on board. I dropped my faded and tattered *lei* into the water as we were rowed out, and now while the "Kinau" lies at Mahukana, doing nothing, I write to tell you that our journey has been fascinating, in spite of prosaic sugar plantations, and that I am yearning to get back to Waimea, where I might stay a month at Samuel Parker's great ranch, and ride his horses about the slopes of Mauna Kea, while indefinite girls of the old-gold variety should hang indefinite garlands round my bronze neck.

Sept. 24. Honolulu again. . . . Now that I look back on

our Hawaiian journey of the last ten days, it seems really a considerable experience, and one new to common travellers in gaiters. If you feel enough curiosity to know what others think of the same scenes, read Miss Bird's travels in the Sandwich Islands. I have carefully avoided looking at her remarks, for I know that she always dilates with a correct emotion, and I yearn only for the incorrect ones; but you will surely see Islands of the soundest principles—travellers' principles, I mean—if you read Miss Bird, who will tell you all that I ought to have seen and felt, and for whom the volcano behaved so well, and performed its correct motions so properly that it becomes a joy to follow her. To us the volcano was positively flat, and I sympathised actively with an Englishman, who, we were told, after a single glance at it, turned away and gazed only at the planets and the Southern Cross. To irritate me still more, we are now assured that the lake of fire by which we sat unmoved, became very active within four-and-twenty hours afterwards. These are our lucks. I never see the world as the world ought to be.

In revenge I have enjoyed much that is not to be set down in literary composition, unless by a writer like Fromentin or a spectacled and animated prism like La Farge. He has taught me to feel the subtleness and endless variety of charm in the color and light of every hour in the tropical island's day and night. I get gently intoxicated on the soft violets and strong blues, the masses of purple and the broad bands of orange and green in the sunsets, as I used to *griser* myself on absinthe on the summer evenings in the Palais Royal before dining at Véfour's, thirty years ago. The outlines of the great mountains, their reddish purple glow, the infinite variety of greens and the perfectly intemperate shifting blues of the ocean, are a new world to me. To be sure, man is pretty vile, but perhaps woman might partly compensate for him, if one only knew where to find her. As she canters about the roads, a-straddle on horseback, with wreaths of faded yellow flowers, and clothed in a blue or red or yellow night-gown, she is rather a riddle than a satisfaction. . . .

To ELIZABETH CAMERON

Apia [Samoa], October 9, 1890.

Well we are here, and I am sitting in the early morning on the verandah of a rough cottage, in a grove of cocoa-nut palms, with native huts all about me, and across the grass, fifty yards away, I can see and hear the sea with its distant line of surf on the coral reef beyond. Natives clothed mostly in a waist-cloth, but sometimes their toilet completed by a hybiscus or other flower in their hair, pass every moment or two before my cabin, often handsome as Greek gods. I am the guest of Consul Sewall, whose consulate is within the same grove, near the beach. . . .

Sunday morning at nine o'clock or thereabouts, the "Alameda" turned a corner of Tutuila, and I saw the little schooner knocking about in the open sea beyond. The day was overcast, threatening rain. From the shore, half a dozen large boats, filled with naked savages, were paddling down with the wind, singing a curiously wild chant to their paddles. La Farge and I felt that we were to be captured and probably eaten, but the cruise of sixty miles in a forty-ton schooner, beating to windward in tropical squalls, was worse than being eaten. We dropt into the boat among scores of naked Samoans, half of them swimming, or clambering over our backs, with war clubs to sell, and when we reached our schooner, we stood in the rain and watched the "Alameda" steam away. That was our first joy. Whatever fate was in store, we had escaped from the steamer, and might die before another would come.

The cutter was commanded by Captain Peter, a huge captain, but little skilled in the languages with which I am more or less acquainted. His six sailors were as little fluent in English as though they had studied at Harvard. Captain Peter talked what he supposed to be English with excessive energy, but we could catch only the three words "now and again," repeated with frequency but in no apparent connection. "Now and again" something was to happen; meanwhile he beat up under the shore into quieter water, and presently, in a downpour of rain, we cast anchor in a bay, with mountains above, but a sand-beach within the coral reef, and native huts half hidden among the cocoanut palms. I insisted on going ashore straightway without respect for H. M.'s mail, and Captain Peter seemed not unwilling. A splendid naked savage carried La Farge, in an india-rubber water-proof, mildly kicking, from the boat to the shore, and returned for me. I embraced his neck with effusive gratitude, and so landed on the island of Tutuila, which does not resemble the picture on the Oceanic Steamship Company's colored advertisement. I found it densely covered with tropical mountains and vegetation, but glad as I was to set foot on mountains and see vegetation, I was soon more interested in the refined hospitality of the cultured inhabitants. We entered the nearest hut, and put on our best manners, which were none too good, for the natives had manners that made me feel withered prematurely in association with the occupants of pig-sties. Grave, courteous, with quiet voices and a sort of benevolence beyond the utmost expressiveness of Benjamin Franklin, they received us and made us at home. The cabin was charming when one looked about it. Nearly circular, with a diameter of some forty feet, its thatched roof, beautifully built up, came within about five feet of the ground, ending there on posts, and leaving the whole house open to the air. Within, mats covered a floor of white corals, smooth and almost soft like coarse sand. Fire was made in the middle of the hut. Only women and children were there. One was staining a tapa-cloth; another was lying down unwell; others were sitting about, and one or two naked children, wonderfully silent and well-behaved, sat and stared at us. We dropped our umbrellas and water-proofs and sat down on the mats to wait for Captain Peter to sail; but presently a proud young woman entered and seated herself in silence after shaking hands. Captain Peter succeeded in making us understand that this was the chief's daughter. Other young women dropped in, shook hands and sat down. Soon we seemed to have a *matinée*. As no one could say more than a word or two in the other's language, communication was as hard as at a Washington party, but it was more successful. In a very short time we were all intimate. La Farge began to draw the Princess, as we called her, and Wakea—for that was her name—was pleased to drop her dress-skirt, and sit for him in her native undress, with a dignity and gravity quite indescribable. The other girls were less imposing, but very amusing. One, Sivà, a younger sister of the Princess, was fascinating. Of course I soon devoted my attention to talking, and, as I could understand nothing, talk was moderately easy; but through Captain Peter we learned a little, and some of the touches of savagery were perfect. I asked Sivà her name—mine was Hen-li—and her age. She did not know her age; even her father, an old man, could not say how many years old she was. I guessed fourteen, equivalent to our eighteen. All her motions were splendid, and she threw a plate on the floor, as Martha Braggiotti would say, like a race-horse. Her lines were all antique, and in face she recalled a little my niece Lulu, Molly's sister. Presently she brought a curious pan-shaped wooden dish, standing on eight legs, all of one block; and sitting down behind it, began to grate a dry root, like a flag-root but larger, on a grater, over the dish. This was rather hard work, and took some time. Then another girl brought some cocoa-nuts full of water, and she poured the water on the grated root. Then she took a bundle of clean cocoa-nut fibre, and seemed to wash her hands in the water which was already muddy and dirty with the grated root. We divined that she really strained out the grated particles, which were caught on the fibre, and wrung out by another girl. When all the grains were strained off, the drink was ready, and we realised that we had got to swallow it, for this was the *kawa,* and we were grateful that in our first experience the root was grated, not chewed, as it ought to be, by the girls. Please read Kingsley's account of it in the "Earl and the Doctor," a book you will probably be able to borrow from Herbert, as it was done for or by his brother Pembroke. A cocoa-nut half full of it was handed to us, and as usual La Farge, who had kicked at the idea more than I did, took to it at once, and drank it rather freely. I found it "not nice, papa, but funny"; a queer lingering, varying, aromatic, arumatic, Polynesian, old-gold flavor, that clings to the palate like creosote or coal-oil. I drank the milk of a green cocoa-nut to wash it off, but all the green cocoa-nuts in the ocean could not wash out that little taste. After the *kawa* we became still more intimate. Besides Wakea and her sister Sivà, we made the acquaintance of Tuvale, Amerika, Sitoa, and Faaiuro, which is no other than Fayaway, I imagine. We showed them our writing, and found that they could write very well, as they proved by writing us letters on the spot, in choice Samoan, which we tried to translate, with the usual result. So evening came on; we had some supper; a kerosene lamp was lit; and La Farge and I began to cry out for the *Siva.*

The *Siva,* we had learned to know at Hawaii, is the Samoan dance, and the girl, Sivà, had already been unable to resist giving us snatches of the songs and motions. Sivà was fascinating. She danced all over, and seemed more Greek in every new motion. I could not understand what orders were given by the elders, but, once they were assured that we were not missionaries, all seemed right. The girls disappeared; and after some delay, while I was rather discouraged, thinking that the Siva was not to be, suddenly out of the dark, five girls came into the light, with a dramatic effect that really I never felt before. Naked to the waist, their rich skins glistened with cocoa-nut oil. Around their heads and necks they wore garlands of green leaves in strips, like seaweeds, and these too glistened with oil, as though the girls had come out of the sea. Around their waists, to the knee, they wore leaf-clothes, or *lavalavas,* also of fresh leaves, green and red. Their faces and figures varied in looks, some shading the negro too closely; but Sivà was divine, and you can imagine that we found our attention absorbed in watching her. The mysterious depths of darkness behind, against which the skins and dresses of the dancers mingled rather than contrasted; the sense of remoteness and of genuineness in the stage-management; the conviction that at last the kingdom of old-gold was ours, and that we were as good Polynesiacs as our neighbors—the whole scene and association gave so much freshness to our fancy that no future experience, short of being eaten, will ever make us feel so new again. La Farge's spectacles quivered with emotion and gasped for sheer inability to note everything at once. To me the dominant idea was that the girls, with their dripping grasses and leaves, and their glistening breasts and arms, had actually come out of the sea a few steps away. They entered in file, and sat down opposite us. Then the so-called Siva dance began. The girls sat cross-legged, and the dance was as much song as motion, although the motion was incessant. As the song or chant, a rhythmical and rather pleasant, quick movement, began, the dancers swayed about; clapped their hands, shoulders, legs; stretched out their arms in every direction and with every possible action, always in harmony, and seldom repeating the same figure. We had dozens of these different motives until I thought the poor girls would be exhausted, for they made so much muscular effort, feet, thighs, hips and even ribs working as energetically as the arms, that they panted at the close of each figure; but they were evidently enjoying it as much as we, and kept it up with glances at us and laughter among themselves. All through this part of the performance, our Princess did not dance but sat before us on the mats, and beat time with a stick. At last she too got up, and after ten minutes' absence, reappeared, costumed like the rest, but taller and more splendid. La Farge exploded with enthusiasm for her, and expressed boundless contempt for Carmencita. You can imagine the best female figure you ever saw, on about a six foot scale, neck, breast, back, arms and legs, all absolutely Greek in modelling and action, with such freedom of muscle and motion as the Greeks themselves hardly knew, and you can appreciate La Farge's excitement. When she came in the other dancers rose, and then began what I supposed to be a war or sword dance, the Princess brandishing a stick and evidently destroying her enemies, one of whom was a comic character and expressed abject cowardice. With this performance the dance ended; Sivà got out the *kawa* dish; Wakea and the others went for our tobacco, and soon we were all sprawling over the mats, smoking, laughing, trying to talk, with a sense of shoulders, arms, legs, cocoa-nut oil, and general nudeness most strangely mixed with a sense of propriety. Anyone would naturally suppose such a scene to be an orgy of savage license. I don't pretend to know what it was, but I give you my affidavit that we could see nothing in the songs or dances that suggested impropriety, and that not a word or a sign during our whole stay could have brought a blush to the cheek of Senator H—— himself. Unusual as the experience is of half dressed or undressed women lying about the floor, in all sorts of attitudes, and as likely as not throwing their arms or their shoulders across one as one lies or sits near them, as far as we could see the girls were perfectly good, and except occasionally for hinting that they would like a present of a handkerchief, or for giving us perhaps a ring, there was no approach to familiarity with us. Indeed at last we were extinguished by dropping a big mosquito netting over us, so that we were enclosed in a private room; the girls went off to their houses; our household sank into perfect quiet, and we slept in our clothes on the floor as comfortably as we knew how, while the kerosene lamp burned all night in the centre of the floor.

The next morning we very unwillingly tumbled into our boat, after a surf bath, and then, for the next four or five hours, we were pitching about, in a head wind and sea, trying to round the western point of Tutuila. Nothing could be more lovely than the day, the blue sea, and the green island stretching away in different planes of color, till lost in the distance. At two o'clock that afternoon we rounded our point, and our boat went ashore to fetch off Consul Sewall and Lieut. Parker on their return from Pango Pango, where they had gone to settle on the new naval station. They came instantly on board, and we four Americans then lay on the deck of that cutter from two o'clock Monday afternoon, till two o'clock Wednesday morning, thirty-six hours, going sixty miles, in a calm, with a vertical sun overhead, and three of the four seasick. You can conceive that we were glad to reach Apia on any terms, and tumbled ashore, in a leaky boat, in the dead of night, only too glad to get shelter about the consulate. Our only excitement at sea was a huge shark that looked like a whale. Once ashore, supper and bed were paradise; but my brain and stomach went on turning somersaults, and I was not wholly happy.

October 12. Sunday here, when it should be Saturday, but Samoa is above astronomy. Time has already made us familiar with our surroundings. I find myself now and then regaining consciousness that I was once an American supposing himself real. The Samoan is so different from all my preconceived ideas, that my own identity becomes hazy, and yours alone remains tolerably clear. I took one day of entire rest, after arriving, and passed it in looking at the sea, and rejoicing to have escaped it. The second day we performed our visits of ceremony. First, we called on King Malietoa, and I assure you that I was not in the least inclined to joke about him. He is not *opéra bouffe,* or Kalakaua. The ceremony was simple as though we were in a democratic republic. We began by keeping his Majesty waiting half an hour while we lounged over our cigars after breakfast. When we arrived at the audience-house, we found Malietoa gone, but he was sent for, and came to receive us. The house was the ordinary native house, such as we were in at Tutuila. We sat on the floor. Malietoa was alone, without officers or attendants, and was dressed as usual with chiefs on state occasions, in an ordinary white linen jacket and trousers. He is an elderly man, with the usual rather pathetic expression of these islanders, and with the charming voice and manner which seem to belong to high chiefs. He talked slowly, with a little effort, but with a dignity and seriousness that quite overawed me. As the interpreter translated, I caught only the drift of his words, which were at first formal; then became warm in expressions of regard for Americans; and at last turned to an interesting and rather important discussion of the political dangers and uneasiness in these islands. He said nothing of his own sufferings or troubles, but seemed anxious for fear of disturbance here, and evidently dreads some outbreak against his own authority unless the three foreign powers execute their treaty promptly, which the three foreign powers seem, for reasons of their own, determined not to do. If you want a lecture on Samoan politics, I am in a fair way to be able to give you one; for though I loathe the very word, and of all kinds of politics detest most those of islands, I am just soaked with the stuff here, where the natives are children, full of little jealousies and intrigues, and the foreigners are rather worse than the natives. The three foreign powers have made a mess, and the natives are in it. Even in case they fight, I do not much expect to be massacred, as Americans are very popular indeed; but I am a great *ali*—nobleman—because all the natives knew the frigate "Adams," and I am the first American who has ever visited the country merely for pleasure; so I feel bound to look grave and let Sewall do the talking. Malietoa was sad and despondent; Mata-afa, the intermediary king, who led the fighting after Malietoa's deportation, and was deposed by the treaty of Berlin, seemed also depressed, but was even more earnest in his expressions of gratitude to America. We made also a ceremonial call on Mata-afa, after we had seen Malietoa, and while we were going through the unavoidable *kawa*, which becomes a serious swallow after many repetitions, Mata-afa talked of his gratitude to America. I won't bore you by explaining why he is grateful. I don't much care myself; and was much more interested in watching the dignity of his face, the modulation of his voice, the extraordinary restraint and refinement of his rhetoric, and the exquisite art of the slight choking in his voice as he told us that his only hope was in Christ and in America. I felt more interest in the art of his civilisation, you understand, than I did in the detail that Bayard and Sewall had saved the islanders from being killed or enslaved. As rhetoricians and men of manners, the great Samoan chiefs, and, for that matter, the little ones too, make me feel as though I were the son of a camel-driver degraded to the position of stable-boy in Spokane West Centre. Aristocracy can go no further, and any ordinary aristocracy is vulgar by the side of the Samoan. For centuries these people have thought of nothing else. They have no other arts worth mentioning. Some day I will tell you of their straw mats, their chief artistic pride; their houses, too, are artistic in their way, and their taste in colors is splendidly bold; but their real art is social, and they have done what in theory every scientific society would like to do—they have bred themselves systematically. Love marriages are unknown. The old chiefs select the wives for the young chiefs, and choose for strength and form rather than beauty of face. Each village elects a girl to be the village maiden, a sort of candidate for ambitious marriage, and she is the tallest and best made girl of the good society of the place. She is bound to behave herself, and marry a handsome young chief. The consequence is that the chiefs are the handsomest men you can imagine, physically Apollos, and the women can all carry me in their arms as though I was a baby.

The chief of Apia is Seumano, the hero of the hurricane, who took his boat through the surf and saved the shipwrecked crews. Our government sent him a present of a fancy whale-boat, very handsome though a little like a man-of-war, requiring about fifty men to move it. Seumano is a giant in strength; his wife, Fatolea, is quite a *grande dame,* and their adopted daughter, Fanua, is the village maiden, or Taupo, of Apia. Sewall got Seumano, who is as warmly American as all the rest, to give us a big Siva dance that we might see the thing properly, and the occasion was evidently one of general interest. In general the scene was the same as at Nua in

Tutuila, but instead of an improvised affair, Seumano gave us a regular party, with the whole village taking part or looking on. Fanua was the centre girl, and had nine or ten companions. Fanua wore an immensely high and heavy headdress that belongs to the village maiden. The others were dressed in the Siva costume, but spoiled their effect by wearing banana leaves round their breasts, in deference to missionary prejudices. The figure is everything in the native dance, and the color counts almost as much as dress with you creatures of civilisation. The banana leaves were as little objectionable as such symbols of a corrupt taste could be, but they reminded one of the world and the devil. Our impromptu at Nua was better, for though some of the girls were more or less grotesque, the handsome ones, with fine figures, were tremendously effective. You can imagine what would be the effect of applying such a test to a New York ball-room, and how unpopular the banana leaf would be with girls whose figures were better than their faces. Nevertheless the Siva was a good one, especially in the singing and the drill. The older women sat in the dark behind the girls, and acted as chorus. Sewall, his vice Consul Blacklock, La Farge and I sat in front, opposite the dancers. Towards the end, when the dancers got up and began their last figure, which grows more and more vivacious to the end, Fanua, who had mischief in her eyes, pranced up before me, and bending over, put her arms round my neck and kissed me. The kissing felt quite natural and was loudly applauded with much laughter, but I have been redolent of cocoa-nut oil ever since, and the more because Fanua afterwards gave me her wreaths, and put one over my neck, the other round my waist, dripping with cocoa-nut oil. . . .

October 17. Yesterday afternoon Sewall took La Farge and me to call on Robert Louis Stevenson. We mounted some gawky horses and rode up the hills about an hour on the native road or path which leads across the island. The forest is not especially exciting; not nearly so beautiful as that above Hilo in Hawaii, but every now and again, as Captain Peter, or Pito, used to say, we came on some little touch of tropical effect that had charm, especially a party of three girls in their dress of green leaves, or *titi*, which La Farge became glowing about. The afternoon was lowering, with drops of rain, and misty in the distance. At last we came out on a clearing dotted with burned stumps exactly like a clearing in our backwoods. In the middle stood a two-story Irish shanty with steps outside to the upper floor, and a galvanised iron roof. A pervasive atmosphere of dirt seemed to hang around it, and the squalor like a railroad navvy's board hut. As we reached the steps a figure came out that I cannot do justice to. Imagine a man so thin and emaciated that he looked like a bundle of sticks in a bag, with a head and eyes morbidly intelligent and restless. He was costumed in a dirty striped cotton pyjamas, the baggy legs tucked into coarse knit woollen stockings, one of which was bright brown in color, the other a purplish dark tone. With him was a woman who retired for a moment into the house to reappear a moment afterwards, probably in some change of costume, but, as far as I could see, the change could have consisted only in putting shoes on her bare feet. She wore the usual missionary nightgown which was no cleaner than her husband's shirt and drawers, but she omitted the stockings. Her complexion and eyes were dark and strong, like a half-breed Mexican. They received us cordially enough, and as soon as Stevenson heard La Farge's name and learned who he was, they became very friendly, while I sat by, nervously conscious that my eyes could not help glaring at Stevenson's stockings, and wondering, as La Farge said, which color he would have chosen if he had been obliged to wear a pair that matched. We sat an hour or more, perched on his verandah, looking down over his field of black stumps, and the forest beyond, to the misty line of distant ocean to the northward. He has bought a hundred acres or more of mountain and forest so dense that he says it costs him a dollar for every foot he walks in it. To me the place seemed oppressively shut in by forest and mountain, but the weather may have caused that impression. When conversation fairly began, though I could not forget the dirt and discomfort, I found Stevenson extremely entertaining. He has the nervous restlessness of his disease, and, although he said he was unusually well, I half expected to see him drop with a hemorrhage at any moment, for he cannot be quiet, but sits down, jumps up, darts off and flies back, at every sentence he utters, and his eyes and features gleam with a hectic glow. He seems weak, and complains that the ride of an hour up to his place costs him a day's work; but, as he describes his travels and life in the South Seas, he has been through what would have broken me into a miserable rag. For months he has sailed about the islands in wretched trading schooners and stray steamers almost worse than sailing vessels, with such food as he could get, or lived on coral atolls eating bread-fruit and yams, all the time working hard with his pen, and of course always dirty, uncomfortable and poorly served, not to speak of being ill-clothed, which matters little in these parts. He has seen more of the island than any literary or scientific man ever did before, and knows all he has seen. His talk is most entertaining, and of course interested us peculiarly. He says that the Tahitians are by far finer men than the Samoans, and that he does not regard the Samoans as an especially fine race, or the islands here as specially beautiful. I am not surprised at the last opinion, for I do not think this island of Upolu very beautiful as these islands go; certainly not so beautiful as the Hilo district of Hawaii; but I shall wait for our own judgment about the men and women. Tahiti and Nukuheva are his ideals, which encourages us with something to look forward to. He had much to say about his experiences, and about atolls, French *gens d'armes,* beach-combers, natives and Chinamen; about the island of Flatterers where the natives surrounded him and stroked him down, saying "Alofa," "love," and "You handsome man," "You all same as my father"; and about islands where the girls took away all his plug tobacco and picked his pocket of his matchbox, and then with the utmost dignity gave him one match to light his cigarette. But the natives, he says, are always respectable, while some of the whites are degraded beyond description. Pembroke, in his "South Sea Bubbles" has scandalised all Polynesia by libelling the chieftainess of one island where he was very hospitably treated, and is said to have behaved very ill. I can easily understand getting very mixed up about Polynesian morals, for I feel that the subject is a deep one, and the best informed whites seem perplexed about it; but I remember how much poor Okakura was perplexed by the same subject in America, and how frankly La Farge and I avowed our own ignorance even among our own people. Stevenson is about to build a house, and says he shall never leave the island again, and cannot understand how any man who is able to live in the South Seas, should consent to live elsewhere.

To ELIZABETH CAMERON

Vaiale [Samoa], 8 November, 1890.

. . . Stevenson returned our call the other day, and passed several hours with us. He was cleaner, and his wife was not with him, for which reasons perhaps he seemed less like W——
E——. He talked very well, as usual, but said nothing that stuck very hard. He will tell his experiences in the form of

Travels, and I was rather surprised to find that his range of study included pretty much everything: geology, sociology, laws, politics and ethnology. We like him, but he would be, I think, an impossible companion. His face has a certain beauty, especially the eyes, but it is the beauty of disease. He is a strange compound of callousness and susceptibility, and his susceptibility is sometimes more amusing than his callousness. We were highly delighted with one trait which he showed in absolute unconsciousness of its simplicity. The standard of domestic morality here is not what is commonly regarded as rigid. Most of the traders and residents have native wives, to whom they are married after the native custom: that is, during pleasure. A clerk in the employ of an American trader named Moors was discovered in too close relations with the native wife of a lawyer named Carruthers. The offence was condoned once, and this lenity seemed very proper to Stevenson, who declared that he had no difficulty in forgiving his wife once, but not a second time. Recently the scandal was renewed, and caused great tribulation. Stevenson was deeply outraged, and declared that he would no longer dine with Moors for fear of meeting the clerk. Moors, who had various wives to say nothing of incidental feminine resources, was also scandalized, and dismissed the clerk, though the clerk was indispensable to his business. Carruthers was painfully saddened. The woman's father, an old native, was worst of all. I have not yet learned the views of Mrs. Stevenson; but we are curious to know why, in the light of their own experience, they could not have suggested the easy device of advising Carruthers to let his wife go, and allowing the clerk to marry her. The unfortunate clerk is the victim of outraged Samoan morality, and is to be sent back to San Francisco where the standard is, I presume, less exalted. This part of Stevenson's talk was altogether the most humorous, and as grotesque as the New Arabian Nights; but Stevenson was not in the least conscious of our entertainment.

Samoa becomes more curious, in this sort of grotesqueness, the more one sees of it. The sexual arrangements are queer enough, and the stories of old Samsoni, or Hamilton, formerly pilot, harbor-master, American Vice Consul, and what not, amuse me beyond description, though they are rarely capable of record. In my last letter, somewhere, I may have mentioned Taele, a native woman who keeps a supervision of our native house. Taele is still young; hardly more than twenty; and unusually pretty. Her prettiness so attracted a recent British Consul, that he married her, after Samoan custom, and she was known as his wife. They had a child, a handsome boy, now five or six years old, who lives with our old village chief To-fai, close by our sleeping-quarters, and is inseparable from the old man. A couple of years ago or thereabouts, the Consul was ordered elsewhere, and went, leaving Taele with a small pension and the hope of his return. Taele waited for him dutifully until she despaired of his return, and then she married a native carpenter who had been a missionary teacher. Very recently I learned from Mele Samsoni that the second husband had gone off to another province and had taken another wife. Taele quietly remains here, much respected and very interesting in the melancholy style of some Samoan beauties; but she is scared into the forest because I want her to serve as a model to draw from. She cannot endure the idea of being painted, even in full dress, covered up to the ears, and is in deadly terror because I wanted her to wear the *lavalava,* or waist-cloth, which every native habitually carries. Yet I have no doubt that Taele will have another husband soon.

In other ways the natives are more inscrutable. Chiefly for want of something to talk about during the interminable visits of native chiefs, I ask questions about the old customs, families and religion. Three times out of four, when I reach any interesting point, I am blocked by the reply that what I ask is a secret. At first I thought that this was only a way of disguising ignorance, but was assured that it was not so. I am pretty well convinced that all matters involving their old superstitions, priesthood, and family history, are really secret, and that their Christianity covers a pretty complete paganism with priests and superstitions as strong as ever. Indeed, To-fai made no bones of telling me, at great length, the whole story, and on his information I have in several cases surprised other chiefs into admissions that they did not intend to make; but I am still convinced that the Samoans have an entire intellectual world of their own, and never admit outsiders into it. I feel sure that they have a secret priesthood more powerful than the political chiefs, with supernatural powers, invocations, prophecy, charms, and the whole paraphernalia of paganism. I care too little about these matters to make any searching inquiry, so they may keep their secrets for anything I shall do; but I never imagined a race so docile and gentle, yet so obstinately secret. They never killed a missionary, but they are just masters in playing the missionaries off. The chiefs especially detest the missionary teachers, who are all common people of no social rank, and who have mostly chosen to become teachers in order to get a position of any kind, which can be done only by undermining the power of the chiefs. . . .

Our lunch today was only remarkable for my having at last tasted *pollolo*, a Samoan delicacy of the repulsive order. The *pollolo* is a curious salt-water worm, or long thin creature like a very slim earthworm; it appears only once a year, just at dawn, at a certain place on the coral reef opposite our Consulate. As the day happened about ten days ago, we all went out to see the show, starting at four o'clock with the first light of dawn. As we bumped and hauled over the coral we could gradually see a dozen or more boats, mostly the narrow native dug-outs, about a distant spot near the outer, or barrier reef. When we came up, we joined them, and, peering into the water, with the growing light, we could at last see one or two long, thin, thread-like creatures swimming near the surface. They had some sense akin to sight, for when I tried to catch them with my hand, they swam away. At last I caught one, and as I looked at him in the hollow of my hand, the little wretch kicked himself in pieces, and I had half a dozen little kicking earwigs in my hand. The same thing happened in the water. As the day dawned, the creatures became thicker, but each soon divided into inch- or half-inch sections, and the top of the water soon swarmed with things, which the boat-people caught with fine hand-nets, or sieves, and turned into pails. Nothing seems to be known of the creature, or why he should come on one particular day of the year, at certain, far distant spots, for an hour before dawn, and should disappear at sunrise. The water was but two or three feet deep on the coral rock, and the creature has ample motive power to come out or go in as he likes, but he comes and goes only by the calendar. The natives eat them raw; but to keep the luxury longer, they cook it with cocoa-nut meat, pounded, and Fatuleia brought some of it for lunch; a greenish, pasty stuff, like fine spinach. I tried it on bread, and thought it rather like *foie-gras*. . . .

To JOHN HAY

Vaiale [Samoa], 16 Novr. 1890.

By this time I had expected to be in Tahiti, but we have found more in Samoa than we expected. Our nasty little pig-stye of a steamer sailed for Tahiti a week ago or so, and will not return for a month. Then perhaps we shall sail, and when

this reaches you on Christmas Day I hope we shall be established at Papeete. I doubt whether it will have much novelty
after Samoa, but it will give a chance for you to join us. By
taking the mail sailing-ship from San Francisco, you can reach
Tahiti in about a month; perhaps less, for what I know.

Your letter of October 10 arrived by the last mail. All my
letters were very satisfactory, yours highly so, except for Som-
brerete, which is sombrereteer than ever. I am brewing a letter
to King which I shall write some day, and it will be a volume,
for I have seen heaps of things that I can tell him what I
don't know about; but the chiefest thing is that a man can
still live on these islands of the South Seas for pure fun. The
Consuls themselves, the greatest men within a thousand miles,
may spend four or five thousand a year. The richest trader
can hardly have more. King Malietoa has not a Chilian quar-
ter-dollar to his back. My neighbor and friend Mata-afa, ex-
king, goes every morning to work in his taro-patch, or to fish
on the reef with the villagers. I have had no little difficulty in
obtaining a thousand dollars to spend here, and I am regarded as fabulously rich. When I staid in Savaii with Aiga,
Malietoa's adopted daughter, my gift at parting was ten dollars; to Lauati, the great orator and chief of Safotulafai, where
we staid three days, I gave twenty, which was equivalent to a
fine mat, the costliest of possessions; and as a token of regard
for Anai, Chief of Iva, I am going—God forgive me—to supply
his little daughter with a year's schooling at the missionary
college at Malua. You see that a dollar still goes a long way
in Samóa, and when I tell you that I pay the extravagant rent
of ten dollars a month for my native house, and that a horse
costs thirty dollars and is not worth riding when he is bought,
you can safely assure King that the South Seas can always
shelter him though Sombreretes fall. Indeed, for that matter,
a great reputation can be made here with mighty small capi-

tal. Darwin and Dana and Wallace have only scratched the ocean's surface. The geologist who can explain these islands, and the artist who can express them, will have got a sure hold on the shirt-tail of fame. If I were twenty years younger, and knew anything to start with, I would try it on. King, who is always young and bloomful, can do it at any time.

The curse of money has touched here, but is not yet deep, though mountain forests, covered with dense and almost impenetrable vegetation, are held at ten dollars an acre, and the poor chiefs, whose only possession is a cocoa-nut grove, have mortgaged it to the eyes. By the Berlin treaty, the whites are not permitted to buy more land from natives, but the whites already claim under one title or another, more land than exists in the whole group of islands. If the sugar cultivation is introduced, the people are lost. Nothing can stand against the frantic barbarism of the sugar-planter. As yet, the only plantations are cocoa-nut, and these are not so mischievous, especially as they are badly managed by German companies which spend more money than the Copra brings. Yet the social changes are steady, and another generation will leave behind it the finest part of the old Samoan world. The young chiefs are inferior to the old ones. Gun-powder and missionaries have destroyed the life of the nobles. In former times a great chief went into battle with no thought of the common warrior. He passed through a herd of them, and none presumed to attack him. Chiefs fought only with chiefs. The idea of being killed by a common man was sacrilege. The introduction of fire-arms has changed all this, and now, as one of the chiefs said with a voice of horror, any hunchback, behind a tree, can kill the greatest chief in Samoa.

Since I wrote to you last, I have made a journey along the coast as far as Savaii, the westernmost and largest island of the group. We were an imposing party. The Consul General Sewall, whose guests we are, was the head of it, and Sewall is extremely popular among the Malietoa and Mata-afa chiefs who consider him to have saved their lives and liberties. Their expressions of gratitude to him and to the United States are unbounded, and they certainly showed that they felt it, for in their strongholds we were received like kings. Our escort was Seumano-tafa, the chief of Apia, Malietoa's right-hand man. You may remember that, in the great hurricane at Apia, Seumano took his boat through the surf, and saved many lives. For this act, our government sent him some costly presents, among others a beautiful boat, perfectly fitted out for oars and sails. On our *malanga,* or boat-excursion, we went with Seu in his boat, and our own boat followed with our baggage and stores. We carried on Seu's boat the Samoan flag; on our own, the American; and our entire party, including servants and crews, was more than twenty men. We were absent some ten days, with fine weather, and visited the most interesting parts of the islands. I felt as though I had got back to Homer's time, and were cruising about on the Aegean with Ajax. Of all the classic spots I ever imagined, the little island of Manono was the most ideal. Ithaca was, even in the reign of Ulysses, absolutely modern by the side of it. As the *mise-en-scène* of an opera, it would be perfection. If I could note music, I would compose an opera, on the musical motives of the Samoan dances and boat-songs, gutturals, grunts and all. You may bet your biggest margin it would be a tremendous success, if the police would only keep their hands off. The ballet alone would put New York on its head with excitement. You would rush for the next steamer if you could realize the beauty of some parts of the Siva. There are figures stupid and grotesque as you please; but there are others which would make you gasp with delight, and movements which I do not exaggerate in calling unsurpassable. Then, if I could close the spectacle with the climax of the *pai-pai*, I should just clean out the bottom dollar of W. W. Astor. The *pai-pai* is a figure taboo by the missionaries, as indeed the Lancers and Virginia Reel are; but it is still danced in the late hours of the night, though we have seen it only once. Two or three women are the dancers, and they should be the best, especially in figure. They dance at first with the same movements, as far as I could see, that they use in many other figures, and as I did not know what they were dancing I paid no special attention. Presently I noticed that the chief dancer's waist-cloth seemed getting loose. This is their only dress, and it is nothing but a strip of cotton or *tapa* about eighteen inches wide, wrapped round the waist, with the end or corner tucked inside to hold it. Of course it constantly works loose, but the natives are so well used to it that they always tighten it, and I never yet have seen either man, woman or child let it fall by accident. In the *pai-pai*, the women let their *lava-lavas,* as they are called, or *siapas,* seem about to fall. The dancer pretends to tighten it, but only opens it so as to show a little more thigh, and fastens it again so low as to show a little more hip. Always turning about and moving with the chorus, she repeats this process again and again, showing more legs and hips every time, until the *siapa* barely hangs on her, and would fall except that she holds it. At last it falls; she turns once or twice more, in full view; then snatches up the *siapa* and runs away.

You must imagine these dances in a native house, lighted by the ruddy flame of a palm-leaf fire in the centre, and filled, except where the dancing is done, by old-gold men and women applauding, laughing, smoking, and smelling of cocoanut oil. You are sitting or lying, with your back against an outer-post. Behind you, outside, the moon is lighting a swarm of children, or women, who are also looking eagerly at the dancers. The night air is soft, and the palms rustle above the house. Your legs are cramped by long sitting cross-legged; your back aches; your eyes droop with fatigue; your head aches with the noise; you would give a fortune to be allowed to go to bed, but you can't till the dance is over and the house is cleared. You are a little feverish, for this thing has gone on, day and night, for a week, and it is more exhausting than a Pan-American railway jaunt. You are weary of travel and tired of the South Seas. You want to be at home, in your own bed, with clean sheets and a pillow, and quiet. Well! I give you my word, founded on experience, that, with all this, when you see the *pai-pai,* you are glad you came.

Of course the Siva, and especially the figure of the *pai-pai*— beautiful thighs—is made to display the form and not the face. To the Samoan, nine tenths of beauty consists in form; the other tenth in feature, coloring and such details. The Samoan Siva, like the Japanese bath, is evidently connected with nat- ural selection; the young men and young women learn there to know who are the finest marriageable articles. Probably the girl who could make the best show in the *pai-pai* would rise in value to the village by the difference of two or three fine mats and a dozen pigs. In such a case the *pai-pai,* danced by a chief's daughter or *taupo*, does not prove license but virtue. The audience is far less moved by it than a French audience is by a good ballet. Any European suddenly taken to such a show would assume that the girl was licentious, and if he were a Frenchman he would probably ask for her. The chief would be scandalised at European want of decency. He keeps his *taupo* as carefully watched and guarded as though he were a Spaniard. The girl herself knows her own value and is not likely to throw herself away. She has no passions, though she is good-natured enough, and might perhaps elope with a handsome young fellow who made long siege of her. The

Frenchman would be politely given some middle-aged woman, more or less repulsive in person, and the mother of several illegitimate children, who would have to be his only consolation for losing the object of his desire. The natives would fully appreciate the joke, and probably nickname the victim by some word preserving its memory.

I have not changed my ideas on the point of morality here. As elsewhere, vice follows vice. We have not sought it, and consequently have not found it. Thus far, no one, either man or woman, has made so much as a suggestion, by word or sign, of any licentious idea. My boatmen probably have license enough, but, as the German Consul warned me, I have none. I might as well be living in a nursery for all the vice that is shown to me, and if I did see it, I should only be amused at its simplicity beside the elaborated viciousness of Paris or even of Naples. I never have lived in so unself-conscious a place. Yesterday La Farge and I snorted with laughter because our boy Charley, a half-caste who acts as our interpreter, informed us that "a girl had just been caught running away with a man." On cross-examination, La Farge drew out the further facts that the pair were literally running, in full sight of half the town, along the main road by the seashore, when they might have dodged into a trackless forest within fifty yards; that the girl was then in a neighboring house getting a scolding from her mother; and that after the scolding she would get a beating. La Farge was so much delighted that he wanted to start off at once to see the girl, with a view, I think, to some possible picture to be called the "The Elopement," but he was hard at work painting a sketch of Fang-alo sliding down the waterfall, for Clarence King's satisfaction no doubt, and he could not leave his sketch.

Apropos to cataracts of girls, they are common as any other cataracts here. Any waterfall with a ten-foot pool at its base, and a suitable drop, is sure to be used both by girls and boys, and by men as well. The difficulty is that the coast is mostly flat; the waterfalls are far off, and few of them are suited to the purpose. The only one near Apia is fully five miles away, in the hills, far from any village; and one must make up a party of girls from here, and devote a day to a regular picnic, in order to see the show. For King's sake I did this last week. My friend Fatuleia, Seumano's wife, the chiefess of Apia, took charge of the affair, and summoned half a dozen of the belles of Apia:—Fanua, the *taupo*; Otaota, whose photograph I must have sent you, a pretty girl standing before the grave-monument of a chief; Fang-alo, whose photograph you also have; Nelly, a pretty missionary girl; and two or three others. We rode two hours through the forest, and clambered down a ravine to the spot, a deep valley, with cliffs overgrown with verdure, and topped by high trees far above us. To my surprise I found that the waterfall was little more than a brook, as far as the water had to do with it, though the fall was steep enough; full twenty feet into a deep pool. For this reason the place is called the Sliding Rock, for the water has smoothed the hard stone, and covered it with a slippery grass or fine slimy growth. The girls sit in the running water, and slide or coast down, with a plunge of ten or twelve feet below. They go like a shot, and the sight is very pretty. La Farge and I were immensely amused by it, and so were the girls, who went in as though they were naiads. They wore whatever suited their ideas of propriety, from a waist-cloth to a nightgown dress; but the variety rather added to the effect, and the water took charge of the proprieties.

The most curious part of our experience here is to find that the natives are so totally different from what I imagined, and yet so like what I ought to have expected. They are a finer race than I supposed, and seem uncontaminated by outside influence. They have not suffered from diseases introduced from abroad. They have their own diseases—elephantiasis is the worst, but skin-troubles and sores are common, and eyes are apt to be affected by blemish—but they are otherwise strong and would shame any white race I ever saw, for the uniform vigor of their bodies. One never sees a tall man who is thin or feeble. Their standard of beauty varies between six feet, and six-feet-six, in height, but is always broad and muscular in proportion. The women are very nearly as strong as the men. Often in walking behind them I puzzle myself to decide from their backs whether they are men or women, and I am never sure. La Farge detects a certain widening towards the hips which I am too little trained to see; and no wonder, for I have taken enough measurements of typical specimens to be certain that a girl of my height, or say five-feet-six, will have a waist measuring at least thirty-three-and-a-half inches, and hips measuring not more than forty-two. Her upper-arm will be 14½ inches in circumference; her wrist, eight; the calf of her leg at least sixteen; her ankle near eleven; and yet her foot is but 10½ inches long, and both foot and hands are well shaped. These are masculine proportions, and the men assure me that the women have nearly the strength of men. Child-birth is an easy affair of twenty-four hours. Every motion and gesture is free and masculine. They go into battle with the men, and, as one of the most famous fighting chiefs, Pa-tu, my neighbor, told me of his own daughter who fell in battle by his side, "she was killed fighting like a man."

Now comes the quality which to me is most curious. Here are these superb men and women—creatures of this soft climate and voluptuous nature, living under a tropical sun, and skies of divine purple and blue—who ought, on my notions, to be chock-full of languid longings and passionate emotions, but they are pure Greek fauns. Their intellectual existence is made up of concrete facts. As La Farge says, they have no thoughts. They are not in the least voluptuous; they have no longings and very brief passions; they live a matter-of-fact existence that would scare a New England spinster. Even their dances—proper or improper—always represent facts, and never even attempt to reproduce an emotion. The dancers play at ball, or at bathing, or at cocoa-nut gathering, or hammer, or row, or represent cats, birds or devils, but never an abstraction. They do not know how to be voluptuous. Old Samasoni, the American pilot here for many years, and twice married to high-class native women, tells us that the worst dance he ever saw here was a literal reproduction of the marriage ceremony, and that the man went through the entire form, which is long and highly peculiar, and ended with the consummation—openly, before the whole village, delighted with the fun—but that neither actors nor spectators showed a sign of emotion or passion, but went through it as practically as though it had been a cricket-match. Their only idea was that it was funny—as, in a sense, it certainly was; that is, it was not nice. Sentiment or sentimentality is unknown to them. They are astonishingly kind to their children, and their children are very well-behaved; but there is no sentiment, only good-nature, about it. They are the happiest, easiest, smilingest people I ever saw, and the most delightfully archaic. They fight bravely, but are not morally brave. They have the virtues of healthy children—and the weaknesses of Agamemnon and Ulysses.

I could babble on indefinitely about them and their ways, but I think you care less about the Archaic than King or I do, and I might only bore you. For myself, I am not bored. I go to bed soon after nine o'clock, and sleep well till half past five. I eat bananas, mangoes, oranges, pineapples and mummy-apples by the peck. I smoke like a lobster. I write, or study water-color drawing all day. The rainy season has begun. Our gay colors and warm lights have washed out into a uniform grey and faint violet. Expeditions are too risky, for one is sure to be drenched, and the rain falls here solid. But we are well, cheerful and dread moving. I ought to take more exercise, but I don't, and time slides as though it were Fang-alo on the Sliding Rock.

Nov. 25. Fine weather again. We are starting on a boat-tour of the island.

To ELIZABETH CAMERON

[*Samoa*] *5.30* A.M. *November 27, 1890.*

. . . We have seen much of Stevenson these last few days, and I must say no more in ridicule, for he has been extremely obliging, and given me very valuable letters of introduction to Tahiti and the Marquesas. He has amused and interested us, too, and greatly by his conversation. Last evening he came at five o'clock, and brought his wife to dine with us. Their arrival was characteristic. He appeared first, looking like an insane stork, very warm and very restless. I was not present, and the reception fell on little Mrs. Parker, who is as delicate and fragile as Stevenson, but as quiet and gentle as a flower. Presently Mrs. Stevenson in a reddish cotton nightgown, staggered up the steps, and sank into a chair, gasping and unable to speak. Stevenson hurried to explain that she was overcome by the heat and the walk. Might she lie down? Mrs. Parker sacrificed her own bed, and gave her some cognac. Stevenson says that his wife has some disease, I know not what, of a paralytic nature, and suffers greatly from its attacks. I know only that when I arrived soon afterwards, I found her on the piazza chatting with Mrs. Parker, and apparently as well and stalwart as any other Apache squaw. Stevenson then devoted an hour to me, very kindly, and was astonishingly agreeable, dancing about, brandishing his long arms above his head, and looking so attenuated in the thin flannel shirt which is his constant wear, that I expected to see him break in sections, like the *pollolo*. He has an infinite experience to draw upon, and to my great relief is not a Presbyterian, but is as little missionary as I am. His sufferings here as a farmer are his latest fund for humor, and he described, with bounds of gesticulation, how he had just bought two huge farm horses, and stabled them in a native house near his; and how at midnight, in a deluge of rain and a gale of wind, he had heard unearthly howls from the stable, and had ventured out with a lantern. As he approached, by the glimmer of the light, he became aware of two phantom excrescences protruding from the stable roof. These were his horses' heads, which, after eating off the roof of the house, were wildly tossing in the storm, while the legs and bodies were inconceivably mixed up, inside. I have stopped to eat a mango, which Stevenson says is a stimulant almost as strong as fluid extract of coco. I hope it is, for I have then a reason for liking them. . . .

Enough of Stevenson. His stories are not for me to tell, and towards eleven o'clock, we summoned our boat crew, and sent him back by water, in the moonlight to Apia. We may never see him again, for he talks of going to Auckland next week, and some day I suppose we too shall go away somewhere. Our parting last night, on the beach, in the Samoan moonlight, was appropriate, and my last distinct vision of his wife was her archaic figure in the arms of my coxswain, trying to get her legs—or feet—over the side of my boat. . . .

To JOHN HAY

Falealili, 7 December, 1890.

This is Sunday in Samoa. I am circumnavigating the island,

with the same outfit I took to Savaii, but without Consul Sewall. My crews have chosen to rest for Sunday at a village—
Vaovai—in the province of Falealili on the south coast, about
half way round. It is afternoon. I have wobbled over the coral
reef in a native canoe with a native hunchback, named
Japhet, and a native youth to paddle me. We have inspected
an island scented with sweet-smelling trees, and happily unin-
habited. I have a bad tooth-ache, though my teeth were carefully put in order before leaving home; but my tooth-ache
is no harder to bear than my wish for statistics from home.
My last mail reached me here at dusk last evening. No letters
at all! I expected none, knowing that they would go to Tahiti; but the Consulate made up for the deficiency by sending
me two newspapers. One contained news of the elections; the
other, of the London panic and the Baring's troubles by telegraph from Auckland. You may imagine my emotions. At best
it is hard to negotiate a draft here, but now I apprehend flat
refusal. I have not a dollar, and owe several hundreds, and
cannot leave Samoa without money. No one at home knows
where I am, to send aid. As far as I can foresee, I am destined
to three months of poverty and imprisonment.

Well! If La Farge can stand it, I can. I shall write to Tahiti for my letters, which will arrive in five weeks. I shall cut
down my expenses, and wait for rescue. Samoa has amused
me for two months; I will marry a *taupo* (on credit), and see
if she can amuse me for two months more. I doubt it, but
will give her the benefit of the doubt. My acquaintance with
taupo is now very considerable, and if all of them came to
breakfast at once, even you could hardly entertain them; but
it is not likely that they can all visit Washington together. My
hostess at this village tells us that most of her neighbor *taupo*
have run off with young men, or in other words, have made
love-matches, rather less permanent than the ordinary mar-

riage. At our last stopping-place the muscular maiden announced her strong desire to run off with me. As yet, their raiment of cocoa-nut oil has proved an impassable barrier between them and me; for I cannot take a bath every time my beloved touches me; but bankruptcy is a powerful motive for a marriage of inconvenience, and I know not what number of pigs and fine mats might save me from starvation. Everyone has his price.

I have been a week absent from Apia, cruising in open boats along the shore of Upolu eastward until we turned the corner and came westward. What I don't know about Samoa is hardly worth the bite of a mosquito. Of its thirty-thousand inhabitants, fully half must have seen us, if I have not seen them. I have flirted with girls in a score of villages, and talked of ancient law with chiefs of hoary antiquity. I have been amused and I have been bored. The amusement has been great; the boredom has not been small. When I come to figure up the balance, I will tell you how it stands; as yet the account is very current. I admit to a great liking for old-gold, but perhaps what I really like most is the limitations, and yet its limitations are a bore. One delights to see splendid men and women, all well made, with rich color, and no clothes; but one grows tired of finding them even more alike than the less romantic inhabitants of Saugus West Centre. Their contrasts, on the other hand, redeem them. Their theory of religion and morality is in constant and enlivening contrast with their practise. They supply the most unexpected and humorous contradictions which keep one's mind from stagnation. They are all as like each other as two casts from the same mould, but they are quite unlike us, and the perpetual cross-purposes at which we all labor, make life very unexpected. Within their limitations, they are a marvelous success, complete all round, and physically a joy to look at. Their social

system is communism so aristocratic as to make our commu-
nists turn green with horror. Their aristocracy is so democratic as to carry a chill to the bones of William Waldorf Astor. Their social, political and religious system is preposterous
to a degree quite incredible, but it has worked well enough to
make them the happiest people on earth for an indefinite
past. They are sweet tempered, gay, full of humor, and astonishingly gentle. Their frequent wars have kept up a high
standard of courage, at least among the chiefs, though I think
them really a timid race. They have a keen sense for grace,
strength and beauty, as you can see in their dances.

Now for the limitations! They are, as far as I can see, the
least imaginative people I ever met. They have almost no arts
or literature or legends. Their songs are mere catches; un-
meaning lines repeated over and over. Even their superstitions are practical. They live in an atmosphere of spirits and
devils that would satisfy the greediest spirit medium in the
United States; but they have no good ghost-stories and no mischievous devils. The best spirit I have found is in Fangaloa
Bay where a woman comes down from the mountain and goes
fishing at night with the villagers. She walks on the water,
and carries a light. The villagers see her as she passes down
the bay, and when she returns they can watch her light as far
as the top of the mountain. She is the sister of a devil who
lives on the mountain, but who was absent in Savaii when I
passed. This is all. Fangaloa Bay is one of the liveliest spots
in creation, and should have a first-rate article in legendary
ghosts, but no legend has grown there. Further away, in Alei-
pata, at the eastern end of this island, I stayed with an old
chief who had a spirit always with him; but it was only that
of his son who was killed in war about two years ago. The
whole village recognised the fact, and knew the spirit perfectly; but though it was so obliging as to come, in the form

of an owl, to announce our intended visit before the news arrived by letter, I could not learn that it did anything unusual for the most commonplace American spirits. Every family, every village, every district and every kingdom, has its spirit; and only two months ago the spirits of Savaii came over in canoes and fought the spirits of aïtu of Upolu, but were perfectly practical about it, and went quietly home when beaten. The only pretty superstition that I found was that of the old kingdom of Atua, at the eastward. There, when going to war, they are guided by the rainbow. If it crosses their path, either before or behind them, they stop. If it appears to the right or left, in a line with their march, they go on, confident of success. You could make a pretty war-song of this. "When Israel, of the Lord beloved."

In the quality of imagination as in physical qualities, they are, as Stevenson assures me, inferior to the Tahitians. Their moralities are another matter, and interest me. greatly, because they certainly have moral standards though the most elusive, not to say delusive, I can conceive. As far as I can see, they are very honest. I have been here two months, and during all that time my things—sometimes money, but always articles valuable to them—have been scattered about, in native houses, boats, and people's hands—without caution on my part; but nothing has been taken. Yet they are so communistic that any present one gives them, even a cigar, will probably pass through a dozen hands—or mouths—before it is used up. The chiefs complain much of Samoan thievery, but this is because they are themselves the police. A fortnight ago the halyards of the consular flagstaff were stolen. The next day, Mata-afa came, as he often does, to our native house, for a talk. You may remember that Mata-afa was king, while the Germans held Malietoa, and still Mata-afa is probably the first man in Samoa as far as reputation goes. We live within a stone's throw of him, and he regards us as under his protection, as well as under that of To-fai, the chief of the village. I mentioned to Mata-afa the loss of the halyards as a joke, without a thought that he would take it seriously, but it seemed to shock him, and he did not recover from it. During the whole visit he was absent-minded, and repeatedly returned to the subject. Whenever a Samoan is put out, he has a way of clucking—Tut-tut-tut—and one always knows what he is thinking of. I found his sensibility rather a bore, for I did not care a cent whether our government lost its halyards or not; but a few days afterwards, early in the morning Sewall heard a lively chattering outside his door, and on getting out of bed, and going out, he tumbled over a man lying regularly trussed and ironed, at his threshold. To-fai had found the thief somehow, and the native judge promptly sentenced him to sixty lashes and six months labor. The fun is that, of course, at Sewall's intercession the sentence was mitigated to three months labor; and now the convict, perfectly unguarded and always smiling, is usually sitting in front of the consulate, supposed to be keeping the weeds down, but really chattering and smoking cigarettes with his friends in the coolest and pleasantest spot near Apia.

With this exception of Mata-afa, I have never seen a Samoan shocked, and often wonder whether they know the feeling. Nothing that we regard as indecent shocks them; yet they observe conventional proprieties with strange strictness. One seldom or never sees a grown Samoan naked, except for some rare reason. The women are never indecent in the way of solicitation. I have not once been annoyed by advances such as I should certainly meet, within ten minutes, by night, in the streets of any large city. They do not always know me, so that the reason cannot always be their respect for the American *ali,* and indeed the girls show familiarity enough in other

ways. Yet, for indecency—*Cre Dieu!* as some Frenchman may
have observed. Indecency is a European fiction strange to a
Polynesian, to whom all facts are equally practical. Some of
their dances have turned my few remaining dark hairs gray
with horror, and are quite beyond description; yet even these
are so simply and humorously expressive that I cannot help
laughing at them. Other dances are indecent without intent.
At one of the last towns we have visited, when I was dozing
off, overcome by sleep, in the drowsiness of the unavoidable
Siva, I was suddenly and completely roused by the funny-man
of the dance, who began on an unmistakeable imitation of the
process of child-birth. It was excessively laughable too. For
twenty minutes or more, the man went through a sort of pantomime, accompanied by monologue, representing the pains
of child-birth, the birth of the child, and the suckling of it, by
an incompetent mother who committed all sorts of extrava-
gances; and we laughed as heartily as anyone, to the delight
of the audience. I own that I laughed till the tears came,
though the acting was realistic in the extreme. I laughed almost as much at another dance by girls, called "Digging Yams
in the Famine," of which La Farge was to a slight degree the
victim. The regular or sitting Siva, is always perfectly proper,
as far as I can see or understand it; but the standing dances
are regular pieces of acting, and one never knows what may
be the subject of the funny-man's humor.

So, too, in the relations of the sexes. I cannot comprehend
their notions of morality, but apparently they have some, ru-
dimentary perhaps, but tolerably clear to them. La Farge was
much delighted by the prattle of one of our crew, named
Maua, who understands and speaks English, and who explained to him that as ours was a European *malanga,* or picnic, the crew did not insist on having women; but that on a
native *malanga,* every man who did not have a woman with

him would be laughed at. Every native *malanga* commonly ends in the running away of half a dozen women with the departing boats; and at one village we were gratified by an illustration of the principle. As we were making ready to leave, we heard a great noise of children laughing and running about outside; and on inquiry we learned that they were making fun of a girl who had been persuaded by one of our crew to run away into the bush, on the idea that our boats would pick her up, on the shore, and take her off. Apparently he had, at last, undeceived her, and she had returned, to be laughed at by the village, as Maua explained, "to make her ashamed." I do not think she was much ashamed, and I was assured that her moral character was not essentially affected by the escapade; but if ours had been a native *malanga,* she would have been taken off as a matter of course. As it was, she probably got a whipping from her father, or mother, or elder sister. Whipping is the only corrective for violations of conventional rules. When a man sends away his wife, and takes another, it is apt to end in promiscuous whipping. The family of the injured wife takes it out on any member of the new wife's family, or on the new wife herself, if they happen to lay hands on her, and in such a case the victim gets an unmerciful thrashing. Only in case the new wife belongs to a higher social rank is the revenge not inflicted.

To ELIZABETH CAMERON

Papeete, 6 February, 1891.

Tahiti! does the word mean anything to you? To me it has a perfume of its own, made up of utterly inconsequent associations; essence of the South Seas mixed with imaginations of at least forty years ago; Herman Melville and Captain Cook head and heels with the French opera and Pierre Loti. Of course I expected something different from what I find, yet the reality fits in, after a fashion. Here is what I find, or at least here is where I am. A cottage of three or four rooms and a verandah. In front, a little garden twenty feet deep, with flowers and vines. Then a paling; then the road; then the sea, or rather the harbor, with small waves flopping on the beach, twenty yards from me as I write on the verandah; then a broad stretch of blue water until, ten miles away, the horizon ends with the soft outline of the mountains of Moorea, another island, which reminds me of Capri, as the water does of the Bay of Naples. La Farge and I have just finished our first breakfast in our new establishment, and I feel highly pleased because it was quite Parisian. Our new cook is a Frenchman, bearing the name of Peraudot. I pay him fifty dollars a month in Chilian money, or about thirty-five dollars in gold; and if you were only here, you would find my new breakfast-table better than at Washington. In an hour we are to go to see the King.

We have been here but two days. . . . Early one morning we entered the harbor of Papeete, and hauled up close to the shore. Atwater, our former Consul, and young Doty, a Georgetown youth, our actual Consul, came on board to receive us, and I asked to what hotel I had best send our trunks. "Well! there is no hotel in Papeete," the two gentlemen rather awkwardly replied. I was a bit staggered, and asked where then I could go. They suggested that I had better take a cottage. Could I find one furnished? "Well! no! probably not. But there were one or two to be had, and I might soon buy or hire furniture." Then and there we stepped on shore and went house-hunting. We shortly learned that there was but one available cottage, and that we must vacate it on the 15th. I wish you could have seen its condition. Fortunately we had no choice, so Doty took us to breakfast, and by miraculous efforts of Awoki we slept in our cottage that night.

So here we are. *J'y suis, mais je n'y reste pas.* Next week we must put our new cooking-stove and our pots and pans in a whale-boat, and move elsewhere. As we never meant to remain in Papeete, we are not annoyed, but rather pleased, and meanwhile have begun a vigorous social campaign, necessarily short, but still to us formidable. Papeete is the strangest little corner of earth you ever invented to amuse Martha. Here is a native King, Pomare, with no functions whatever except to drink. His divorced Queen is of course a Teva, since the Tevas are the true princes of Tahiti, and equally of course she is a Brander by connection. Please consult Miss Gordon-Cumming's book on these family matters. Then comes the French Governor who is a Martinique negro. I am gratified to learn that some governments are stupider than our own. The French actually send here a full corps of West India negroes to govern a people almost as high-blooded as Greeks. Society now consists, as far as I can learn, of the Branders and their connection. These are four or five sisters, daughters of a deceased London Jew named Salmon, who married the Teva heiress and created a princely house of Salmon. As my letters are likely to be filled with Salmons or Salmonidae, please grapple at the outset with the following consanguinity:

One of Salmon's daughters married King Pomare, and a few years ago got a divorce. She now lives in a house behind the Consulate.

Another daughter married Atwater, our Consul, and lives a little way behind the town.

Another daughter married Brander, a Scotchman of good family, and had nine children. Brander died of softening of the brain, and some years later she married another Scotchman named Darsie, and has had three more children. She now lives in the country, two or three miles behind here.

I won't bother you with the other sisters, who can wait. So

can the brothers, Tati and Narii Salmon, gentlemen of the first importance here, of whom I shall probably have much to say hereafter. As yet we have called only on the Queen that was; Mrs. Darsie, and Mrs. Atwater; and found only Mrs. Darsie and Mrs. Atwater at home. They are both women of a certain age, decidedly Polynesian, rather handsome. We liked them. They talk excellent English, and are familiar with America and Europe.

If there were a Court, these would be it. Pomare's sale of his royal rights to the French, and his pleasant vice of royal drunkenness, have left Tahiti courtless. The nicest royalty was said to be the Princess Moe, wife of Tamatua, another brother, once king of the neighboring island of Raiotea, but expelled for potting his subjects with a rifle when drunk. You have read of the Princess Moe in the Earl and the Doctor, where "that unutterable cad, Pembroke," according to Stevenson, gave an account of her that exasperated everybody in these regions, and quite broke up poor Moe, who, in consequence, never would visit Europe. Miss Gordon-Cumming, too, had much to say of her. Stevenson adored her, and gave us a letter of introduction to her; but our first news on arrival was of Moe's death, which happened a month ago. Her husband Tamatua died before her. So that chapter we found closed.

Now then! Of all the female Salmonidae, Mrs. Brander-Darsie and her twelve children are naturally the most pervasive. Everything social in Papeete is Brander. The nine Brander children are now grown. Five of them are handsome young men; and they are chiefly to be found about our Consulate, where we tumbled headlong among them, howling for houses, beds, cooks, laundresses, social instruction and general advice. The howls were very obligingly responded to; and from Doty we learned much of the private history of these youths. It is rather interesting. Their father, Brander, was the great merchant of these seas. His plantations produced cocoa-nuts by the million; his pearl-fisheries sent tons of shell to Europe; his ships carried all the trade of the islands; his income was very great, and his wealth estimated by millions. He sent all his sons to Europe to be educated as royalties, and the boys duly coronetted their handkerchiefs and their Gladstone bags, and bore themselves so as to do credit to their uncle-cousin, the King of Tahiti. They were English subjects, and were Scotch gentlemen, so they went to Universities, and I've no doubt were howling swells, as all bloods-royal should be. Then their father died, and his estate, when settled, shrank to the modest amount of a million dollars. The widow took half, leaving half a million to be divided among nine children equally. The boys who were educated on the scale of a million apiece, were reduced practically to nothing, or just enough for a modest bachelor's establishment in Papeete. Here they are, very gentlemanly young Englishmen. They want careers, and they find our Consulate convenient.

Socially speaking, I have now described Papeete. No one else exists here except the occasional French naval officer, who is not specially at home among the Salmonidae. The Martinique governor and his adjuncts are still less favored. Apparently La Farge and I are welcomed, but you can judge of the number of travellers from the fact that literally Papeete has no hotel. Even Apia, small as it is, had more than one tolerable hotel, but Papeete has no accommodation of any kind for travellers. Yet the shops are fairly good—much better than in Apia, and European customs are very long fixed. I get an excellent French cuisinier at European wages, but I cannot get a cottage with a sitting room. The same queer contradictions run through the whole place. The little town, with its suspicion of French provincial queerness, and its streets running under shade-trees along the water-wall, is sweetly pretty.

Neat schooners, in two or threes, are hauled up, stem and stern, against the sea-wall. There is no perceptible tide. Occasionally a man walks by. Sometimes he drives a pony in a chaise or cart. Quiet reigns except when broken by the frigate's regular calls. The air is like that of Naples. In the evening nothing stirs; by ten o'clock the silence is tremendous. There is a little club, and my first act was to sit down on the verandah and play dominoes; it seemed so obviously the correct thing to do; and at other tables half a dozen Frenchmen also played dominoes. To me the atmosphere is more than tinged by a South Sea melancholy, a little sense of hopelessness and premature decay. The natives are not the gay, big, animal creatures of Samoa who sang and danced because their whole natures were overstocked with life; they are still, silent, rather sad in expression, like the Hawaiians, and they are fearfully few in number. I catch myself always wondering what their towns will be like; but their towns, at least hereabouts, are thin and uncared for, and their houses seem never to belong where they stand. Even within ten years, life has fast drained away. There is far less sense of activity, less society and less gaiety, than ten years ago. Probably I like it better, but then it is not what I expected. Melancholy in such air and with blues so very ultramarine, has charm, and if La Farge could catch it in color, he would do something uncommon delicate; but behind the melancholy there is disease, and the old Hawaiian horror crops up here to make one sick with disgust. Except in the remoter places, the poor natives are all more or less diseased. They are allowed all the rum they want, and they drink wildly. They are forbidden to dance or to keep any of their old warlike habits. They have no amusements, and they have *gens d'armes.* . . .

Tahiti is very—very old; seamed and scarred by deep valleys, with mountain ridges sharp as knife edges, and not forest-covered, like Samoa, but showing great stretches of red earth or jungle-like grass-land. It is bordered by the same broad coral reef as in Samoa, with a broad edge of surf. As in Samoa, the low shores are covered with cocoa-nut palms, but the phylloxera has been introduced, and has turned its attention so vigorously to the palms that they are all yellow, diseased and dying. Mango trees grow everywhere, and we are revelling again in their turpentiny lusciousness. You can see from all this that we have found nothing very new or startling to us; only a sort of half-way house between Hawaii and Samoa. . . .

To MABEL HOOPER LA FARGE

Papeete, 9 February, 1891.

I've got all your letters at last. Two big ones were waiting for me here. After all, La Farge came with me, and we have been here since the 4th. We were a week on board the steamer, and I was even miserabler than usual. How I do hate the ocean, and what a lot of ocean I have got to travel! We have done more than six thousand miles already, on this trip, and I expect to do twenty thousand more before I get back to America. That means about four months of solid seasickness even if I manage to do it all by steam, but here the steamers are very small, very hot, and very slow. They go about two hundred miles a day, and never are quiet. Yet I don't hanker after sailing in a schooner, which is our next fate.

Anyway, here we are, and a very out-of-the-way place we've got into. After reading about Tahiti since I was a child, I feel half angry to find that it's a real place, and not a pantomime. As yet we've seen only Papeete, which is a little French provincial town, pretty as can be, but neither Polynesian nor European, and quieter than any town you ever imagined. The natives wear clothes and look commonplace, after

Samoa. They are, I think, a shade deeper in color, and I rather believe them to be a little more refined in features, and perhaps in figure, than the Samoans; but the difference is small, the language is much the same, and the only wonder to me is that the Samoans are so much like the Tahitians, and the Tahitians still more like the Hawaiians. There are lots of funny and mysterious things about these South Seas. How the people ever got here is a mystery; for, even with steam we were a week coming, and a strong trade-wind, right against us, made me seasick all the way. Yet they got here, and, what is more, they got to Hawaii; and must have done it at least a thousand years ago, when even in Europe there were no vessels fit for such long voyages of discovery. Then the islands are queer and mysterious; all old volcanoes, but some, like this one, so very-very old that it seems wrinkled as Methusaleh or old Betsy. The soil is nothing but decayed lava, strong red in color, and the mountains are sharp like knife-edges, so that one can sometimes walk up their sides on a narrow platform only three feet wide, with a sheer precipice on each side for hundreds of feet. What could make such sharp spurs? Not rain, for rain levels. Something has planed away the sides as though a knife had cut them. Then the tides are quite uncanny, for they are always the same; every day at noon and midnight the tide is high, and never changes its hour. Then the island is full of ghosts. I never saw nearly so many ghosts anywhere else; and many varieties, some of them quite unusual. Then there are centipede fish; and poisonous fish that are sure death to eat; and wonderfully colored fish, and more coral of outrageous purples and yellows and reds than you would dream of. I've not begun to find out all the queer things here, but already I feel as though it were the oldest and most unreasonable corner of creation, and that we are rather guilty of an impertinence in coming here at all.

In other places something always moves; but nothing moves here, not even the tides or the children, except to fire off crackers on the Chinese New Year, which is now; and where else in Christian countries do boys keep the Chinese New Year! I think nothing has ever moved here since the last volcano shut up, and that must have been about the time that the world began. Everything is decrepit with antiquity, including your dear uncle Henry who is rapidly getting to think himself as venerable as the volcano. Nothing ever came here except a few men, and they are fast getting tired and dying out.

Of course it is pretty. Indeed it is beautiful. I enjoy it in a way, but I am altogether upset by its unlikeness to what I expected. Not that I know what I expected, but that the result isn't like it. The difference from Samoa is wonderful, yet the two places are quite alike. This is nonsense, but true. Samoa was cheerful even under six inches of rain; Tahiti is melancholy even when the sun is brightest and the sea blue as glass. I don't mean that the place is gloomy, but just quietly sad, as though it were a very pretty woman who had got through her fun and her troubles, and grown old, and was just amusing herself by looking on, without caring much what happens. She has retired a long way out of the world, and sees only her particular friends, like me, with the highest introductions; but she dresses well, and her jewels are superb. In private I suspect she is given to crying because she feels so solitary; but when she sees me she always smiles like my venerable grandmother when I was five years old.

This is very silly, no doubt, Miss Pollyamiable, but just you come here and see if it's not true. If I were La Farge I would paint it. As I'm not, and can paint nothing except what I don't want to paint, I give it away to you. If you were here, you would be as puzzled as I am about it. Neither the residents nor the natives seem to feel at home here, or to understand what business they have. There is a King, named Pomare, but he has abdicated. We called on him; he wore green goggles; smiled kindly, and was at the club the next evening, very drunk and noisy. There is a Queen, a pretty, ladylike woman, named Marau, but she could not stand it, and got a divorce. There is a French governor, but he is a Martinique negro. There are two or three thousand residents, but no one of them seems to have a nationality in particular. There are four or five thousand natives, or whatever the number may be; but they do nothing except get drunk and die. They don't even seem amused. Evidently something is the matter with the place. It has a sort of Rip van Winkle flavor, as you can see in the photograph enclosed, looking up from Papeete into the mountains. The curious peaks just in the centre, closing the valley, are called the Diadem. The second photograph shows its shape when nearer. The Diadem is not the highest mountain here, but it is the queerest, and for once I think it rather well named, as though some one were sitting in there, and one never saw anything of her but her crown. . . .

To ELIZABETH CAMERON

[*Tahiti*] *Tuesday, February 12* [*1891*].

. . . I never saw a people that seemed so hopelessly bored as the Tahitians. The foreign residents here avow it with unnecessary energy, and the natives express it in every look and attitude. Rum is the only amusement which civilisation and religion have left them, and they drink-drink-drink, more and more every year, while cultivation declines, the plantations go to ruin, and disease undermines the race. The melancholy of it quite oppresses me, though La Farge, being at last very well, seems unconscious of it. Last Sunday afternoon at five o'clock we strolled up to hear the native band play, in the little square before the unfinished building meant for a royal palace. All the books talk of this band-playing, from Charley Stoddard's to the last newspaper correspondent's letters in the New Zealand Daily Polynesian, if there is one. I expected a gay little crowd with some French vivacity, but I found only a dozen men walking up and down by threes and fours, and about twice as many native or half-caste women in the usual cotton night-gowns, sitting on benches or on the wet ground, and appearing as little amused as myself. A few vehicles were drawn up by the side of the street, and the ex-Queen Marau with her sister Manihini drove up and down the road in a somewhat dilapidated pony-wagon. . . . From Papara I propose driving on, across the isthmus of Taravao, as far as the district of Tautira. There Stevenson staid, as the guest of the chiefs Ori and Arié, and was adopted as a brother by Ori, and "given a name," as you can see in the dedication of his new South Sea poem: "The Song of Rahéro." "Giving a name" is a serious matter here, like giving a title of nobility in Europe, only more so, because a real name, or title, is here a fixed thing, and goes with certain lands. In fact, to "give a name" is a regular feudal enfeofment; and Mrs. Salmon, as head chiefess, was by no means pleased with Ori for giving Stevenson a serious distinction of the kind. . . .

February 13. La Farge has settled down to painting, varied by his usual mania for collecting photographs. I call it a mania because with me it has become a phobia; and he is almost afraid of telling me about his photographs because I detest them so much. Not that I blame him; for in my own line of manuscripts I did the same thing, and had to collect ten times what I could ever make useful; but I hate photographs abstractly, because they have given me more ideas perversely and immoveably wrong, than I ever should get by imagination. They are almost as bad as an ordinary book of travels. . . .

I was delighted to see that some one was attacking my Vols. v and vi, in the *Tribune,* not that I wanted to know what he had to say in the way of attack, for I like abuse as little as other men do; but that I felt sure at last that I had one unknown reader. Till then I doubted greatly whether a hundred copies of the book had been sold. I still doubt, but am a little more hopeful. Really I think I do not much care, for I feel that the history is not what I care now to write, or want to say, if I say anything. It belongs to the *me* of 1870; a strangely different being from the *me* of 1890. There are not nine pages in the nine volumes that now express anything of my interests or feelings; unless perhaps some of my disillusionments. So you must not blame me if I feel, or seem to feel, morbid on the subject of the history. I care more for one chapter, or any dozen pages of *Esther* than for the whole history, including maps and indexes; so much more, indeed, that I would not let anyone read the story for fear the reader should profane it. . . .

To ELIZABETH CAMERON

Papara [*Tahiti*], *8 April* [*1891*].

. . . Very unwillingly we shall probably leave Tati's hospitality tomorrow. Our visit here has been one of the bright spots of our travels. If I struck such episodes often, I think I should travel indefinitely, yet I hardly know what it is that we find so pleasant. As long as the women were here, we had society, for they would be interesting persons in any country-house. The old lady, Hinari or Grandmother, is a very fine type indeed; quite a royal person in her island way. Naturally I have treated her for what she is; that is, next to Mata-afa, altogether the most interesting native figure in the whole

Pacific. Apparently she felt that I meant what I said, for she was very good-natured and open with us. She told us freely her oldest legends and traditions, and took a motherly interest in us. My adoption into the Teva clan by Ori was rather a joke. Indeed I had sent word to the old Chiefess through Tati, a month ago, that I should not think of accepting such a relationship without her formal and express approval. I supposed she would have given it on our arrival here, but she did not; nor did she ever call me Ori, as she should naturally have done if she approved, so that I rather inferred that she did not like the adoption, as she was said to have been displeased by that of Stevenson. I was quite upset, last Monday morning, just before they all went away, when the old lady with a certain dignity of manner, drawing a chair near mine, sat down and made me a little formal speech in native words, which of course I did not understand, and which Marau, who was in the secret, instantly translated. The speech was, I believe, the proper, traditional and formal act of investiture, and conferred on me the hereditary family name of Taura-atua, with the lands, rights and privileges attached to it. The compliment from such a source was so great as to be awkward. To be sure, the lands attached to the name of Taura-atua are only about a hundred feet square, a few miles from here; but the name is a very real thing, and was borne by Tati's ancestors, and is actually borne now by his second son. To give it to me was a sort of adoption. Of course, I expressed my sense of the honor, and got Marau to speak for me; after which she turned to La Farge and repeated the same form to him, conferring on him another name, also real and hereditary. The whole thing was done simply but quite royally, with a certain condescension as well as kindness of manner. For once, my repose of manner was disturbed beyond concealment. So I am now Taura-atua and Ori-a-ori; a member of both outer and inner Tevas, and a close relation of Tati himself. La Farge also is Teva by double adoption, and I suppose we are both brothers of Mrs. Stevenson. The adoption was the more formal because it was done in the presence of Tati, Marau, and all the family then here, and they had been consulted beforehand. I was glad of this, because I like them all, and especially took interest in Marau, the queen, who is a woman very much out of the common. She is, I imagine, somewhere in the thirties, and her face and figure have grown heavy and somewhat Indian, as is rather the rule with the women here. If she was once handsome, certainly her beauty is not what attracts men now. What she has is a face strongly marked and decidedly intelligent, with a sub-expression of recklessness, or true old-goldishness, that always charms me and Clarence King when it is real. One feels the hundred generations of chiefs who are in her, without one commoner except the late Salmon, her deceased parent. Hebrew and Polynesian mix rather well, when the Hebrew does not get the better; and Marau, like her brother Tati, is more Tahiti than Syria. At all events she is greatly interested in Tahiti history, poetry, legends and traditions, and as for ghost-stories, she tells them by the hour with evident belief in them, and entire confidence in the independent evolution of native ghosts and ghost-seers. As everyone here does in his heart believe in all the old native spiritual faiths; and Christianity is just one more, only successful because Jehovah is biggest and has licked Taaroa and Oro, there is nothing really strange in Marau's frank outspokenness; but it is entertaining all the same. Marau has the same big, Richardsonian ways that her brother Tati has. She always seems to me to be quite capable of doing anything strange, out of abstraction; as she might mistake me for her small child, and sling me on her arm without noticing the difference, such as it is, in size.

She is good-natured, I should say; easy, indolent, and yet, like her race, capable of committing any kind of folly, and of going to the devil like a true Polynesian for sentiment or for appetite, for love, jealousy or ennui. Luckily she is now pretty well past her *jeunesse outrageuse*. The next generation is the one now in trouble, and of that I hear much, but see little. Poor Pree has had to go to Papeete to see her doctor again, and I fear her cough is worse. La Farge has made a little drawing for her album, and I have written in it a metrical translation of a dozen lines from the Odyssey. Manini is a true girl, with no formed character. All of them went away on Monday, leaving us alone with Tati and his wife. Tati's wife is shy and avoids us, probably because she speaks none of our languages, and is neither a Pomare nor a chiefess in her own right. Tati does everything. This afternoon he drove us in the farm-wagon a mile or two through the woods to see my duchy, Taura-atua. Apart from the personal interest in my estate of six orange trees and a mango or pandanus, I was interested in the glimpse of history. Some fifteen generations ago, old Taura was a great warrior. I imagine him like Pa-tu in Samoa. He was military chief of the two districts here, and must have led several thousand men, but never owned any land except the hundred feet square on which his house stood. There Tati showed us the stones which limited the low platform or terrace on which the house stood. As Taura-atua I had also a private Marau and the right to order human sacrifices. I took investiture of my duchy in the shape of an orange. On our way back we spied sharply for the cave in the cliff where the heads of Tati's ancestors are hidden, and which Tati himself does not know. The old man, whose hereditary duty was to take up the heads and keep them oiled and fresh, can no longer climb up there, and has no son to succeed him, and is bound by oath to tell the secret to no one else. The family must lose its heads. Tomorrow we bid Tati good-bye. He is a dear fellow.

To ELIZABETH CAMERON

Opunohu [*Moorea*], *19 April, 1891.*

. . . Tahiti is lovely; the climate is perfect; we have made a sort of home here; and I never shall meet another spot so suitable to die in. The world actually vanishes here. Papeete was silent and sleepy; Tautira was so remote that existence became a dream; but Opunohu is solitude such as neither poetry nor mathematics can express. Now that I have seen this little island—Moorea or Eimeo—I see that it was once a big volcano, enormously long ages ago. The crater was on the level of the sea, but its walls rose, like those of Kilauea and Haleakala in the Sandwich Islands, several thousand feet above the floor of the crater. Peaks, sharp as knives and toothpicks, still remain three or four thousand feet high. We are in the old crater, and need imagination to know it, for it is two or three miles long, and instead of being a great pit, like Kilauea, it broke its sides out in two places into the sea. So it now makes an irregular amphitheatre, looking out on the ocean through the Opunohu bay, and the neighboring Cook's Bay, each some two miles long, while the valley behind us, which was the crater, extends back still greater distances till it abuts against walls of lava-rock worn and colored by time. Geology breaks down in measuring time here. Nothing has ever changed. The seasons are all summer; the tradewind has always blown; the ocean has always been infinite about it. Moorea is the oldest spot of earth I ever saw. Compared with it, Tahiti is a younger brother. I believe it has stood here since time began, and oceans cooled. At all events, I defy geology to prove the contrary; and have my private opinion of Darwin and Dana, as by this time you know. If Tahiti was sad, Moorea is sadder. Man somehow got here, I think about a thousand years ago, and made a society which was on the whole the most successful the world ever saw, because it rested on the solidest possible foundation of no morals at all. . . .

To ELIZABETH CAMERON

Hitiaa, Tahiti, 4 June, 1891.

Our last day on Tahiti. I breakfasted with my family [the Tevas]. The old chiefess never sits at table, she hates such Europeanisms, and she had to go to church to pray for Pomare and the sick; a special prayer-day on account of the epidemic of fever and dysentery which has been ravaging the island ever since we arrived. So Marau presided, with her brother Nari, just from the Paumotus. By the bye, Nari, who is as charming as Tati in his way, showed us, at La Farge's request, a box of pearls which was the total result of fifty tons of pearl-shell. The shell is worth about a hundred dollars a ton, I think—or a thousand—or a hundred thousand—I neither know nor care which, and my love of inaccuracy, and want of memory drive La Farge half mad. He is—don't laugh! —phenomenally accurate and precise. No one will believe me, but I tell what I know, when I say that he is as systematic, exact and conventional as he thinks he is. The world altogether misunderstands us both. He is practical; I am loose minded, and looser still in my management of affairs. He is to be implicitly believed wherever facts are in question; I am invariably mistaken. *Revenons à nos perles!* Nari's box contained half a dozen pearls—or seven—or five, or, in short, a small number. He valued them at an average of about a hundred dollars, gold, apiece; his consignee, the animal Jorss, estimated them at less than half. None were worth buying. . . . Besides Marau and Pree and Nari, all the Brander

boys were at table: Aleck, Norman, Arthur and Winny; and
we had a gay breakfast; but I cared much less for the gaiety
than I did for the parting with the dear old lady, who kissed
me on both cheeks—after all, she is barely seventy, *va!*—and
made us a little speech, with such dignity and feeling, that
though it was in native, and I did not understand a word of
it, I quite broke down. I shall never see her again, but I have
learned from her what the archaic woman was. If Marau
only completes the memoirs, you will see; and I left Marau
dead bent on doing it.

So Taura-atua and Terai-tua y Amo drove away from the
home of their nobility, and left forever the scenes where they
had been great warriors and splendid lovers. I wrote poetry
then. Marae-ura was her name, and she lived at the pae-pae,
among the bushes. I had to leave her because *my* family objected; but I immortalised her in verse. That was a century—
or two—or three—ago. Time goes so fast! Four months seem
now an eternity—just the time I have been here, and must
take to get elsewhere, counting from one o'clock yesterday
afternoon when we started from Papeete on our drive to
Hitiaa. We need not have made the journey, but we wanted
to see the east side of the island, which is almost prettier
than the west. The road, much of it, is a narrow and rough
wagonway cut in the cliff, and not safer than it should be; but
it always skirts the big ocean—such a big ocean!—and when it
wanders a few rods away, it runs through a grassy avenue of
forest—not tropical, as one imagines it, but much as it might
be in England, if England produced palms and breadfruit besides oaks and ash.

After rambling four hours or more among this somewhat
bumpy but all the more beautiful road, we arrived towards
sunset at an ideal Tahitian village—Hitiaa—where I am now
writing, on the green turf, or at least grass, before the hut,

with the surf close behind me, and the big trees above. It is almost the prettiest spot we have seen. To the southward, twenty miles or so across the bay, we see our old quarters at Tautira, and our little steamer lies three miles down the shore, loading with oranges. The season is mid-winter. The temperature has fallen several degrees, and is now about eighty. The ocean is rough with the trade-wind, and looks as blue as I feel at going again upon it. The people are as friendly and mild as ever, and, for the moment, are not drunk. Tati, who has the oranges to ship, received us with open arms, as big and handsome as ever. I wish you knew him, for he is to me quite fascinating, with the sort of over-flow of life that made Richardson so irresistible. If he ever stays with me at Washington, you and I will have him to our-selves, and not let the natives misunderstand him. His wife, a sweet-presenced native woman who speaks no foreign jar-gon, and ripples out from time to time only with *tiritara-tauauteve,* or something like it—for these sounds mean every-thing—bids us *iorana* which is good-morning, or good-day or good-night, like the Samoan *alofa;* and then tells the small baby Tita, *haremai,* which means *come;* or, to pacify La Farge I will say *go;* and that is all we know about it. Our native house is perfectly clean, and has a floor, and beds, and the host and hostess think it their duty to watch us undress, and dress in the morning. My bath in the river is a levee. *Aue!* 't will all be over tomorrow. . . .

To ELIZABETH CAMERON

Tuesday, September 8, 1891.

We landed at Colombo [Ceylon] at eight o'clock Sunday evening, in a temper and with feelings of the most depraved sort. Although we were the only passengers to Colombo, the Messageries officers, stewards and all, totally neglected us, gave us no notice when, where or how to land, and after causing us to lose two hours of light, deliberately let us go off at last as we could, at our own expense, in a native boat, handling our own luggage, without apology, although our situation was again and again, with the utmost civility made known to them, with the request, not for aid, but only for information. I do not think we do this sort of thing in America, but it has happened twice to us since leaving Brisbane, and is, I think, the rule in the east. Steamers do not land passengers, but forget them. Had I been in my usual form, I should not have cared, but I had a cracking headache and a cold, and could not eat all day, and was exhausted by the moist heat, and generally felt more like a dead beetle than ever before I bade you goodbye. When we got to a hotel, I crept to bed, and tried to find a spot on my pillow where my head would lie without cracking open, and so dozed till morning with the prospect of the long-expected fever at last. In the morning the headache departed, but I was left very weak, and terribly oppressed by the damp heat of Colombo—a rice-field heat—which has made me think that if Bishop Heber had known more of the matter he would have made an improvement in his poetry, and would have altered it to: "What though the ricey breezes, blow damp o'er Ceylon's isle!" Spice, I know not, but Colombo is in a big rice-swamp, and I felt as though I were in a Turkish bath, and could not get out. All this was owing, I am sure, to something eaten on the "Melbourne"—I suspect the Camembert cheese—and to being obliged to pass the nights on deck with little sleep and no comfort. Steamers in the tropics are made just like steamers in Greenland. I have not yet seen one—except the American line to Australia—constructed with any reference to the passengers' comfort, or any means of making them comfortable; and if I could hang a few constructors, I would certainly do it in memory of the suffering I have seen them cause to women and children; but the stupidity of the European man is quite radiant, and no one proclaims it louder than the officers who are condemned to command European ships. Between French cheese and French cabins, my life was not worth taking; but my life is a trifle; and I wanted to take some Frenchman's when I saw what happened to others. A delicate little English girl, about Martha's age, was on board; colorless and thin, like all these tropic birds, but talking broken Malay, and rather interesting. On our last night on board, the heat in the cabin was great, the child was taken very sick, and while her mother was examining her, at the table in the saloon, by the light, the little creature fell flat on her face in a dead faint. She was not seasick, but exhausted; and the mother was not allowed to change cabins, or to have air, or to give the child any relief, though the ship was empty, until in a state of ferocity, she went to the Captain. She was howling furious about it, and I gave her what sympathy my sufferings tended to rouse.

Of course our first act, Monday morning, was to seek the Consulate, which I found at eleven o'clock in charge of a small native girl who was then sweeping it, but who seemed to divine my character, for she pointed to a pigeon-hole where I found letters. . . . Ceylon is certainly the most interesting and beautiful island we have seen, taking its many-sided interests into account. In one way, Hawaii is grander; in another, Tahiti is more lovely; but Hawaii is a volcano and Tahiti a dream; while Ceylon is what I supposed Java to be, and it was not—a combination of rich nature and varied human interest, a true piece of voluptuous creativeness. We have seen nothing to approach the brilliancy of the greens and the luxury of the vegetation; but we have been even more struck by the great beauty of the few girls we have caught a glimpse of; especially their eyes, which have a large, dark, far-off, beseeching look, that seems to tell of a coming soul—not Polynesian.

September 10. Kandy is pretty—very; and the surrounding country is prettier still, full of hills and valleys, flowers, elephants, palms and snakes. Monkeys are here also, but I have seen none wild. Another Paradise opens its arms to another son of Adam, but the devil of restlessness, who led my ancestor to the loss of his estate, leads me. I cannot stay three days contented. Socially Kandy seems as impossible as are all these colonial drearinesses, and intellectually man is indubitably vile, as the bishop justly says. In all Ceylon I cannot buy or beg a book on the Ceylon art, literature, religion or history. Of all that has been published on India, not even a stray volume of Max Müller have I seen here, except in the little library of the Sacred Tooth, the Buddhist Temple where the true faith is now alone taught by aid of our master's Tooth, or Tusk—for it is said to be ivory. Of course we visited the famous temple at once, for here is now the last remaining watchfire of our church, except for Boston where Bill Bigelow and Fenollosa fan faint embers. The Temple—Dalada Maligawa, Palace of the Tooth—was a sad disappointment after the Japanese Temples. The art is poor, rather mean, and quite modern, and even the golden shrine of the Tooth had little to recommend it except one or two cat's-eyes. Occasionally a refined piece of stone carving—a door-way or threshold—built into a coarse plaster wall, shows where some older temple has been used for modern ornament, and gives an idea that Ceylon had refinement in the thirteenth century. Hence our tears, or rather our restlessness; for photographs tell us of immense ruined cities in the jungle, a day or two distant; cities as old or older than our æra, where Buddhism flourished like the wicked, more than two thousand years ago. To get there, we must travel day and night in ox-carts; but what of that? We swallow the oxen more willingly than the fevers, snakes, leeches and ticks, with which the deserted cities are said to be now inhabited. So we start tomorrow for Anuradhpura, and, if possible, for Polonnaruwa, and shall return only just in time to take our steamer, the seventeenth. . . .

Anuradhpura, Sunday, 13 Sepr. The ox-cart was funny, but not bad, if one must pass nights in these hot regions. We have come about eighty miles from Kandy, and have passed portions of two days inspecting this very sacred city, which is very much out of the world, in a burned jungle, with perfect roads, an excellent government inn, or Rest-house, and a poor native village, much fever-stricken, infested by jackals, with no whites except government officials in the whole district. I wanted to see the island, and this is it, I suppose, or at least the dry part of it, and sufficiently undisturbed by Europeans, of whom only a few travellers ever come here. I have looked through the inn-book, and found not a name known to me, during a record of eight or ten years; but, for that matter, since leaving San Francisco I have come across no one I ever knew before, so I could not count on finding them here. Yet Ceylon is a place where vast numbers of travellers come— or at least pass—and these ruined cities are the chief interest of the island; so they are visited by about one Englishman a month, thank Buddha, and praise to Siva and Vishnu, not even the photograph fiend is here. As for the ruins, they are here beyond question, and we have duly inspected them. Imagine a great plain, covered with woods. Dumped on this dry plain are half a dozen huge domes of solid brick, overgrown with grass and shrubs; artificial mounds that have lost their architectural decorations and their plaster covering, but still rise one or two hundred feet above the trees, and have a certain grandeur. Each of these dagobas represents an old temple which had buildings about it, stone bathing-tanks, and stone statues of Buddha, chapels and paved platforms decorated with carved or brick elephant-heads, humped oxen, lions and horses. When Buddha flourished here, two thousand years ago, vast numbers of pilgrims came to worship the relics supposed to be hidden under the dagobas, but still more to pray at the sacred bo-tree, which is the original shoot brought here more than two thousand years ago from the original bo-tree under which Buddha attained Nirvana. This then, was Anuradhpura; the bo-tree; six dagobas with relics; and one or two temples more or less Brahmanic, that is, rather for Siva or Vishnu than for Buddha, though Buddhism ran here a good deal into Brahmanism. As long as Buddhism flourished, Anuradhpura flourished, and the kings went on building tanks, both for bathing and for irrigation, some of the irrigation tanks being immense lakes, with many miles of embankment. When Buddhism declined, the place went gradually to pieces, and nothing but what was almost indestructible remains. Of course we cared little for the historical or industrial part of the affair, but came here to see the art, which is older than anything in India, and belongs to the earliest and probably purest Buddhist times; for Anuradhpura was the centre of Buddhism even then. I expected—never mind what—all sorts of things—which I have not found. To my surprise and disappointment, all the art seems to me pretty poor and cheap. Compared with Egypt or even with Japan, Ceylon is second rate. The huge brick dagobas were laid out on a large scale, with a sense of proportion that must have been artistic, but the want of knowledge or use of the arch makes the result uninteresting. The details are not rich; the stone carving is not fine; the statues are not numerous or very imposing even in size; and all the stone-work, even to the bathing-tanks, is so poorly and cheaply done, without mortar, rivetting or backing, that it can't hold itself up. I have hunted for something to admire, but except the bigness, I am left cold. Not a piece of work, big or small, have I seen that has a heart to it. The place was a big bazaar of religion, made for show and profit. Any country shrine has more feeling in it than this whole city seems to have shown. I am rather glad the jackals and monkeys own it, for they at least are not religious formalists, and they give a moral and emotion to the empty doorways and broken thresholds. Of course we went at once to the sacred bo-tree, which is now only a sickly shoot or two from the original trunk, and under it I sat for half an hour, hoping to attain Nirvana. . . . I left the bo-tree without attaining Buddhaship. Towards evening we got an ox-cart; a real cart with two wheels, and two slow, meditative, humped oxen, who are also sacred cattle, and who have the most Buddhistic expression in their humps and horns that ever was reached by God's creatures. The cart was hooped over with thatch, and we put two chairs inside, and were slowly driven by a naked Tamil, as though we were priests or even Hindu deities, through the woods, every now and then clambering out to inspect some stone tank or temple among the trees, and in secret deadly terror of ticks, leeches and cobras, not to speak of centipedes and scorpions. Dusk came on just as a family of monkeys scampered up the trees and jumped across above our heads. I felt no sense of desolation or even of remoteness; sensations have palled on me; but the scene was certainly new, and in a way beautiful, for the evening light was lively, and the ruined dagobas assumed a color that art never gave them. This evening we resume our travelling ox-cart, with the dainty little trotting oxen, more like deer than cattle; and travelling all night, we reach Dambolo in the morning, where we have to look at some rock temples. I have no longer any hope of finding real art in Ceylon; even the oldest looks to me mechanical, as though it were imported, and paid by the superficial area; but we want to be sure we have seen all the styles, and the rock-temple is a style. I would rather travel by night than by day, even when packed tight in a cart, with my boots sticking out behind. The moon is sweet, and the air exquisite, jackals and all.

September 15. Before leaving Anuradhpura, we had a dance, after the traditional style of Ceylon. Four men, ornamented with brass arm-plates, silver bangles, and other decorations belonging to their profession, and making music for themselves by thrumming small hand-drums, danced for us, before the Rest-house. They danced well, their training was good, and the dance itself was in a style quite new to us, with a good deal of violent physical exertion at times; but it did not interest me much, and I could see no trace of meaning in it; not even the overlaid, solemn elaboration of Chinese or Japanese movements, which no one can any longer explain. We paid what seems here, among these terribly poor people, rather a high price for the show—fifteen rupees, or a little more than a sovereign; but we always encourage native industries. At about eight o'clock in the evening, our mail-cart came for us, and we started on the return journey. I think the night travel amused me more than the ruins did. The night air is pleasantly cool, and the moon was bright. We lay on our backs on a mattress, with just room—and barely—for us two. Our little white oxen, with their mystical straight horns, and their religious sacred humps, tripped along, sometimes trotting and sometimes running, their bells tinkling in the quaintest way; and the two wheeled cart, which luckily had springs, tipped about, as though it enjoyed the fun. I slept a good deal, smoked a little, and watched the moonlight on the road and the jungle. We did twenty-eight miles in seven hours, and reaching a Rest-house at three o'clock in the morning, where we had to change into a less comfortable horse-coach. We knocked up the keeper of the Rest-house, and while he boiled water and made tea, we sat in the dark on the porch, listening to the creak of ox-mills, and to the weird cries of the jackals, which seemed to fill the woods, and which are the uncanniest night-sound I ever heard. We were on the road again long before dawn, but at six o'clock we reached Dambolo, and climbed up to the rock temple, about a mile away. When we got there, the priest and the keys were away, and we had to send back for them, while we sat on the rocks and looked over miles and miles of forest jungle, to distant mountains. The cave temples were an exasperating disappointment, mean outside and stupid within. Not stupid, La Farge insisted, but priestlike; long rows of dirty cotton curtains ran round each temple, carefully hiding the statues, in order, no doubt, to extort money for showing them. The statues or figures have no merit as art, but are only conventional Indian Buddhas, sitting or reclining, and coarsely colored; their only value is as decoration, and of course their effect was not only lost but caricatured by concealing them. I think La Farge was angrier than I; but anyway I should not have cared much for the temples which are mere rough holes, without architecture or form. We hurried back to the Rest-house, and kept H. M.'s mail waiting for us till we had breakfasted; then at eight o'clock were on our way again, and at two in the afternoon were in Kandy, which seems deliciously cool and moist after the dry, hot, weary parchment of the plains. We like Kandy as much as though we were children, and it were assorted. The walks and drives are charming, and the peace is almost as ideal as that of Papeete. . . .

IV

UNITY VS. MULTIPLICITY

1891–1907

IT WAS during the years after his return from the South Seas and before his completion of the *Education,* in 1907, that Adams's mind took on its final and most familiar cast. All the tendencies toward nihilism, mechanism, and pessimism that had been with him from the beginning were now more and more confirmed, even hardened, by such experiences as the financial panic of 1893, the international tensions of the decade, his own study of the newer physics, and a visit to the Hall of Dynamos at the Paris Exposition in 1901. Meanwhile Adams had discovered an at least imaginative refuge from the frightening multiplicity of his own time by his discovery or rediscovery of the glories of medieval architecture on a visit to Coutances, Mont-Saint-Michel, Chartres, and other such spots in 1895. In 1904 he published privately, as the tangible fruit of this passionate interest, *Mont-Saint-Michel and Chartres*; and three years later had finished and printed, again privately, the most famous of his books, *The Education of Henry Adams.* Much earlier, in 1893, he had printed, in the same manner, a memorial of his stay on Tahiti, the *Memoirs of Marau Taaroa, Last Queen of Tahiti.*

His winters continued to be spent mostly at his house on H Street in Washington, where his life took the form of a rather accessible seclusion—accessible to the men and women who interested and diverted him—and from the late nineties until 1914 he regularly passed the summers in an apartment on the Avenue du Bois de Boulogne in Paris. He made no journeys so ambitious as that to the South Seas, but his travels continued, sometimes strenuously. In the winter of 1894–1895 he was in Mexico with Chandler Hale; in 1898 he made another journey to Egypt, which was followed by a stay in Greece, Turkey, and Hungary; in 1899 he was in Sicily and elsewhere in Italy; and in 1901, with the Lodges, he traveled to Bayreuth for the Wagner festival and then journeyed on through Austria and Poland to Russia. After parting with the Lodges in St. Petersburg, Adams himself traveled on alone into Scandinavia, and did not turn back southward until after reaching Hammerfest in Norway, within the Arctic Circle.

To ELIZABETH CAMERON

Paris, 29 December, 1891.

. . . To change the atmosphere I went down to the table-d'hôte, which is ghastly but quick; and hurried off to the Opéra Comique to perform an act of piety to the memory of my revered grandfather. Some people might think it a queer place for the purpose, and the association of ideas may not be obvious even to you, but it is simple. A century ago, more or less, Grétry produced his opera, Richard Cœur de Lion. A century ago, more or less, President Washington sent my grandfather, before he was thirty years old, as minister to the Hague, and my grandfather was fond of music to such an extent that, if I remember right, he tried to play the flute. Anyway he was so much attached to Grétry's music that when he was turned out of the Presidency he could think of nothing, for days together, but *"Oh, Richard, oh, mon roy, l'univers t'abandonne"*; and as I had never heard the opera, I thought I would see it now that it has been revived at the Opéra Comique. Nothing more de-

lightfully rococo and simple could well be, than the music of
Grétry. To think that it was fin de siècle too—and shows it in
the words—and led directly to the French Revolution. I tried to
imagine myself as I was then—and you know what an awfully
handsome young fellow Copley made me—with full dress and
powdered hair, talking to Mme. Chose in the boxes, and stopping to applaud *"Un regard de ma belle."* Unluckily the Opéra
Comique, which used to be the cheerfullest theatre in Paris, is
now to me the dreariest, and poor Richard howled mournfully
as though time had troubled him. Unluckily for me, too, the
next piece was the Lakmé by Delibes, modern enough, no doubt;
but if I abhor the French more in one genre than in another,
and find their fatuity more out of place in any other part of the
world than in that where I happen to be, my abomination of
them is greatest when they try to escape from themselves, and
especially when they become oriental. I forgive them for making me wring my teeth with despair at their Greeks and Romans,
their English and Americans; but I cannot stand them when they
get south of Marseilles and the Suez Canal. After sitting through
a bayadère dance that ground me into the dust, I came away
with the last verse in my ears: *"Dieu protège nos amours!"* As
far as I can see, this is all God has to do in Paris anyhow. . . .

4 January. Luckily I have exhausted all the Paris I can do
single-handed, and can devote myself conscientiously to reading. I call it a poor day when I don't finish at least one volume. Imagine my state of happiness, surrounded by a pile
of yellow literature, skimming a volume of Goncourt, swallowing a volume of Maupassant with my roast, and wondering
that I feel unwell afterwards. These writers have at least the
merit of explaining to me why I dislike the French, and why
the French are proper subjects for dislike. Even I, who do
not love the French, and who, as you know, have never been
able even to swallow my friends' Frenchmen, should hesitate

to believe that human nature, except in the Solomon Islands, could be quite so mean and monkey-like in its intellectual cruelty as the naturalists and realists describe their fellow-countrymen to be, unless I read every day in the police-reports the proof that they do not exaggerate. At every interval of years I come back here with a wider experience of men and knowledge of races, and always the impression becomes stronger that, of all people in the world, the French are the most gratuitously wicked. They almost do me good. I feel it a gain to have an object of dislike. At least that is real, and I can kick it. Next to having an object to like, I am duly grateful for having an object to detest. . . .

January 7 [*1892*]. In my journey of eighteen months round the world, among the remote and melancholy islands where I have been for four months at a time imprisoned, unable to escape, never have I felt anything like the effect of nightmare that I have got from four weeks in Paris. Talk about our American nerves! they are normal and healthy compared with the nerves of the French, which are more diseased than anything on earth except the simple Norwegian blondes of Mr. Ibsen. In all Paris—literature, theatre, art, people and cuisine —I have not yet seen one healthy new thing. Nothing simple, or simply felt, or healthy; all forced even in its effort to be simple—like Maupassant, the flower of young France—all tormented, and all self-conscious. . . .

To ELIZABETH CAMERON

[*London*] *Jan. 23* [*1892*].
. . . So the time has come for closing and sending off my last letter. On Monday I go down to Yorkshire to pass the week with Gaskell, and on my return I shall have only a day here to close up and go. London is still quiet, muddy and dark. Last night I went to Sir Charles Hallé's concert with Augusta

Hervey and a friend of hers. The hall was only half full, and the big orchestra seemed a majority. I believe I have done all my social duties as far as the season and the influenza allow. The little society I have found has offered a curious contrast to my former experiences here, when the days were hardly long enough to meet the engagements. Now I seem to be the oldest inhabitant, and forgotten by time. I should not mind except that sometimes the feeling of being less than half my old self becomes rather trying. I have seen nothing worth buying, which is another great change; and have heard of no one whom I care to meet. Still, London is in its way rather pleasant and quieting. I am not anxious to get away, and the absence of clatter and fashion is on the whole pleasanter than being surrounded by a swarm of society that is wholly strange. Tomorrow, as usual on Sundays, I lunch with Harry James, who is chiefly excited by the marriage of his friend Rudyard Kipling with the sister of another friend, Balestier, an American who was half publisher, half author, and whose sudden death at Dresden a month ago, was a sad blow to James, who depended on him for all his business arrangements. I imagine Kipling to be rather a Bohemian and wanderer of the second or third social order, but he has behaved well about his young woman and has run in the face of family and friends who think him a kind of Shakespeare, and wanted him to marry the Queen or the Duchess of Westminster. I believe his wife is a perfectly undistinguished American without beauty or money or special intelligence. They were married very privately and almost secretly last week. James had confided it all to me last Sunday, which is the cause of my happening to know about it. James also confided to me his distress because Sargent, the painter, had quarreled with a farmer down at the place, wherever it is [Broadway in

Worcestershire], where the Abbey-Millet-Parsons crowd now pass their winters, and after riding up and down his fields of spring wheat, had been wrought to such frenzy by being called no gentleman, that he went to the farmer's house, called him out, and pounded him; for which our artist-genius in America would certainly get some months of gaol, and may get it even here, which much distresses Henry who has a sympathetic heart. This too was confided to me, and has not yet got into the newspapers. As Sargent seems not to distress himself, I see no reason why James should do so; but poor James may well be a little off his nerves, for besides Balestier's death, the long, nervous illness of James's sister [Alice] is drawing slowly to its inevitable close, and James has the load of it to carry, not quite alone, for Catherine Loring is here in charge of the invalid, but still the constant load on one's spirits is considerable. I wish I could help him. His sister now keeps her bed, and is too weak to think of anything but her nerves. I sat two hours with Miss Loring yesterday.

I suppose that the *Teutonic* will somehow get me across that dreary ocean and land me at New York in due time. I think about it as little as possible, and shall certainly be much surprised at finding myself there. . . .

To JOHN HAY

1603 H Street [*Washington*], *18 Oct. 1893.*

Your letter from Paris, October 5, reached me yesterday on my return from Chicago where I have just passed a fortnight. For a poor old ghost like me, just barely hovering on this earth for which my ethereal nature unfits me, the Midway Plaisance was a sweet repose. I revelled in all its fakes and frauds, all its wickedness that seemed not to be understood by our innocent natives, and all its genuineness which was under-

stood still less. I labored solemnly through all the great buildings and looked like an owl at the dynamos and steam-
engines. All the time I kept up a devil of a thinking. You
know the terror of my thought, so I will not spare you; but if
we ever write those Travels of ours, I've a volume or two to
put in for the Fair. I want to talk among other matters about
the architecture, and discuss the question of the true relation
between Burnham, Attwood, McKim, White, Millett, etc.,
and the world. Do you remember Sargent's portrait of Mrs.
Hamersly in London this summer? Was it a defiance or an insult to our society, or a rendering in good faith of our civilization, or a conscious snub to French and English art, or an
unconscious revelation of the artist's despair of reconciliation
with the female of the gold-bug? I say the female, because
the male has been the butt of the artist for centuries. Well!
the Chicago architecture is precisely an architectural Mrs.
Hamersly. I like to look at it as an appeal to the human animal, the superstitious and ignorant savage within us, that has
instincts and no reason, against the world as money has made
it. I have seen a faint gleam of intelligence lighten the faces
even of the ignorant rich and almost penetrate the eyes of a
mugwump and Harvard College graduate, as he brooded, in
his usual stolidity of self-satisfaction, on his own merits, before the Court of Honor. Never tell me to despair of our
gold-bugs after this; we can always drown them. Burnham,
Stanford White, Millett, and the rest, are a little more violent
than I. They rather want to torture the very Chicago gold-
bugs who have given them the money, beginning with Hig-
ginbothem. As for me, I was always humane. I would only
drown them without torture, or electrocute them with their
own dynamos, painlessly. The mugwump, I admit, is a difficulty; death cannot end his self-esteem; but even Gilder
ought to be treated without vindictive feelings. Besides, he

has already been flayed alive by the *Sun* and the *Tribune,* and really means well, and is a cherub.

I came back at midnight, Monday evening, to plunge into a bath of boiling politics. You never lost so much as in missing this silver fight. During the fortnight of my absence, matters have grown irretrievably worse. Cleveland has driven on the passions of the Senate until we are in a really dangerous temper. I fully expect that someone will be killed, unless the situation is immediately relieved. My dear democracy is all in pieces; not a rag of decency is left. Every debate is a four-sided fight; the republican attacks the democrat; the eastern democrat flies at the throat of the western democrat; all three then attack Cleveland. Yesterday John Sherman just danced on Morgan and Hill, while Morgan and Hill were rolling around, gouging each other; and all of them were wild to burn Cleveland alive. The poor mugwumps are the unhappiest of all. They have, with their accustomed simplicity of soul, chosen poor Van Alen as their peculiar grievance, and we are told that Schurz has forced Harper's *Weekly* to declare war on Cleveland for this awful iniquity—after swallowing Garland and Joe Quincy and Maxwell, and the Lord only knows what iniquities of patronage to buy Voorhees and his brother Senators. Wall Street and its various ramifications are howling for a *coup d'état* in the Senate. Cleveland is trying to effect one. The silver men challenge it. Oh, cock-a-doodle-doo! if I were not a pessimist and a fatalist, a populist, a communist, a socialist, and the friend of a humanist, where would I be at?

As I can see nothing but universal bankruptcy before the world, whatever way it turns, and whatever standard it prefers in which to reckon the balance-sheet of its insolvency, I take little stock either in gold, silver or paper, except that I want all I can get of them all; and most cool men, like those who run the *Sun,* the *Tribune,* and such conservative sheets, seem to hold the same view; but with Cleveland for President, and Populism as my only refuge after he has licked me out of the Democratic party, my toes are getting cold with a very familiar sensation of being shut out-doors in the blizzard.

Socially, too, I am likely to be left alone. You are gone. During my absence at Chicago, Mrs. Sherman died, and Mrs. Cameron returned only yesterday from the funeral at Cleveland. I have not yet had time to talk with her, but I've no doubt she will go to St. Helena for the winter. Arnold Hague has convulsed society by announcing his marriage on the 14th November next to Mrs. Walter Howe, or something of that kind; a widow of New York, known to Teddy [Roosevelt] and the wives of various people; said to be well off in gold and interest-bearing bonds; and a drowned husband at Newport two years ago. So Arnold is lost. Ward Thoron is dropped the next day; so my sole young lover disappears from my stage. Even Rebecca Rae has migrated with all her live-stock to Annapolis to teach school at the Academy. Except Loonatic Phillips and Loonatic Teddy and Senator Loonatic Cabot, I have no one left; and these three Loons do not make a winter.

Of King I hear nothing. His bank busted with the rest, and I fear he has gone under. Frank Emmons, too, is busted. The Fortieth Parallel always had the devil's bad luck and yet Arnold Hague marries. The ruin has, I fear, not yet fairly begun, and will not be fully known till the Chicago Fair is closed, and business becomes settled on the bottom-mud.

I have looked into your house to see your windows [by La Farge], which are exquisite. Perhaps after all, I will accept your offer, and move into your house, just to live with the windows. Better than widows anywhere.

If not that, you may see me any day. If you will go with me to the Taj, telegraph, and I will start within four-and-twenty hours.

To CHARLES MILNES GASKELL

Washington, 28 April, 1894.

I found your letter of April 11 awaiting me here last Monday, when I arrived at my house after four months absence in
the south. The spirit of unrest which drives me from one form
of seasickness to another has hunted me this season through
Cuba and the Bahamas, regions mostly new to me, and with
much that has amused me immensely. One effect of years I can
now take as constant. I love the tropics, and feel really at ease
nowhere else. A good, rotten tropical Spanish island, like Cuba,
with no roads and no drainage, but plenty of bananas and brigands, never bores me. . . . Every time I come back to what we
are pleased to call civilized life, it bores me more, and seems to
me more hopelessly idiotic; and, as I do not care to imitate
Carlyle and Ruskin and Emerson and all the rest of our pro-
testing philosophers by trying to make a living by abusing the
society of my time, nothing remains but to quit it, and seek another. I am satisfied that [Charles Henry] Pearson is right, and
that the dark races are gaining on us, so that we may depend on
their steadily shutting down on us, as they have already done in
Haiti, and are doing throughout the West Indies and our
southern States. In another fifty years, at the same rate of movement, the white races will have to reconquer the tropics by war
and nomadic invasion, or be shut up, north of the fortieth
parallel. I know that with our fatuous self-esteem, our newspapers admire themselves too much to admit their own possible inferiority to niggers without newspapers; but as I rather
prefer niggers to whites, and much prefer oriental art to European, I incline to make the most of the tropics while the white
is still tolerated there.

My return here is not of a sort to discourage these notions. If
ever one saw an enormous exhibition of imbecility, we give it
here. We don't know what is the matter with us, yet we all ad-

mit that we have had a terrific shock of some sort. We see no reason at all for assuming that the causes, whatever they are, which have brought about the prostration, have ceased, or will cease, to act. On the contrary, as far as we can see, if anything is radically wrong, it must grow worse, for it must be in our system itself, and at the bottom of all modern society. If we are diseased, so is all the world. Everyone is discussing, disputing, doubting, economising, going into bankruptcy, waiting for the storm to pass, but no sign of agreement is visible as to what has upset us, or whether we can cure the disease. That the trouble is quite different from any previous experience, pretty much everyone seems to admit; but nobody diagnoses it. Probably in a year or two, we shall pick ourselves up again, and go ahead, but we shall know no better what hit us. To judge from what I can gather from the *Economist* and other European sources of financial wisdom, Europe is rather more in the dark than we are. Europe and Asia are used to accepting diseases and death as inevitable, but to us the idea is a new one. We want to know what is wrong with the world that it should suddenly go to smash without visible cause or possible advantage. Here, in this young, rich continent, capable of supporting three times its population with ease, we have had a million men out of employment for nearly a year, and the situation growing worse rather than better. Society here, as well as in Europe, is shaking, yet we have no bombs, no violence, and no wars to fear. I prefer my Cuba, which is frankly subsiding into savagery. At least the problems there are simple.

Thus far I have not suffered. As well as I know, I have not lost a dollar either in capital or income. Of course this cannot last. Probably within another year, I shall feel the shrinkage. At present I feel it only through others, and chiefly in the form of physical collapse. All my brothers have gone, or are on their way, to Europe for rest. They need it. Men of sixty wear out fast under steady anxiety. Edward Hooper has also gone over, probably for the same reason, although he says nothing of his health. My friend La Farge is with him, also for health, although collapse in his case is not due to finance, I suppose. Clarence King woke up one day to find himself in Bloomingdale Asylum. He stayed there some weeks, till the congestion of his fifth or fifteenth or fiftieth vertebra subsided, and then went with me to Cuba. He is still with me, never better, but dreading return to New York and care. These private instances of the collapse would not bother me so much except that I feel the same unhealthy excitability and worry in society, high and low, rich and poor, industrial, financial and political. Moreton Frewen is rushing about, quite out of character, with feverish activity to cure creation. Spring Rice is furious with Frewen. Sir Julian Pauncefote has taken to gout and worry. . . . My favorite girls, too, have all got married—which is a bore.

Never mind! We have had our little day.

I agree with you about [J.R.] Lowell's letters. They are deadly. But what letters are not now? Do tell me of a new book.

To CHARLES MILNES GASKELL

Washington, 18 June, 1894.

. . . Thousands of Americans are now abroad, mostly for economy, which is my reason for staying at home. It's a bore, for I've nothing to do. In despair, I've taken to reading history again, and as our world seems to have gone to the devil—at least in art and literature—I have taken up the story of that greater world, the Roman Empire, which went so inexplicably to the devil before us. I find it very entertaining, especially in its bearings on our droll assumptions of superiority. How much Petronius could give Zola, and yet need no odds! I am now preparing to start into the Rocky Mountains for the summer, hoping to pitch my camp all through the Yellowstone and

Teton range, far beyond sight or hearing of white men until snow begins to fly, which, out there, is in September; and I am going to carry with me a small library of the Roman decadence. The contrast should be entertaining.

Naturally I have no news to offer you, which would be worth your hearing. Public affairs are all on your side. We seem to have settled only one point, and that is that we shall henceforward be more protectionist and exclusive than ever before. I shall not be surprised if within another five years, we clap on a hundred per cent duties on every foreign product, and go over to the silver standard besides. The reaction against European influence is terrific. Nothing short of total non-intercourse seems quite to satisfy our people, and the next elections are likely to sweep the old democratic free-trade doctrines simply out of existence. I look forward to them with a certain curiosity, though it is chiefly the curiosity of a monkey on a hand-organ. I want to break it, to see what is inside. To me personally nothing seems to matter much,—unless perhaps we too take to bombs. . . .

I will try to read [Benjamin] Kidd, since everyone is talking about him, but on these matters I have my own prejudgments, and hate to see half-treatment, like Pearson's, etc. We know too little yet to make a science of history. Another fifty years will do it, I've no doubt. I can wait. It will do no one any good. Did you ever read Karl Marx? I think I never struck a book which taught me so much, and with which I disagreed so radically in conclusion. Anyway, these studies of morbid society are not so amusing as Petronius and Plutarch.

We are now in the midst of a spasm of virtue, the outcome of hard times. Everywhere we are rubbing our noses in filth with high delight. After all, it is nothing much, to one fresh from later Rome. A few bribed policemen and speculative legislators make the whole harvest.

To SIR ROBERT CUNLIFFE

Cuautla, Mexico, 8 January, 1895.

Why you should suddenly occur to my mind just now, I do not know; but my conscience, which has been dull enough of late, wakes me up this morning with an order to write to tell you something—I don't know what. *Pax!* I trust all still goes well in your pilgrimage. As I have been wandering, since December 1, where letters could not follow me, and where telegraphs were little useful, I know not what news may wait my reappearance in the world. All news, at our time of life, is bad news. So I thought three months ago, when on coming out of the Rocky Mountains, my only letter told me that my eldest brother was dead. So I think now, when I try to imagine whether any possible news that may await me, can be good news. My best prayer for you and yours is that you have no news to send.

Certainly I have none to send you. What does Petrarch say in that forgotten, but very much 'fin-de-siècle' sonnet beginning *'Dell'empia Babilonia,'* and continuing *'aqui me sto solo'*? (unless my Spanish has mixed itself with what little Italian I once thought I knew). At any rate, here I am passably solitary. For a month I have been drifting about Mexico, until mules and mountains so wearied me that I have stopped at this small town to rest, and to cure an obstinate cold. I do not know that you feel even a gleam of curiosity to know where the town is, and I am not, myself, quite sure of its latitude and longitude, but, as I came here, it stood about a hundred miles, more or less, to the south of the city of Mexico. I came here because it was the way to Acapulco where I was trying to get, and where I found I could not get, at least in time for the steamer; so after riding a hundred and fifty miles on mule-back, in a sugar-loaf hat, leather jacket and trousers, and spurs that weigh many kilos, I dropped back here, under the slopes of Popocatapetl, and lie all day on my bed, looking at the red Poinsettias and oleanders and hybiscus flowering in the garden, and the eternally blue sky over the snow of Popocatapetl, and wondering whether the dust and the dirt and the heat of midday, and the cold of midnight and the bad food and the general beastliness will let me stay quiet another day. Do you know that I have travelled to every place on earth which travellers have described as most fascinating, in the hope of finding one where I should want to stay or return, and have found that Faust had a sure horse on the devil in his promise about the passing hour: *Bleibe doch, du bist so schön!* Three days in any place on earth is all it will bear. The pleasure is in the movement, as Faust knew when he let the devil in to the preposterous contract. Mexico is exceptionally amusing, not in the romantic way I expected, but in a prosaic, grimy, Indian, scarlet-vermilion way of its own, impossible to describe, and disappointing to realize. It is another money-making machine, like the United States or England or Italy, but uses peculiar and rather successful processes of its own, remnants of the Roman Empire, which still survives here in full flower. As far as I could judge, living as I have done, in their mud huts, and eating their *tortillas* and *chile* by their side, among the pigs and hens and dogs that fill the interstices of their cabins, I saw nothing whatever that I should not have seen in a like journey in the Spain of Hadrian. Every detail of the pottery, the huts, the mule-trains with their loads, the food, the clothes, and the roads where no wheel had ever passed, might have been Roman, and the people have the peculiar look, though all really Indians, that the Roman empire left forever on its slave-provinces. Thanks to its silver coinage Mexico is now flourishing, chiefly at the cost of the United States and England. Agriculture, manufactures and mines are all splendidly successful, and the poorest labor is well employed. I see the country at its best, and admit that it is right, and we are the failures. Mexico can lose nothing, for it is at the bottom in respect to its wants. She is bound to clean us out.

Artistically the old Mexico both ecclesiastical and secular was charming, and has astonished me much.

I have done with it now, and in a week expect to be in Havana, hoping to reach the Windward Islands through Porto Rico, having failed to get round through Panama. Towards April I should drift northward again, and hope then to find a letter from you.

To MABEL HOOPER LA FARGE

Paris, 1 Sept. '95.

Two days ago, on arriving here, I got Looly's and Fanny's letters, which gave me all the news in the world, or at least all I am likely to get, for no one else writes. By the time you get this, summer will be waning. My own passage is taken for October 12, and by the 20th I hope to be running the house at Washington. . . .

We all left London on Sunday, the 18th, and, with lovely weather, crossed to Amiens where we passed Monday in the Cathedral. Of course I had been there often, but it is always newer and more wonderful every time, and it never seemed so fresh as now, or so marvellously perfect. Then we went on to Rouen and passed Wednesday there, also on old ground, but interesting, and we might well have stayed longer. We kept on then to Caen, Thursday, which was new to me, and full of William the Conqueror and his buildings. On Friday we stopped some hours at Bayeux to see Matilda's tapestry and another early church; and we had time at Saint-Lo to bag another curious early Cathedral, still reaching Coutances in time to see the sunset from the top of the Cathedral there.

We thought Coutances the most charming of all these places, but perhaps it was only a surprise. The Norman Cathedral there was something quite new to me, and humbled my proud spirit a good bit. I had not thought myself so ignorant or so stupid as to have remained blind to such things, being more or less within sight of them now for nearly forty years. I thought I knew Gothic. Caen, Bayeux, and Coutances were a chapter I never opened before, and which pleased my jaded appetite. They are austere. They have, outside, little of the vanity of Religion. Inside, they are worked with a feeling and a devotion that turns even Amiens green with jealousy. I knew before pretty well all that my own life and time was worth, but I never before felt quite so utterly stood on, as I did in the Cathedral at Coutances. Amiens has mercy. Coutances is above mercy itself. The squirming devils under the feet of the stone Apostles looked uncommonly like me and my generation.

On Saturday we came on to Mont Saint Michel, among a mob of tourists. About Mont Saint Michel I can say little because it is too big. It is the Church Militant, but if Coutances expressed the last—or first—word of Religion, as an emotion of self-abasement, Mont Saint Michel lifted one up to a sort of Sir Galahad in its mixture of sword and cross. We passed two days there, in the most abominable herd of human hogs I ever saw at the trough of a table-d'hôte, but the castle was worth many hogs. When Rafael painted Saint Michael flourishing his big sword over Satan, he thought no doubt that he had done a good bit of religious painting, but the Norman architecture makes even Rafael vulgar. The Saint Michael of the Mount is as big as Orion and his sword must be as high as Sirius, if Sirius in these days has any Faith, which may be doubted; and if stars anyway are of any use, which is more questionable still, both stars and swords being now better understood, or more antiquated, than in the eleventh century. So we bade good-bye to Sir Galahad Saint Michael, on Monday, with the proud thought that we could smash him with one cannon-ball, or the gold resources of a single Wall Street Bank, and we rode and we rode and we hunted and we hollowed till we came to Vitré to sleep, and there too we saw what is left of a very old town, and walls, above a green valley, and a great Castle of the Tremoilles, grands seigneurs s'il en fût; and the old Château of Mme. de Sévigné, a few miles off, untouched, and for all the world exactly like our Scotch castles. From Vitré to Le Mans, with another Cathedral; and, last of all, two long hours at Chartres on a lovely summer afternoon, with the sun flaming behind Saint Anne, David, Solomon, Nebuchadnezzar, and the rest, in the great windows of the north transept. No austerity there, inside or out, except in the old south tower and spire which still protests against mere humanity. I've a notion that you saw Chartres, and know all about it. If so, I can drop it. If not, I hope to take you there. Of course I studied the windows, if only for La Farge's sake, and tried to understand their makers. On the whole, as a combination of high merits, religious and spiritual; artistic, as architecture; technical, as engineering; for color, form, and thought; for elevation of idea and successful subordination of detail; I suppose Chartres is now the finest thing in the world. At least that would be my guess; but I've no confidence in it; and if you say you prefer Saint Paul's or Saint Peter's, so let it be. It does not matter much now-a-days. I believe a vast majority prefers the Houses of Parliament and the State Department at Washington. You can take your own line.

The same evening we came on to Paris, and here we are: Hôtel des deux Mondes, Avenue de l'Opéra. Mr. and Mrs. Lodge, the two boys, and I, occupying one apartment. We have not quarrelled or differed, and our journey since leaving New York has been highly successful. I hope they have enjoyed it as much as I have. I find the Cunliffes here, which is another joy to me. The Luces also, our other sister, are here, and two thousand million Americans sitting at every café, with penetrating

voices proclaiming that they only wish they were in New York.
I wish they were, and I further still, for I love Paris only so
very little that I would not quite utterly destroy it, as I would
destroy London; but would leave the Louvre, and Notre Dame,
and the Café Riche or Véfour's. The only real objection I have
to France is that there is no good Champagne in it. Otherwise
it is a tolerable place enough, except for the Jews and Americans. . . .

To ELIZABETH CAMERON

Tours, 18 September, 1895.

. . . Sister Anne [Mrs. Henry Cabot Lodge] came down here
with us last Sunday, and at once had a desperate cold which has
prevented her from going with us anywhere. Of course we
have to go without her, and I do not think she has lost very
much, so far. Decidedly the Loire is a violently over-admired
country. After Mont Saint Michel and the churches of the
north, nothing here seems much worth while. I do not love
the Valois or their art. I have made that remark before. They
are very earthy. They feel gilded, and smell of musk. They
strike attitudes, and admire themselves in mirrors. Francis I
and Henry VIII are brothers, and should have been cooks. They
look it. Their architecture looks it, just in proportion as it loses
the old military character. In soul, it is mercantile, bourgeois
and gold-bug. When I look at it, I am homesick for Mont Saint
Michel and Coutances. The ancient Gauls were noble in comparison, and I yearned to live in the stone-age.

Not a single character or association seems to lend dignity
or character to all this country. Rabelais, Balzac, civil wars,
massacres, assassinations and royal mistresses are pretty much
all it can show. Between Louis XI and Mr. Terry of Chenonceau or Herr Siegfried of Langeais, I have no great choice.
None of them seems to answer my Sphynx. The old Châteaux

never had much meaning, and now hardly point even a moral. I cannot find even a Mme. de Sévigné to fill them. Diane de Poitiers, whom I rather imagine to have been of the same somewhat *cuisinière* order as the rest of the Court, seems to be highest deity of Touraine. They all belong to the *Contes Drolatiques*. They are sensual, coarse and greedy. They are gold-bugs.

My single keen pleasure is the few glass windows still left in the Cathedral here. There are a dozen or two very exquisite and perfect ones, as good, I should think, as those at Chartres, and with rather more variety of design, if I can remember right. These are a joy. I am not quite sure that there is much religion in glass; but for once I will not require too much. The ultimate cathedral of the 13th century was deliberately intended to unite all the arts and sciences in the direct service of God. It was a Chicago Exposition for God's profit. It showed an Architectural exhibit, a Museum of Painting, Glass-staining, Wood and Stone Carving, Music, vocal and instrumental, Embroidering, Jewelry and Gem-setting, Tapestry-weaving, and I know not what other arts, all in one building. It was the greatest single creation of man. Its statuary alone puts it with Greek art. Its religious conception, by uniting the whole Pantheon of deities in one system, gives it a decided advantage over the Greeks. The more I study it, the more I admire and wonder. I am not disposed to find fault. The result was beyond what I should suppose possible to so mean an animal as man. It gives him a dignity which he is in no other instance entitled to claim. Even its weaknesses are great, and its failures, like Beauvais and Le Mans, are because man rose beyond himself.

So I accept the glass, as I do the reliquaries and embroidered vestments and tapestries.

Thursday morning, 19th. We went yesterday afternoon to Chinon, a superb old military ruin, of a type like Windsor, but without architecture other than the usual military construction. It is not a Mont Saint Michel, but the dirty little town is very Gustave Doré, Rabelais and Balzac. The view from the Castle is the best and most imposing we've seen. The weather is divine, but the drought and dust are bad, and even the heat is still no very bad joke for the season. In the afternoon glow, the broad valley and river were as rich and succulent as the grapes.

Cabot and I are discussing whether Cleveland may not have to call Congress for the 1st of November. The situation is critical, and even the harvest may not save the Treasury now. If he does, I may have to give up my stateroom to the Lodges, and take theirs, which would delay me a month. For me, it is much better to be out of it. The behavior of our government and monied-men irritates me, wears on my nerves, and makes me talk much more than is wise or virtuous. Away from America I am always more human;—a trait not wholly peculiar to me.

Paris, 25 September, 1895.

. . . I wrote rather abusively about Touraine last week. I ought to make one exception. The Château of Blois is very beautiful. At least, the fragment which contains the staircase, making one side of the court, is perhaps the best thing I have seen in its way;—not quite so dignified and broad as the corresponding court of the Louvre, but even more original and refined. It is a charming and altogether an ideal spot, for it contains the best political murder ever made. The Valois kings were true artists, and they never did anything artistically half so brilliant elsewhere, as to build the Château de Blois in order to murder the Guises in it, with a *mise-en-scène* and a list of actors that would have put to shame all the resources of the French stage in its best days. In the room where De Guise lay dead, and the King came in to look at him, and kick him a bit, I understood for the first time the very inferior, not to say plebeian affair at Holyrood, which was but a Scotch attempt to be as artistic as France. The Scotch did fairly well. Mary Stuart was not a bad variation on Catherine of Medici. Compared with the coarse brutality of Henry the Eighth, who undertook also to be an artist in the same way, the Scotch were very superior; but after all, they were imitators. The great scenes at Amboise and Blois were original compositions, and, as art, stand beyond rivalry. I know of nothing since the tragedies of Aeschylus so splendid, and so grandly immoral. No history, Greek, Roman or modern, contains contrasts so dramatic and so gorgeously tragic, as the contrast between the Cathedrals of the 13th and the Châteaux of the 15th centuries. After the ecstasies of Chartres and Amiens, the elevation and passion, the absorption of every act and thought in an ideal of infinite beauty and purity, we sit down with a bump on the thrones of Francis and Henry. As if this shock were too much for our nervous systems, we are not only forbidden to conceive the tragedy in the grand Greek way, but we are also condemned to listen to the unutterable cant of British morality, which makes the ghastliest cynicism seem a relief and a religion. May the Lord, in his infinite mercy, forgive himself for creating British moral and historical writers, and the Church of England. This reflection is wrung from me by the British writers on French history.

Well, well! when I get quite wild with England, I read Ruskin and Carlyle, or Matt Arnold or Shelley and console myself by thinking of their lifelong martyrdoms, so inglorious, so grimy, and so mean. At least I can love Jeanne d'Arc. We crossed her path again at Orléans where we passed a day. I suppose the British shop-keepers did not burn her. But it is a singular coincidence that she was burned—by the British. She is a dear creature, and it was almost worth while to be burned like her, rather than be suffocated like us. At least, *her* protest was effective, as far as it went.

Of all the places we saw, the only one which seemed to unite everything was Chaumont. I do not know that an atmosphere of Catherine de Medici and Diane de Poitiers combined in one room is very healthy, but at Chaumont one seems to breathe and see without effort. Even the great military towers and the drawbridge do not scare one. If it were not for tourists, Chaumont would be still a dignified country-place. Perhaps the Broglies think it is so anyway. They seem to live there quietly enough, and to bear with tourists, republic and Diane, while at Chenonceau the Terrys—Cubans of the Cienfuegos sugar epoch—war on tourists, and shut their doors, so that we did not get there. I could not blame them. To be a tourist is to lose self-respect and to invite insult. Quentin Durward was evidently taken for a tourist when Tristan wanted to string him up, on his appearance at Plessy les Tours. Nothing saved him but being a Scotchman. Had he been an American, we must have applauded his execution, and if an Englishman we should have helped to string him up.

In spite of Blois and Chaumont, Touraine cannot compare with Normandy. It leaves a greasy taste; a mercantile and gold-bug trail, even on the architecture and the murders. I turn back to my dear Coutances and my divine Mont Saint Michel with the relief of an epicure who has had to eat pork. . . .

27th. I have passed an hour with Rodin in his studio looking at his marbles, and especially at a Venus and dead Adonis which he is sending to some exhibition in Philadelphia, and which is quite too too utter and decadent, but like all his things hardly made for *jeunes personnes* like me and my breakfast-table company. Why can we decadents never take the comfort and satisfaction of our decadence. Surely the meanest life on earth is that of an age that has not a standard left on any form of morality or art, except the British sovereign. I prefer Rodin's decadent sensualities, but I must not have them, and though rotten with decadence, I have not enough vitality left to be sensual. Victoria and I and our age are about equally genuine. We are beyond even vice. . . .

I am losing interest in public affairs now that you say you are out of it, and as our country must inevitably declare itself insolvent within a year, I have ceased to care much about the process; but probably Frewen has written to you that Balfour is hatching a silver scheme for us to swallow. Being a gold-bug myself, and wishing for a cataclysm, I trust that any English scheme will fail.

To CHARLES FRANCIS ADAMS, JR.

Washington, 21 February, 1896.

I send you by express my copy of the rebel organ in London.

In many ways our father was a singular man. He remains an unsolved problem to me in the fact that he never seemed conscious of being bored, or of the world being different from what he wanted it to be. Although I have no doubt that he was more in his element in London than at any other time in his life, he never seemed aware of it, and showed it only by the momentary expansion of his interests. Perhaps in this quality he was like the earlier men. Jefferson did much the same. J. Q. Adams did not understand why he was bored. Indeed none of the old crowd was very self-conscious. Yet all our father's contemporaries in Boston—Sumner, Palfrey, Winthrop, Hillard, Ticknor, Motley, and Lowell—secretly or openly showed that they were hungry for something they could not get. The trait of restlessness has been marked in all the rest of the family, with few exceptions, before and since. Our father was not lazy, yet he never much cared for change. He was reflective, yet not self-conscious. He was logical, yet never carried a line of thought beyond a conventional conclusion. He was so complete, as far as he went, that I shall never understand why he went no farther.

This is all I can answer to your question. I've no doubt that what you say is true, but I doubt whether he would have thought so. My impression is that he thought he wanted to be in Mt. Vernon Street, polishing his coins. What is more extraordinary, I believe he continued to think so even after he had entered again the solemn portal of No.57.

He was a happy man.

To ELIZABETH CAMERON

Athens, 10 April, 1898.

. . . I make desperate efforts to hear and think as little as possible about the situation, but, do what I will, I hear and think too much, and as I sit on the platform of the Pnyx, or wander over the hills at Phaleron or Eleusis, my mind wanders terribly fast between Salamis, where Xerxes is before my eyes, and Key West where our ships are waiting orders. The moment is perhaps a turning-point in history; in any case it can hardly fail to fix the lines of a new concentration, and to throw open an immense new field of difficulties. The world is abjectly helpless. It is running a race to nowhere, only to beggar its neighbors. It must either abolish its nationalities, concentrate its governments and confiscate its monopolies for social economics, or it must steadily bump from rock to rock, and founder at last, economically; while it will founder socially if it does concentrate and economise. Even so weak and wild a political member as Spain or Turkey has the power to pull down the whole fabric of the world, and the whole of Europe quivers with terror if she threatens to use it. Germany, Russia and England can agree in nothing but a division of thefts, and a tacit understanding that no part of the world shall be exempt from the exercise of their power. Behind it all, there lies an economical war which is vastly more fatal in its effects than any ordinary war of armies.

Slowly and painfully our people are waking up to the new world they are to live in, and I am, as you know, for these five years past, so absorbed in it that it gives me nervous dyspepsia, insomnia and incipient paralysis if I have to face a crisis. . . .

So I dread coming west, and dread still more the thought that I may be obliged to come west. I am too glad to remain here, and to haunt the poor, old, ridiculous, academic, pedagogic, preposterous associations of Attica. What a droll little amusing fraud of imagination it was, and how it has imposed its own valuation of itself on all respectable society down to this day! Fifty years of fortunate bloom at a lucky moment,—a sudden flood of wealth from a rich silver mine, the Rand of that day,—was all that really dazzles us; a sort of unnatural, forced flower, never strong, never restful, and always half-conscious of its own superficiality. So ridiculous a city, without excuse for existence, and without land to cultivate, water to drink, or trade to handle, no historian ever saw elsewhere. Aristophanes and Lucian are the only people who really understood it. Still, it had a certain success that I could wish had been commoner. Without being a superstitious worshipper of Athenian art, I shouldn't mind if a little of it could have survived. My brother Brooks says,—'No! It cannot be! man is made to be cheap, and Athens was costly.'—After all, other and greater arts have gone; —Chartres and Amiens are as dead as Athens, and Michael Angelo deader than Phidias. It is a comfort to find one city that never kept shop, and where art never smelt of per-centages. I, prefer it to Venice.

Rockhill and I roam all over the place, for Mrs. Rockhill and Dolly have gone to Olympia for three days, and left us here. One afternoon we passed at Eleusis, really an exquisite spot. All day today we have rambled along the seashore of Phalerum and the Piræus. We haunt low quarters where I bargain for coins with dirty pawn-brokers and greasy Greek peddlers. As they

sell me for a dollar or two the same coins which the shops and
collectors at Athens will not sell for less than ten or twenty or
a hundred dollars, naturally I prefer their friendship. My coin-
collection is becoming weighty. I must have bought more than
a hundred since Assouan, and they afford me not only much
amusement but lots of instruction. A new king turns up every
day or two, of whose existence I never heard, but whose head is
a medallion that all the Caesars since Julius have never been
able to approach—unless it be Napoleon, who did pretty well
on medals as on some other rivalries with classic triumphs. But
of course the only real charm of Athens, as of all these other dry
countries, is the color and the water, the mountains and the
sea. . . .

April 13. Poor dear old McKinley stands like Olympian Zeus
with his thunder-bolt ready, and Sir Julian Neptune [Paunce-
fote] with the lesser Gods offering him burnt-incense. I only
hope he will keep it up. The real issue is now European, and, to
me, a veritable turning-point of the hinges of Hades. If we only
get round that corner safely—and that corner means the Kaiser
Willy to me! Then they can pick up the pieces of various shat-
tered empires at our leisure. To think that the gold-bugs, instead of squeezing us into obedience, have squeezed Paris and
London till they howl, and have forced the Bank of England to
put up its rate to four per cent. In order to borrow more of our
money when she can't pay what they already owe! . . .

Ah! I've been thinking so long of this crisis, and have cast up
so many columns of figures, not to speak of our prodigious
Cameron Reports of the Senate Committee, on which, as far as
I can see, the President and Congress have taken their stand.
After all, it was you and I who did all the real fighting against
the odds when Olney went back on himself and us. It was a
mauvais quart d'heure, the Christmas holidays of '96, and poor

Willy Phillips never lived to see the fight recovered. If only this week holds out right!

Meanwhile I have become an Athenian, and have half forgot that countries exist without dust and Greece. I live mostly at Rockhill's, and do little of anything. Our plans are now settled. We are all to start Saturday (16th) for a week's trip to Mycenæ, Corinth, Delphi, etc.; and on our return, as soon as possible, we go to Constantinople; from there to Bucharest, ending up at Belgrade, probably about May 20. I shall then strike for Vienna, and Rockhill will return here to his family, for the ladies do not go with us to the north. . . .

Athens, 20 April, 1898.

. . . After some delays, I got Mrs. Rockhill and Dolly to or-ganise a *partie carrée,* with a Greek gentleman of the Foreign Office named Soutzo, to visit Mycenæ. It is no simple matter even now, to visit these Greek places, though Cook has nomin-ally conquered Greece. I left little Mrs. George Eustis setting out with her friends to drive to Delphi, three days by land. I hope she is enjoying the days. She will be in Venice within a week, and will tell you her adventures. You can compare them with mine, and if she liked the days, you can ask about the nights.

As for us, the descent to Mycenæ was easy. Distances here are absurdly small. We left at seven o'clock in the morning; changed cars at Corinth, and reached the Mycenæ station at about two, where we had ordered a carriage and drove up to Mycenæ. Of course I was greatly interested. Yet the thing was very nearly what I expected. Except that the art was in certain ways much higher, Mycenæ is uncommonly like a ruined castle *quelconque* on the Dee or the Don. It is the citadel of a highland chief whose tastes are developed by contact with

Indian Moguls. I was glad to clear my mind about it. Homer became easy, and even a little modern, as though he knew rather less about his ancient predecessors than I did. After my winter's travels Mycenæ seemed neither very old nor very difficult to understand, although its forms are different from those of Egypt and Asia Minor. I felt quite at home with Clytemnestra and Orestes and the whole lot of them, even with Odysseus. Then we drove down the valley to Argos, which is nothing, and to Tiryns, which is Mycenæ over again as a sea-port, with only the changes that a sea-port would make. Finally, at sunset, we reached our night-quarters at Nauplia.

What rattles one most in Greece is the food. As a rule I can eat anything, even Greek food, but I don't hanker for it. Rockhill, who hates to stir, had gone back on us, and stayed at home. Soutzo was used to the customs of his country. I was tolerably hardened to tastes and smells. Mrs. Rockhill could go hungry. But when Dolly struck goat's milk, or meat fried in goat's milk butter, she wilted and went to bed. The water and the wine are mostly as bad as the goats. Even I caved in when required to drink the resin wine, and was dangerously near sea-sickness. Dinner was therefore a modified success, but we pulled through and went to bed. The Devil, having marked us for victims, had fixed that Saturday evening for the Resurrection of Christ according to the Greek rites, and in raising Christ, the Greeks seem to think that their religion requires them to raise the Devil. Such an infernal *vacarme* I never heard. All night the little square rioted with shouts, music, processions, pistol-shots, fire-crackers, singing, howling and bells. To enliven me, I found that no little energy was necessary to clear out various previous occupants of my bed, which at least gave my midnight hours of wakefulness a useful object. Mrs. Rockhill and Dolly looked out of their window and laughed. I know not what Soutzo did. He was angelic and devoted and would have suppressed the church, had he been able, in order not to show an undignified Greece to strangers, but Easter beat him, and we passed the night as we could.

The sun came at last, and we swallowed gaily some coffee—without milk—and started off again in a carriage three hours into the mountains, just like a dry and purple Scotland. The scenery was striking, and the road fair; the breeze reasonably cool, and the world our own. History lay about so thick that we stopped noticing it. Mrs. Rockhill and Dolly chaffed Soutzo, and I tried in vain to divine whether he was really hunting Dolly or was prospecting imaginary gold mines. I liked him, but he is Greek, and unintelligible to an American mind. Mrs. Rockhill and Dolly were as curious and doubtful as I, and chiefly amused to think of what would happen when the imaginary gold mine should disappear. Poor Soutzo, very gentlemanly, obliging beyond measure, and good-natured as an angel, made himself a slave for us, and did everything except black our boots, so that I am sure he made it possible for us to do what we did; and in fact we got along most smoothly, thanks to him and a general determination to enjoy. He it was who dragged us up to the great Temple of Æsculapius, a sort of Greek Carlsbad, though so Greek, and—oh, so little German! We passed the day there, lunching under the olive-trees, and dozing in their shade; rambling over the ruins, and wondering how much better the Greeks understood health-resorts than we. The theatre was the finest in Greece. The race-course and the little opera-house and the groves of columns and statues, the reservoirs and the buildings raised by Emperors and Vanderbilts of the time, amused us awhile, though only their foundations remain. Then we drove down again to Nauplia and renewed the struggle with dinner. The night was better. Soutzo had invoked the police to stop the pistols.

Monday was eccentric. I did not care to go back to Athens

without finishing my sights. Mrs. Rockhill knew that if she went back without visiting Delphi, she would have a desperate chance of ever getting there. The great Soutzo enjoyed taking us about. He undertook to get us to Delphi. Without returning to Athens, it was not easy. We had to return to Corinth, and catch a steamer which passed through the Corinth canal after midnight. Any ordinary guardian would have depended on ordinary means, but Soutzo was not ordinary. He carried us by rail to the eastern end of the canal, put us into a cart with two wheels, and carted us to the house of the Superintendent, Prince Caratheodori, and dumped us on him for the day and for dinner. It was peaceful, though not exciting, and after dinner we were put to bed till midnight, when we were put on board a tug, which intercepted the steamer, and so, at one o'clock in the morning we found ourselves on one of the dirtiest and smellingest steamers I ever saw, with one room to sleep in for the four. Soutzo, whose sense of propriety was correct, kept outside. As for me, I turned into my bunk in my boots, and Dolly into hers next to me, and Mrs. Rockhill on to a couch—for fear of insects—a foot too short for her; and we slept till the sun rose and we rose with it to land at Itea, the port for Delphi.

Rather to my surprise, Mrs. Rockhill and Dolly made violent faces at the little inn at Itea. They said they objected to the smell. To me the smell was a trifling objection compared to what I had feared, and we calmed down and started for Delphi leaving orders to have the whole house washed out in our absence. Luckily we had it to ourselves. A day later, it would have been packed by Cook's tourists, or some other tourists, who come in groups, sleep four in a room, and drive eight in a carriage if necessary. There are French tourists in bands, and German in cohorts, all worse than the Americans; and English, like the insects, in the interstices. We luckily slipped in between several gangs, and had Bœotia all to ourselves. Bœotia was worth it. *Si j'étais roi,* I should think fairly well of myself. The drive up to Delphi is very striking, and, as the road is now excellent, that part is easy as the forest of Marly. At the end of two or three hours, one finds oneself hanging to a mountain-side, two thousand feet above the valleys, and surrounded by the paraphernalia of a Greek city—temples, theatres, walls, race-courses—which all seem plunging down the hill into space. I felt oracular. Greek temples are never religious, mysterious, or very serious, and they are not even—don't quote me—very imposing. At a small distance they look small. Unlike Egyptian temples or Gothic cathedrals, they suit very well as jewel-boxes for Aphrodite, who is very much at home in them, but they suggest too much, as Aristophanes remarked, or should have remarked, when he wrote *Lysistrata* and gave it to Réjane to act, and scandalised even me. Fortunately you did not see her in it, but other Americans did, and as a rule do not mention it. She was very Greek. So is the play. So is the Parthenon. So was Delphi, I should think, perhaps the Greekest thing of all. It comes nearest being serious, and is charming; a transparent and elegant fraud that no one more than half believed in except when it suited them, but that was artistically satisfactory and scenically perfect. 'Nothing too much,' was its motto—'*Mesure en tout,*' as the French say, or don't say. '*L'excès en tout est un défaut.*' There is no excess at Delphi. The horror of the priestess' cavern is unseen and quite imaginary. The mountains are just imposing enough. The valleys are just far enough off, and the olive gives the tone of color. I was immensely pleased with the wonderful taste of it, as I always am with everything Greek. Only Delphi was the loftiest experiment they made, and the most daring. It was packed dense with colonnades and statuary. Rome and Byzantium filled their streets with its marbles and bronzes. The French have just spent one or two hundred thou-

sand dollars in digging it out again, but have found little that is
perfect. Only a few fine marbles,—some very archaic and singularly interesting,—and a quite wonderful bronze of early
Sicilian art, supposed to be Hiero of Syracuse, and which fasci-
nated me more than a thousand Aphrodites could, with weird
speculations about the beauty of that Sicilian world whose coins
are my delight, and whose life was more Grecian than Greece
itself—this was all. The place itself, plastered against the mountain, is hotter than a radiating steam-heater. In summer one
must have burned there till one envied the Pythoness in her
hole. Mrs. Rockhill and I toiled wearily up and down the mountain, over wastes of ruins without one patch of shade, and invoked every demon in the Pantheon to confound Greek theatres
and race-courses. One could not find a spot level enough even
to lie down on.

Practically this closed our adventures. We drove back to Itea
and improvised a dinner. We slept peacefully and sound. We
were, at seven o'clock, on our way to Athens in another of the
nastiest Greek steamers that heart could wish; and we reached
the Legation here soon after five o'clock in the afternoon. . . .

To BROOKS ADAMS

Grand Hotel Hungaria, Buda-Pest, 7 May, 1898.

. . . So I have worked up to Hungary, where I find a very different situation, and one which gives me much food for reflection. I was always puzzled to understand why the best electric
street-car system was called the Buda-Pest. In ten minutes after
arriving here, I caught on to it from merely seeing the streets.
Buda-Pest and Hungary itself are a new creation.

Just now I'm not writing history, and still less a guide-book,
and if Buda-Pest detains me twenty-four hours, it is not because

I enjoy either its art or its industry; but I make the note for your future use. Buda-Pest is the first place I have struck that really leads to Russia and the future. When you make your journey there, you had better take in the lower Danube.

As far as I can see, the present Hungary is the child of State-Socialism in a most intelligent and practical form. In principle there is no apparent limit to its application. The railways, etc., are all, or nearly all, designed, built, run and owned by and for the State. The forests, the mines, the banks, the very street-cars, and, for all I know, the babies and the pug-dogs, are, or might be, in principle, made, bred and educated solely by and for the governing commissions or committees. What is more curious, the result seems to be reasonably consistent with a degree of individual energy and character. As one form of future society, it deserves a little attention, especially in connection with Russia; and, as it represents to me the possible future with which I sincerely wish I may have nothing to do, I recommend it to your notice. To me it seems to demonstrate that the axiom of what we are civil enough to call progress, has got to be:—All monopolies will be assumed by the State; as a corollary to the proposition that the common interest is supreme over the individual.

Enough of that! I touch on it only with reference to the next Presidential campaign, which, if you feel obliged to take part in, you must lift off from silver, and lift in to Socialism. Not that I love Socialism any better than I do Capitalism, or any other Ism, but I know only one law of political or historical morality, and that is that the form of Society which survives is always in the Right; and therefore a statesman is obliged to follow it, unless he leads. Progress is Economy! Socialism is merely a new application of Economy, which must go on until Competition puts an end to further Economies, or the whole world becomes one Socialistic Society and rots out. One need not love Socialism in order to point out the logical necessity for Society to march that way; and the wisdom of doing it intelligently if it is to do it at all.

To BROOKS ADAMS

Surrenden Dering, Ashford [Kent], 6 July, 1898.

The week's news, since you sailed, will occupy your time and thoughts sufficiently without comments from me. We are still anxious about the casualties, but have heard of no losses among friends. As for the rubbish of the newspaper correspondents, I think you may safely skip it all. The true centre of interest is now Madrid. Of the situation there we know nothing, and if you can pick up any information in Paris, pray let me have it. Now that the boys have had their fun and fighting, I suppose diplomacy will have an inning, and normal conditions will tend to return. It is time. The economics are much more serious than the politics. The exchanges are most abnormal and, as far as I know, without precedent. Europe is steadily drifting on some unknown shore which I want to see before I die.

If I were to talk about the doings at St. Iago, I should probably talk as foolishly as the newspapers; so I hold my tongue. The lessons of the war are staggering for Europe. To Germany, they seem to me almost a *coup de grace*. They give England enormous confidence. The coal-business is at last likely to be understood; and Chamberlain's foreign policy will doubtless take the conscious direction of a war which is indispensable to its ends. The Indian Ocean will become a British sea. Russia will take the north of Asia; England the south; and Africa will necessarily be the central bearings of the British empire. France must follow Spain to the seclusion of local interests; and Germany must merge in Russia. So we can foresee a new centralisation, of which Russia is one pole, and we the other, with England between. The Anglo-American alliance is almost inevitable. The idiocy and tom-foolery of the Kaiser Willy have given an impulse to the Anglo-American business which seems already beyond control. You know what an Anglo-American alliance means to gold-bugs, and what an ocean of corruption we shall sail into. Unless the war spreads, and we have some years of violence, the economic movement will be rapid, and we shall have a social struggle of the gayest kind. The gold-bug will, as usual, breed the anarchist.

You will find Europe several stages worse than when you left. The situation seems now to be one simple, military, police cohesion. Representative government is everywhere suspended or in suspense.

In England the economic situation is worse. The exchanges have again turned against her, and the Bank expects a severe squeeze this autumn. We alone can help them by increasing our imports again.

As soon as you have disposed of your work in Paris, we shall be happy to see you here, where we keep a sort of American hotel on the Paris highroad. I expect Hitty on Saturday to stay till she sails on the 14th. Mr. and Mrs. Cameron are your official hosts, but as you will be my guests, you need not feel shy. We keep in as close relations as possible with the embassy and the passing statesmen. Your assistance will be valued. After all, the world is not an absolutely rosy soap-bubble, and even America is not beyond occasional anxieties, which we may help to allay. I suppose you'll not stay in Paris later than August 1.

As for me, I am very lazy, and pass my time either lying on my back, or sitting on the back of a staid and venerable cob, in these Kentish lanes. Occasionally I go to London for a night, but never to do anything worse than order groceries. Wendell Holmes is in town. So are many others.

To ELIZABETH CAMERON

Girgenti, Tuesday [*23 April, 1899*].

Is it April 23 or 24 or 25? I have kept no run of the month, but it is certainly Tuesday, and so life gets done. Another stitch picked up, and my last Greek cities running off like the time-machine! Here I am at last, looking down over the temples and the Mediterranean, where for nearly forty years I have meant annually to come, and now it is done, and another small object in life wiped out. Of course it's not worth while. One Greek temple is just like another, when it is ruined. Girgenti as a landscape is Athens with improvements. Two thousand, or twenty-five hundred years ago, it must have been immensely charming, like Japan in its prime, but now it is a landscape with hardly ten lines of history, and no art. So we will turn it down and catalogue it. Please consider Cabot and Bay and John and Winty Chanler as having reached Palermo punctually Sunday morning, and taken me to see the mosaics which I came for, and which make another old bird-of-travel flushed and killed. When I came to Palermo in June, 1860, I came to see Garibaldi and a fight. There was a barricade at every fifty yards on the main street, and I chatted with the red-shirted hero in the Municipal town-house as he supped with his staff. I could see no sights but that. All the brigands in Sicily seemed to be in the streets, and the fleas were thick as dust. If Garibaldi were Hannibal, he could not seem further away now, and if I were Empedocles and Matt Arnold to boot, I could not be older; but at last I saw Monreale and the mosaics, and, for a wonder, these were worth while. They make even Ravenna modest. Also some Greek metopes from Sergeste [Segesta?] or some other old ruin, which we struck in the Museum seemed to me of the very first class. To bag two first-class art-works in one place, when I know so few in the world, was a triumph. I was glad I came, and after all, Girgenti is typical; altogether the most beautiful Greek ruin I know; far more charming than Athens or Corinth or even Delphi or Smyrna, and of course out of all comparison with places like Ephesus or Alexandria. I've done fairly well, therefore, and game has been good.

Of course our party has been amusing and pleasant, rather young for me, but almost as much so for Cabot, and old enough to make allowances for each other and the universe. Winty Chanler makes most of the fun and the go, and keeps us properly mad. We have seen no one worthy of being called even pretty, though the boys are of an age to find beauty in a harpy, and naturally we have seen no one that is good, or at least good enough to notice. The weather is cool—almost cold. A fire in the evening would never be out of place. I am rather shivering right now, before an open window, at seven o'clock in the evening, in my heaviest winter clothes. I think I had better get ready for dinner, and at the same time get warm. Tomorrow night we expect to reach Syracuse.

Messina. Saturday morning. Prompt we are! Cabot rattles us through, on time, tourists such as Cook should love; but I don't much mind now. Nothing matters much, except money, I judge; even in the best days of the Greek Gods, money seems to have paid for all. We are now very learned about our Greeks; we have done our Syracuse and we understand our politics and economics as well as though we lived in 415 B. C. and had a hand in the Peloponnesian War. Even Bay [George Cabot Lodge] admits that our Greeks were somewhat wanting as economists and politicians, but on the other hand we are quite overwhelmed by their superiority as landscape gardeners. Girgenti and Syracuse were interesting studies in that profession, but yesterday came the climax at Taormina. Nothing in Japan compares with the vigor and genius which the Greeks put into this poor little colonial mountain-side, to make every inch of beauty count for its utmost value. For the hundredth time I flung up the sponge and stopped chattering before my Greek. It's no use to talk. The fellow's genius passes beyond discussion. Taormina in itself is one of the most beautiful spots in the world. I've seen most of the great landscapes, including the slopes of Fujiyama and Kilauea and Orizaba and Popocatapetl and Turquino. They are all divine, but the Greek is the only man who ever lived that could get the whole value out of his landscape, and add to it a big value of his own. His share counts for almost as much as the share of nature. The wretch was so complete an artist that big or little was equally easy for him to handle, and he took hold of Etna just as easily as he did of the smallest lump of gold or silver to make a perfect coin. . . .

To ELIZABETH CAMERON

Paris, 23 October, 1899.

. . . What you tell me of the Dewey movement troubles me a little. Setting aside the question of party, about which I am not violent, there remains the personal question which is rather serious to me at Washington. How the deuce I am to get on, with Hay and all my friends on one side, and you and Brooks and that dear John McLean and Emily, on the other, I don't know. In fact, I can't do it. Inevitably I must lose something. Generally I have been able to keep clear of these passions, but this time all of you are too deep in the mud. Hay and Cabot, and such-like as Teddy, have too much to lose. Your temper, like mine, is becoming too bitter with age. It is likely to be a scrimmage wanting in the commonest decency of manners. I dread going home to it all the more because there is not a vestige of principle involved, and I can only sit on the very uncomfortable fence, indulging in the luxury, which is long ago a faded joy, of entertaining the deepest contempt for you all. Balanced by the loss of relations, the gain on my part is small. As a con-

vinced, conservative, Christian anarchist, the turning out a
set of cheap politicians in order to put in a cheaper, seems to
me scavenger's work, necessary but low, at least as compared
with the bomb, which has some humor in it, and explodes all
round, making an effectual protest against the whole thing. Altogether I am not comfortable about it. As for mixing with the
Gorman-McLean-Whitney-Croker crowd, they wouldn't let me
in if I asked. I don't mind Bryan, who is just an ass, but
these eastern democrats are intelligent and exclusive. They
know an anarchist when they see him. They are not as bad as
Cleveland was, but practically, for me, they would make Washington equally impossible.

It brings me blue. Apparently I must abandon Washington
altogether, and on the whole, while I am about it, the simpler
and pleasanter solution seems to be to clear out of the planet
once for all, as it is a question of brief importance anyway.
Washington was the last tie. It is now a very weak one. Little
will break it, but less will break me, who only keep going by a
sort of constant tours-de-force, and prestidigitation. You are all
drifting from me; I feel it and see it daily; and I know that the
currents ahead are going to be violent for two winters to come.
I can't choose a current, for that would at once throw me out. I
can't drift with the current, for that is only possible in quiet waters. I can't even run away without cutting myself off from
communion. So I linger in Paris, and bask in the warmth of
the twelfth century, and write letters about nothing, as much as
possible. You know my badge; not that of Valentine: '*Rien ne
m'est plus; plus ne m'est rien,*' but 'Nothing matters much.'
How would it be in Valentine's French: '*Beaucoup ne vaut
Rien.*'

The twelfth century has been active this week. I went to
Chartres last Tuesday and passed a long day studying it out so
as to square it with the books. I passed Wednesday in running

out to Chantilly and driving about three or four miles across to St. Leu d'Esserent, a very beautiful church, high on a terrace over the Oise, with a stone *flèche* of the most delightful original-ity and grace, and the ruins of the Abbey Farm about the church, most pleasing. . . .

One gain I got. The sixth of my party was St. Gaudens. By-the-bye, I hope to manage for him—and her—a medallion head, which Curtis seems to want. St. Gaudens was going down to Amiens on Friday with two Frenchmen, and offered to take me. Naturally I went. The two Frenchmen were like all the Frenchmen I see, bourgeois of the timid type—one an architect, one a lawyer—afraid of everything, conventional as death, seri-ous as a French *noces,* but very nice, courteous in the bourgeois style, and friendly. Of course I had for once to rattle French, which was hard on them; but we were met at Amiens by an-other bourgeois, the *archiviste,* who acted as guide, and we did the town under his direction. Of course Amiens is far from new; it is almost as old as I am. If I did not know the Cathedral intimately, I had at least a bowing-acquaintance with it, these many, many years. If it is as old as I am, it has the advantage of not showing its years. Nothing was ever younger or fresher, and I went all over it again, officially as it were, with more in-terest than ever. Curiously enough, it was new to St. Gaudens. As for the French lawyer, he had never even seen Saint Denis. I found it impossible to be *ingenu;*—not to patronize them. Is one odious! How can one help it? These *boutiquiers*—I except the architect and the *archiviste*—belong to a weird world of childish information about like Marco Polo. Anyway I learned much, and enjoyed it greatly. As for Saint Gaudens, it was a new life. It overpowered him.

My photographs too are an occupation, and by the way a fairly expensive one. The mere *clochers* and *flèches* number hundreds in the Monuments Historiques series alone. Your rooms are becoming a school of romanesque architecture. Volumes lie about the floor. Last evening Joe [Trumbull] Stickney and St. Gaudens dined here, and floundered in architecture on all the chairs. . . .

To BROOKS ADAMS

Paris, 19 December, 1899.

I am sorry to hear of your anxieties. Whether they are harder to bear in one place than another I do not know. One always hopes that home is best in trouble; but I never found it to make much difference. What one really wants is youth, and what one really loses is years. Life becomes at last a mere piece of acting. One goes on by habit, playing more or less clumsily that one is still alive. It is ludicrous and at times humiliating, but there is a certain style in it which youth has not. We become all, more or less, gentlemen; we are *ancien régime;* we learn to smile while gout racks us. We make clever speeches which rhyme with *paresis,*—or do not, for paresis has a short ĕ. We get out of bed in the morning all broken up, without nerves, color or temper, and by noon we are joking with young women about the play. One lives in constant company with diseased hearts, livers, kidneys and lungs; one shakes hands with certain death at closer embrace every day; one sees paralysis in every feature and feels it in every muscle; all one's functions relax their action day by day; and, what is worse, one's grasp on the interests of life relaxes with the physical relaxation; and, through it all, we improve; our manners acquire refinement; our sympathies grow wider; our youthful self-consciousness disappears; very ordinary men and women are found to have charm; our appreciations have weight; we should almost get to respect ourselves if we knew of anything human to respect; so we affect to respect the conventions, and we ask only to be classed as a style. . . .

To ELIZABETH CAMERON

[*Washington*] *12 March, 1900.*

. . . . Sister Anne is still away. Mrs. Hay is a tower of strength as a support, but she is not active in motion. No one else has come in to the ring. The effect is to make me feel more and more indifferent to the world. The indifference is rapidly becoming difference. Positive antipathy lurks round the corner. The want of illusion in this happy and ideal society is painful to the eye and ear. French society is like a Watteau that has been cleaned and scraped down to the canvas. American society is a kind of Whistler that never had any atmosphere to scrape, but shows the paint crude. The women especially get on my nerves. The Daughters! oh, Lord, the Daughters!

The nieces took me to Philadelphia to hear [Milka] Ternina as Ysolde, and Looly [Louisa Hooper] taught me what to say about it. To you, the formula doesn't matter. To me, the singular part of it was that the music of Ysolde should be interpreted to me by two young and perfectly pure girls. Another Americanism! I could not even hint to them what it meant, and they couldn't have hinted it to me if they had known. The twelfth century had the audacity of its passions, and Wagner at times talks almost plain twelfth century language. Ternina put into it all she dared. I wish she had sung in Paris. . . .

To CHARLES MILNES GASKELL

Washington, 29 March, 1901.

For weeks I have been on the point of writing, but held back in order to be precise; and now your letter arrives of the 17th and I have still nothing precise to say.

The devil has raged very terribly since I returned here, and has by no means let me loose yet. He strikes, one after another, all my special weak spots. He has struck Clarence King and driven him south in a critical condition. He struck John Hay, whom I found very down, and who looks to me still far from fresh, though I do not know how serious his staleness is, nor he. Suddenly, last week, the fiend jumped on my brother-in-law Edward Hooper, and laid him low, probably for life; and as Hooper's life was extremely important to all his family, this blow greatly embarrasses me. Finally, when all my plans had been laid to sail on May 1 with the Cabot Lodges, the President suddenly announces that he is going to stay with the Lodges on July 1, in Massachusetts, and so sits on my party.

What I am now to do, I cannot decide, but it may end in my coming to London in May. My apartment in Paris has got me into an exasperating situation with an 83-year old landlord, which makes me sick with white fury, as is always the case in dealing with the French, who cannot help doing things in the style of the civil and religious wars, and must massacre the Huguenots or rob the Church, when they don't worry the foreigner. On the other hand, much as I would like to see you and the other old friends, I am dreadfully afraid of making myself disagreeable, quite without intention; for though I believe my ideas do not at all differ from theirs, and as far as they are concerned I should not probably be more offensive than God pleased to make me, I could hardly go into administration circles without betraying criticisms that would raise blisters; and you can imagine me talking with Joe Chamberlain in the shades of night, over cigars in his own conservatory at Birmingham. Silence would be worse than dispute. We should end by throwing flower-pots at each other. I don't mean that we should quarrel about South Africa. That is not my business but his; and if he chooses to wreck himself and the empire in order to assert a nominal and futile supremacy over a wilderness in the remote interior of the planet Uranus, I've no right to find fault, although apparently the principle he asserts requires him to recover by force his authority over Massachusetts, and to

hang in chains the bones of all my defunct ancestors. Still, he
is welcome to hang up the old gentlemen, if he can, and me
too, if he will do it efficiently and intelligently. We should not
quarrel about a trifle like that. Where we should infallibly
quarrel would be on the larger field of reciprocal blundering;
—China, Canada, Nicaragua, and so on; questions of empire,
where his schemes of imperialism come across ours. There, as
far as I can see, neither agreement nor silence would be possible. I know him well enough to know that he has no idea of getting out of our way. On the contrary, he will exhaust every
means of maintaining his empire where it happens to be in our
way. On the other hand, our Senate is just dancing for a fight
with him. To keep peace is to get cuffed on one side, and kicked
on the other. Chamberlain has now got Lansdowne into the
Foreign Office, and they are a pair. Lansdowne is as bad-tem-
pered as Chamberlain, and hopelessly stupid, which Chamberlain is not. I suppose the Cecils have some intelligible idea of
politics which leads them to take a hopeless failure in one great
branch of administration, and put him at the head of precisely that other in which his defects would be still more mischievous; but I have quite enough to do in fretting over the
blunders of my own government to spare me a loss of temper
over yours.

So I rather dread going to London, where I should infallibly
have to talk. I dread it chiefly because I have nothing to say.
We here have just now no thought in life except to keep up
with the caravan. Our rate of speed is terrific. The mere money-
making has little to do with it; the fun has far more. We like to
go fast. We like to run things on a great scale. In New York I
seriously think that they manage business as they would sail a
yacht, and crack on everything for the fun of seeing how much
she will bear. God only knows what will break first; but we

can't now take in sail, or wear, or get into port. I think it possible we may run somebody down, but that will hardly be in my time. For the next fifty years we are compelled to go on with a momentum and a speed, which, if suddenly checked, will break more necks than any of the old-fashioned convulsions, on the small scale of Europe, ever did.

Certainly, when I return here after six months in Europe, my poor old senile brain whirls and whizzes for weeks. I do not any longer keep up a pretence of knowing where I am. My country in 1900 is something totally different from my own country of 1860. I am wholly a stranger in it. Neither I, nor anyone else, understands it. The turning of a nebula into a star may somewhat resemble the change. All I can see is that it is one of compression, concentration, and consequent development of terrific energy, represented not by souls, but by coal and iron and steam. What I cannot see is the last term of the equation. As I figure it:—$1830:1860::1890:X$, and X always comes out, not 1920, but infinity. Or infinity minus X.

All this is just to explain nothing at all—why I am so vague and strange. It is not my fault. Half the year burrowing in twelfth-century art and religion; the other half, seated here in the very centre of the web, with every whisper of the world coming instantly to my ear, and all my friends in trust of power so great that the poor old Mandarin, whose button was the problem of the eighteenth century, has to be stated now in terms of hundred millions, really I become dazed and at times almost hysterical. I cannot understand how the other fellows carry the responsibility, and I stick my head, every summer, deeper in the sand.

Nevertheless I want once more to hear Ternina sing Brynhilde, and I may come to London to risk it in May. If so, I shall come down to see you, wherever you are.

[219]

To JOHN HAY

Paris, 7 Nov., 1900.

. . . This by way of compliment to your success. Of personal matters I have very little to say. The Exposition is closing. To me it has been an education which I have failed to acquire for want of tutors, but it has been an immense amusement and only needed you to be a constant joy. It has brought me so near the end that I hardly care to wait for the last scenes. There are things in it which run close to the day of judgment. It is a new century, and what we used to call electricity is its God. I can already see that the scientific theories and laws of our generation will, to the next, appear as antiquated as the Ptolemaic system, and that the fellow who gets to 1930 will wish he hadn't. The curious mustiness of decay is already over our youth, and all the period from 1840 to 1870. The period from 1870 to 1900 is closed. I see that much in the machine-gallery of the Champ de Mars. The period from 1900 to 1930 is in full swing, and, geewhacky! how it is going! It will break its damned neck long before it gets through, if it tries to keep up the speed. You are free to deride my sentimentality if you like, but I assure you that I,—a monk of St. Dominic, absorbed in the Beatitudes of the Virgin Mother—go down to the Champ de Mars and sit by the hour over the great dynamos, watching them run as noiselessly and as smoothly as the planets, and asking them—with infinite courtesy—where in Hell they are going. They are marvelous. The Gods are not in it. Chiefly the Germans! Steam no longer appears, although still behind the scenes; but one feels no certainty that another ten years may not abolish steam too. The charm of the show, to me, is that no one pretends to understand even in a remote degree, what these weird things are that they call electricity, Roentgen rays, and what not. The exhibitors are dead dumped into infinity on a fork.

So my solitude prepares itself for heaven, with a constant eye to the London exchanges. With an humble and contrite heart, I prostrate myself before the Major [William McKinley] and the dynamos, and wait for the day of judgment much as I did in the reign of St. Louis. St. Thomas Aquinas and you are my only friends. . . .

To ELIZABETH CAMERON

8 April, 1901.

. . . He [Hay] is amusing about it all, and we are not in the least depressed by facing the grand climacteric or the doctors, who, as Hay justly remarks, have a way of looking at one, when one wants to know, and of implying: 'Well, you old imbecile! What the H— do you expect? To live forever?'

After all, this private *impasse* of grand-climatism is not a bit more troublesome or perplexing than the public one. Whether we are going straight into fits, or are getting safe ashore, no one knows; certainly not the Kaiser or the Czar, who are both in fits already; or Salisbury, who expects fits daily; or Hay, whose vision goes no further than mine. None of them has the glimmering of an idea whether we are on our heels or heads. Two months of close observation here have satisfied me that the European governments are just like boys on rafts, floating down a stream. The last performances of Russia and Germany in China prove it beyond doubt. It is a strange discovery to me that all the little so-called foresight in the world should be confined to America, and is not more than a phosphorescence even there; but the behavior of everyone is only to be explained on the theory that governments are children—and pretty dull and naughty at that.

Such a chaos! Wall Street goes quite wild, while Lombard Street is dead broke, and living on French charity. London and Berlin are standing in perfectly abject terror, watching Pierpont Morgan's nose flaming over the ocean waves, and approaching hourly nearer their bank-vaults. England, if figures have value, is walking straight into bankruptcy, and goes on drinking herself stupid. Russia is in convulsions, and yet flings explosives all over the place. For two years I have been shivering in a ghastly panic because every possible line led to a tremendous convulsion, and only infinite caution and harmony could prevent some enormous collapse, and now we are so near as to touch it, and no government except ours makes a pretence of wanting to avoid it. England persists in her boorish insanity; Russia plays monkey-tricks with the live coals; Germany deliberately impedes all hope of agreement; all grab, and grab, and grab; and the reign of anarchy neither conservative nor christian, is what they deserve.

I am inclined to hope they will get it. They are, in many worse ways, as hopeless as the French society of my friend Mme. de Pompadour, and without her taste or wit. Yah! they are on my nerves, their Cassinis, and Hollebens and Hengenmüllers.

If you are bored by politics I will give you some science. Last Friday I had a geological dinner. Frank Emmons brought his colleague Van Hise, and his chief, Walcott, and a young Canadian named Adams, to dine with me. But I am old, you may put up a margin on that! When I was young, geology began with fossils and shells and the signs of life. Nowadays it ends there. Not one of these four men, whose names are all of the highest authority all over the world, will look twice at a fossil except to throw out the rock they find him in. All they touch is granites and things that lie at the bottom. There they have about five times as much rock as there is above it, and all they study is to know what made it. The youth from Canada has been squeezing it like butter. You should have heard Van Hise lecture us on the Lake Superior ore-beds! All the same, it's a mighty interesting subject, what between Calumet copper and

Steel-trust ore. Most of our present boom is in it. Unluckily, I am not!

Last night [Samuel P.] Langley came to dinner, alone, and we had more science of another sort. Langley is more entertaining than geologists, but nowadays men cannot afford to be entertaining. Langley is old-fashioned. He is still at work on the engine of his flying machine, but I think at heart he much prefers his beaver at Rock Creek. Also I have seen Wayne and Mrs. MacVeagh, who have returned from Palm Beach. As Hay says, Wayne is never so funny as when he is serious. I find him very funny just now. When he starts in to lecture on the situation he is as droll, at the very least, as Chauncey Depew. Really he believes he could run it.

Truly this world is heaps of fun! Hay and I called both on Sister Anne and on Mrs. MacVeagh, and then came back to our hot lemonade with Mrs. Hay. Singular how few people I meet, or hear of, at the houses I go to, which should be much sought by the refined and cultivated! They talk of no one. Spencer Eddy has been here, and gone back,—a weird tale of Muscovy which I had better not write. Harry White arrives this week. So do Brooks and his wife. There is a new Attorney General [Philander C. Knox], not pretty to look at, they say, and sodden with corporation briefs. We are beyond that shame. After us the deluge—or even before!

To ELIZABETH CAMERON

Bayreuth, 26 July, 1901.

After all, I did leave Paris! I began to think I never should. For two summers, I never have; but at last here I am, and how droll it is. . . . Monday morning I rambled on, through Heidelberg, up the Necker to Würzburg, and into the heart of primitive Germany where I tumbled over the Lodges at a little railway junction and we went on to Rothenburg. There we paused and slept.

When I came first abroad in '58, all the towns were Rothenburgs. Antwerp, Nürnberg, even Strasbourg, looked just as mediaeval, or nearly so. Inside, they were much more so. I felt as though I must have been really thirteenth-century, and all but me departed. The young and happy brides—I allude also to my sister Anne—who were with me, enjoyed immensely their first sense of tiled roofs and gabled houses, and I did what I could not to spoil their sport. Really, too, there is some very excellent carving, in astonishing good condition, at Rothenburg, in the churches, and even three large windows of good fourteenth-century glass. There are some interesting houses, and bits running back to the 12th and even the 11th, so that I was not wholly abandoned. To be sure, it is not French, but very near it; and it made me wonder once more that in my own golden day, even Germans and English were almost as artistic as other people, and in the same exact simple style with which I [was] wont to delight myself.

After a rainy day at Rothenburg we came direct to Bayreuth, and, with a desperate struggle, settled into lodgings. I have Bessie and Bay under my wing in the upper story of a house in the suburbs, with an almost 12th century Jewish landlady; but the house is new and clean, and I rather prefer the Jewess to the German. Yesterday we went to the first spectacle, the *Rheingold*. I was nearly asphyxiated, and thought the performance rather mediocre. Of course I did not say so. My companions were very enthusiastic; the older habitués much less so. Between me and Wagner, we rather think we are both a little given to humbug. As I am necessarily a judge of literature rather than of music, I am still ruffed all over by Wagner's clumsy want of clean literary lines and of form, both in thought and expression. This is always obtruding itself between the music and the scene, till I feel like to throw rocks at the singers. Today comes a long session with the *Valkyrie*. I hope I shall get through without express profanity; but I am quite clear that for a delicate digestion like mine: with a tendency to insomnia, the Wagnerian beer-and-sausage should be taken in short gulps, and at concerts. The literary-dramatic expression gives me the same spasms that a Church-of-England Bishop does, in the pulpit. . . .

Nuremberg, 3 August, '01.

So Bayreuth passes! We have finished our cure, and are on our way again. All went well and merrily. All was easy and archaic. Except that I am rather ashamed never to have done it before, I feel that virtue is rewarded. Not that I have got particular pleasure out of it, or that I am more Wagnerian than of old. I got more pleasure, by far, from the regular theatrical performances. I felt my Wagner much better in bits. Too much of him, or of any other artist, gives dyspepsia. His faults get on the nerves. As for Wagner, his German bad taste becomes the only thing I see, at last, and in *Parsifal*, it culminates in a mass of flabby German sentimentality which passes patience, and makes me indifferent to what John Lodge assures me is the highest point he ever reached in music. Of course I have learned a lot about motifs, and all sorts of things, but on the whole, except to have seen it all, without cuts or abbreviations, I do not think I am better off. My conviction that such a monstrosity of form is simply proof of our loss of artistic sense, is stronger than ever.

Germany deepens it. Forty years have added another layer of bad taste to all that went before. It sickens me to think that this is the result, and all the result, of my life-time. I saw the same thing in Italy, but there the effort has not been so gigantic. Here in Nuremberg I feel it the more because this was one of my first delights in art, way back in '59. It makes me happy to think that I shall never see it again. Altogether, Germany gives me the sense of hopeless failure. In fact, I have had more than enough of Europe altogether, and I'm afraid my appetite for America is not voracious either. The world has lived too long. So have I. One of us two has got to go. For the public good, it had better be the world that goes, for at least I am harmless. . . .

To ELIZABETH CAMERON

Moscow, August 21, 1901.

Done! Wipe out Moscow! We have seen the Kremlin at last, after I have said, since the year 1858, regularly every day or two, that really I must go there. What a comfort to meet my end with my task accomplished and wrapped in the appropriate napkin! It is true that, for pleasure, one ought to come here early in life, and especially before visiting Constantinople and Ravenna; one ought to start from Petersburg and pass down through here to Kiev and Roumania, and so to Byzantium and the rest and best; but anyway I've got it done, and it leaves a queer taste like caviar and vodka, semi-barbarous and yet *manqué*. Even barbarism is sometimes weak. The Kremlin is more than half barbarous, but it is not strong; it is Byzantium barbarised. The bulbous domes are weak. The turnip with its root in the air is not so dignified as the turnip with its root in the earth. The architecture is simply ignorance. The builders built in 1600 as they built in 1200 because they knew no more. They had no building-stone. Gold was their only idea of splendor. Crude blue and green was all their decoration when they had to stop on red. They had no fund of taste in themselves; no invention or sense of form or line or color. Where on earth did our tenth-century French get all these? Charlemagne was about on a line with Ivan the Terrible who reigned here somewhere about seven hundred years afterwards, and, I can see no ghost of a reason why art should have had seven hundred years of wonderful wealth after Charlemagne, and should have stayed dead after Ivan. It is a fact, I can't see much anyway. You knew it already. This is only for the benefit of Martha's education. Decidedly I incline to advise her not to marry a Muscovite. The conclusion is rather broad compared with what led to it; but the more I see of Russia, the more terrific the business of Russianising becomes. Moscow is, *à la fin de la fin, une ville manquée*.

The Sunday High Mass at the huge new church, or cathedral, gave me almost a sensation. As I watched it from the gallery, above the dense crowd, I thought that a crusader of the twelfth century who had drifted into Sta. Sofia at Constantinople would have seen so nearly the same thing that he could have stood by my side and told me all about it without a sign of surprise; and I was almost ready to try and remember a little of Villehardouin to start a conversation. The Russian Mass is a marvellous composite of the Jewish tabernacle and the First Crusade. The robes are those of St. Louis, Godfrey of Bouillon, Solomon, Justinian,—I don't know who not—and the ceremonies those of Solomon's Temple. I never saw anything more fascinating. Except the Athanasian Creed I know nothing more Greek.

What lends power to the illusion is the wonderful tenth-century people, whose formal devoutness goes beyond what I imagine ever existed in western Europe, and whose process of crossing themselves is a very curious mathematical combination of gestures lasting a considerable time, so that, as they cross themselves before every street shrine, they keep at it pretty steadily. The men show more persistence than the women, and make the bulk of the audience at Mass. When the whole congregation happens to cross themselves simultaneously, the effect is curious. In some ways, I feel sure, the Russian of today is more primitive than the Frenchman or German ever was, if you call this passive attitude of subjection primitive. I never met with it in any primitive race I have struck before, and even a monkey shows occasional scepticism. I find my chief interests in watching the people in the churches and shrines. What I can't make out is whether the attitude is as completely passive as it seems, or whether there is an occasional gleam of fanatical fire. Thus far I've seen not a sign of individuality. All are run in the same tallow, more or less.

All these observations count on the general question which interests us all, whether we are going to be whacked, or not, by Europe, in the long run. Now, in the long run, the passive character exhausts the active one. Economy of energy is a kind of power. Russia and Asia may clean us all out, especially if Germany helps to run her. What will happen in five hundred years I can't even guess; but I'm clear that we've at least a hundred years' start, and that Martha, if she insists on marrying a Russian, had better keep him at home, and not come here on speculation.

At the same time I judge that the average Russian would make a very docile husband, obstinate only in small matters, and quite a baby always. He will need to be told what to do. Perhaps that may not suit Martha; at least not so well as it would suit some women I have read about.

To ELIZABETH CAMERON

St. Petersburg, September 1, 1901.

Alone again in a mighty cold world! The Lodges started for Berlin yesterday afternoon, leaving me, who am not wild about Berlin or eager to return to Paris, waiting here till Wednesday for a boat to Stockholm. I was sorry to part. We have been six weeks together, without trouble or disagreement. We have got used to each other, to a certain degree. I don't need to murder Cabot here half so often as I do at Washington, and Sister Anne has been as good a sister as you make. Indeed, she has been at times almost pathetic. Curiously enough, I have come to think that the clue to her character is timidity and want of self-confidence. She is easily scared.

We have put in our week of sight-seeing here with as much energy as the holidays and the weather allow. The weather is worse than the holidays, but apparently it has been gay old weather everywhere. Here we freeze in overcoats and all our winter clothes. We went to Peterhof on Friday and saw in the distance the Czar's yacht start off, over a wintry sea of Finland, to carry him his first stage to Paris;—it was like leaving Boston in November, always one of my happiest recollections. As for Peterhof, it is a pretty, rather quaint, arctic sort of Versailles-Marly paradise, with a pleasant palace, furnished in the usual modern taste,—German taste of the fifties,—which the universal German royalty has inflicted on most of Europe. Not quite so bad as Balmoral, but only redeemed by what is left of Mme. de Pompadour and Mme. du Barry! Chiefly their Chinese pleasantries. Not so amusing as Wilhelmina's rococo fun at Bayreuth, but at times really fine, as in the water-works and fountains. A part of Marly is more or less intelligible at Peterhof. Even the name is kept.

The Peterhof palace is a delight, compared with the Winter Palace here, which contains not one room, picture, chair or detail that you or I would live with, if we could help it. The rooms of the Czar Alexander II who was killed in 1884,— if it wasn't some other year,—are kept exactly as he left them, down to his pocket-handkerchief; and I looked with care at every inch to see whether he had about him any object that would have given me pleasure. Not one, small or large! All was ordinary, cheap, such as you would expect in a third-rate German squire's country-house. The furniture was English; the photographs were Cleveland, Ohio; the pictures, bronzes, books, were all bourgeois. You have more taste in your single room at No. 50 than I could find in the whole Winter Palace. Acres of cheap white-and-gold plaster decoration, but not one handsome thing. Apparently everything at St. Petersburg, except one church and one palace, has been done with the object of covering the most space at the least expense. It is the small German principality enlarged. The architecture is all magnificently laid out, and meanly executed. It makes me homesick for the court of the Louvre.

So too with the Hermitage gallery, which is far and away the best thing in the place. There is nothing first-rate in it, except the Dutch. Peter the Great was a flying Dutchman. His idea of style was Dutch. He built Petersburg to imitate Amsterdam. He built a house to duplicate a Dutch cabin. He stamped Dutch on everything he touched, and the stamp has stuck. When Catherine and Elizabeth came to finish his work, they kept the Dutch flavor. There are thousands of Dutch and Flemish pictures in the public and private galleries, but I don't know that there is one touch of Michael Angelo.

You who know my sentiment for Dutch art and Dutch taste can conceive exactly what enthusiasm I feel here.

The Herbert Peirces have been devoted to us, and besides showing us everything, have had us twice to dinner. At the last, they put me next an elderly prince Kilkof—or something of the sort—who is at the head of the railway construction, and who told me heaps about Russian and Siberian railways, complaining all the time that he was hampered by the conservatism and scepticism of the public. I paid him all sorts of compliments on his railways, which are really, I think, the best in Europe, and admirably well kept; and in return he told me some of the difficulties they had to meet in developing the country. Truly I am glad not to have that contract to execute, but it is a big one, and an exceedingly entertaining one, and not more costly than it would be with us. The fun is that the government has to do it all, for the people don't care and won't try. This year has been difficult, but now Witte has got some more French gold; the Czar has gone to France; and stocks have jumped up. So the Siberian railway will soon be finished, and the four thousand miles, equipped, will cost two hundred million dollars. They spend more every year on the army in pure waste of energy. . . .

Alvensleben has come here as [German] ambassador, but him I shall not see; nor do I expect to see anyone else whom I ever knew before, though Petersburg and Sweden must be full of them. No one cares to meet old acquaintances; one's object is to meet new. After all, I've got what I came for; I've done my Bayreuth, and retouched my Austria, and scraped the varnish off Russia here and there; and now, as I don't like shivering with cold, I might as well wander somewhere else. The sum of my certainty is that America has a very clear century of start over Russia, and that western Europe must follow us for a hundred years, before Russia can swing her flail over the Atlantic. Whether she can do it then is no conundrum that I can settle. I imagine that my grandpapa, sitting here in his study ninety years ago, could see ahead to me now, better than I can see ahead to the year 2000; and yet it was not easy guessing even for him.

To ELIZABETH CAMERON

50 Avenue du Bois, Paris, September 28, 1901.
. . . My last was mailed at Trondhjem, wasn't it? on the morning of the 17th. It raced me on the way down, but it can hardly reach you before next week, while I am well here since yesterday afternoon. I came very slowly too. A long, long day from Trondhjem brought me only to a little railway inn at a

station called Tonsaet where I supped with two **Oxford Eng-**
lishmen who were there shooting, as usual. Does an Englishman ever do anything but shoot? Then a still longer day
brought me to Christiania and finished the scenery business.
Another stop at Göthenberg to inspect economy, and so an end
to Sweden and Norway. I take pride in having discovered those
countries which are, from my Yankee point of view, worth all
Europe else. The health, energy and intelligence of all these
Baltic people, whether Finns or North Germans or Swedes or
Danes, are good to see. They've no art or manners or poetry,
but they have go; and as I've long since made my funeral ser-
mon on art and manners, all that remains is go. The Russians
have neither energy nor art nor manners, that I can detect.

So I crossed to Helsingör where Hamlet's father's ghost
was sitting on his terrace waiting for King Oscar of Sweden
who crossed with me; and I stopped a day at Copenhagen to get
my letters and look over the town, which I had not seen for
forty years; and on Sunday I came on to Kiel where I put in a
day to see the Krupp ship-yard and the Kiel Canal. Tuesday I
came on to Hamburg where I applied to six hotels which were
all full, owing to some medical congress, and, having, by that
time, seen enough of Hamburg, I took the night train to
Bremen and slept there. To keep you posted, I sent to Martha
a post-card from Bremen, as I did from Christiania; and so,
after a morning at Bremen, I ran on to Cologne; and after a
morning at Cologne I went on to Namur; and after a morning
at Namur I came on to Paris; passed half an hour scuffling for a
porter at the douane in a wild swarm of arriving or returning
travellers; and at five o'clock was received by Paddy at No.
50, which looked as pretty and fresh and gay in the charming
September sun as though it were its own mistress.

Ten weeks I have been away. Twenty-one hotels I have slept

in, besides steamers. A huge sweep of territory new I have visited. In all that time I have hardly made a new acquaintance, and since leaving Stockholm have scarcely spoken, except to servants and such. The solitude of travel in these days is hor·rible. Forty years ago we made acquaintance with everybody. Now I can travel for weeks with people like the Lodges and Hays, and they never exchange a word with a hen.

Still I have seen much, and reflected more, and find Mr. Maeterlink's remarks on bees very highly instructive. This is a rum world. If our views of today are correct, what view must one take of yesterday and tomorrow? What are our views anyway? I take it that we are economists, for since Russia I've seen no religion, and no art; but you give me, as a last comfort, the mild corrective of assassination.

When I travelled forth in 1858, we looked for moral improvement. I have very likely found what we looked for; but it comes in so queer a shape that I don't know it. It takes the form of police. Anyway, I find all Europe, to the Vistula, now Americanised. That is the work of fifty years.

With that, and the conviction that it is, and must ever be, second-rate Americanism, I shut the book. . . .

Your fears that I might be affected by losing poor dear old McKinley show a susceptible heart, not in me but in you. The Major was a person as completely outside of my personality as any of his recent predecessors. His methods were as bad as possible. His function was that of a very supple and highly paid agent of the crudest capitalism. To do him justice, he served industrial capital rather than the Jews, but he would have served it in any form, consciously or unconsciously, if the times had with us reached that stage. To murder him was a gross absurdity that makes me despair of anarchy. The true person to kill was Hanna,—the senator! . . .

To ELIZABETH CAMERON

[*Washington*] *Sunday, 12 January, 1902.*

Slowly the legs that had gone to sleep have begun to tingle and get the blood moving again but it's not a particularly exhilarating process, and it aches. The only real satisfaction is to count up the number of statesmen I've buried, and the graves of notorieties I have outlived. I want now to outlive the present crowd and am counting my symptoms to figure out four or five years more for myself, so that I can bury the heroes of the Spanish War with those of the Mexican War who were my first admirations here fifty years ago. Even Theodore has not the face to pasture his charger in front of the White House as Zachary Taylor did in 1850, when my father took me to the White House first.

When was my last dinner at the White House? Before you were born! In 1878! Under the reign of Mrs. Hayes. Though it was the happiest time of my whole life, associated with everything—and the only things—I ever cared for, that dinner between Mrs. Carlisle and Mrs. Conger is still a nightmare; but it is curious that the Hays were also there, and that last Friday evening, Mrs. Hay and John stopped in their carriage to pick me up and take me across to the slaughter-house. Mrs. Hay was not—to say the least—more sprightly than I, though we were none of us bubbling, but we all played square, and shirked none of the cards.

That the house is to me ghastly with bloody and dreary associations way back to my great grandmother a hundred years ago, seems no particular reason why it should always depress me, or why it should seem to entomb a little family party of very old friends, in the private dining room, and up-stairs afterwards to smoke in the cheery octagon; but it did. We were only eight; Cabot and Nanny Lodge and a Mrs. Selores of Minnesota, whom I must have known in the Hayes epoch, and who came on me like a ghost. We waited twenty minutes in the hideous red drawing-room before Theodore and Edith came down, and we went in to dinner immediately with as much chaff and informality as though Theodore were still a Civil Service Commissioner. We chattered round talk; Cabot was bright; Hay was just a little older and a thought more formal than once we were; Edith was very bright and gay; but as usual Theodore absorbed the conversation, and if he tried me ten years ago, he crushes me now. To say that I enjoyed it would be, to you, a gratuitous piece of deceit. The dinner was indifferent, very badly served, and, for some reason, nothing to drink but a glass of sherry, and some apollinaris. Theodore's talk was not exactly forced or unnatural, but had less of his old freshness and quite as much of his old dogmatism. None of us had improved. When I think of what has passed I see no reason why I should expect improvement. Even cognac will not impart much after sixty years of ripening.

One condition is clear! Hay and I are shoved up to a distinct seniority; we are sages. I feel it not only in Hay's manner, but in Roosevelt's too, and it is my creed now that my generation had better scuttle gracefully, and leave Theodore to surround himself with his own Rough Riders. He will do it anyway before long, and would do it immediately if he had the men; but his two appointments thus far have betrayed weakness in material, for one is a third-rate lobbyist rejected by McKinley as below proof, while the other is an unknown quantity, very problematic to Wall Street. Theodore is eager to change everything everywhere but his suggestions are all more or less inadequate. The only effect would be to substitute his man for McKinley's man. We outsiders rather lose than gain.

Really, Theodore is exasperating even to me, and always was. His want of tact hurts Congressmen and Senators more than it does me, but what annoys me is his childlike and infantile superficiality with his boyish dogmatism of assertion. He lectures me on history as though he were a high-school pedagogue. Of course I fall back instantly on my favorite protective pose of ignorance, which aggravates his assertions, and so we drift steadily apart.

But the most dangerous rock on Theodore's coast is Cabot. We all look for inevitable shipwreck there. . . .

To BROOKS ADAMS

Inverlochy Castle, Fort William, 10 August, 1902.

. . . I can see no reason why everybody's business should not now run satisfactorily, for the entire world ought to be starting in for a prodigious development, with no longer any resistance that I can see, except their human limitations. Of course, the problem that bothered us so much between '93 and '98 is now settled. The returns of our iron production are alone decisive about that, and our country is established for at least a century as the centre of human energy. As for western Europe and England, I do not think they are likely to give more trouble for a long time to come. They are very rich in accumulated wealth, and very poor in natural resources, but England has had her bumptiousness knocked out of her, and has settled down to work. She will last our time, no doubt, in her attitude, and we need not expect any further great change for the present. If my calculations were near the mark, they never proved that England was running behind-hand more than one, or at most two hundred million dollars a year, and at that rate she can run on for fifty years without perceiving it. On the Boer War alone, she wasted twice as much. . . .

In any case, the chapter seems to be over, and I imagine it to be the last in my lifetime. . . . I see no one, except the 'captains of industry,' who seem to have the smallest importance.

To BROOKS ADAMS [*1903*]

The most brilliant men of my time have died, like Bret Harte, without rousing a ripple. Lord Salisbury dropped out the other day without exciting a remark. There is not now a politician in the world whose name is likely to be remembered a dozen years, unless it is Chamberlain,—*et encore.*

I apprehend for the next hundred years an ultimate, colossal, cosmic collapse; but not on any of our old lines. My belief is that science is to wreck us, and that we are like monkeys monkeying with a loaded shell; we don't in the least know or care where our practically infinite energies come from or will bring us to. For myself, it is true; I know no care at all. But the faintest disturbance of equilibrium is felt throughout the solar system, and I feel sure that our power over energy has now reached a point where it must sensibly affect the old adjustment. It is mathematically certain to me that another thirty years of energy-development at the rate of the last century, must reach an *impasse.*

This is, however, a line of ideas wholly new, and very repugnant to our contemporaries. You will regard it with mild contempt. I owe it only to my having always had a weakness for science mixed with metaphysics. I am a dilution of Lord Kelvin and St. Thomas Aquinas. . . .

To BROOKS ADAMS

1603 H Street [Washington], 2 May, 1903.

Welcome home! glad to hear that your journey has been satisfactory!

My own winter has been as amusing and agreeable as a child-like nature like mine can ask. The game plays itself out. You will have ample time to pick up the tricks, and to measure the results when you settle for the summer. When you have leisure from the Greeks and Persians you can study the dynamic theory of gases. There you can repose your mind on nature, and build up your laws on a Crookes' tube. The only question of serious interest to the world is the atom. What is the atom? Is there an atom? I hold, as a working hypothesis, that an atom is a man. His conduct is singularly alike in each case. Hydrogen is uncommonly Greek. How hydrogenic the American may be, I do not venture to decide, but he is now preparing for a general election, and you will probably find your hydrogenic qualities called into play. You and your brother Charles will both be quite sure that Clerk Maxwell's demon who runs the second law of Thermo-dynamics ought to be made President. I think so too, but the party conventions will have to come to you to find him, and I'm afraid that you would disagree even then, as to the devil in question.

You, like little Quentin Roosevelt, will think me "very silly," but I have passed my life among the snorting demons, and the little cusses amuse me. Their antics are as lively as ever they were in the days of Aristophanes, and almost as expensive. Still, four months of constant attendance at Barnum and Forepaugh's circus tends to satisfy one's immediate appetite, and I am very ready to be seasick at sea.

Accordingly I expect to sail next Wednesday, and to haunt an attic in Paris for a season. I presume that there or thence I shall see another variety of Barnum and Forepaugh, and shall be solitary besides, but I am well used to it all, provided the atoms keep on dancing; and the best scientific authorities lead me to think that they will dance into the fourth dimension with me. They seem as ready as ever to amuse me. . . .

As for the future, I've no views, beyond my well-known solid conservative Christian anarchistic principles. These are becoming common property. In five years, before I fade out, I shall put up a statue to myself as the original conservative anarchist. Roosevelt shall make the oration.

To HENRY JAMES

Paris, 18 November, 1903.

Although you, like most men of toil, hate to be bored, I can hardly pass over your last work without boring you to the extent of a letter. We have reached a time of solar antiquity when nothing matters, but still we feel what used to be called the law of gravitation, mass, or attraction, and obey it.

More than ever, after devouring your William Story [*William Wetmore Story and his Friends*], I feel how difficult a job was imposed on you. It is a *tour de force,* of course, but that you knew from the first. Whether you have succeeded or not, I cannot say, because it all spreads itself out as though I had written it, and I feel where you are walking on firm ground, and where you are on thin ice, as though I were in your place. Verily I believe I wrote it. Except your specialty of style, it is me.

The painful truth is that all of my New England generation, counting the half-century, 1820-1870, were in actual fact only one mind and nature; the individual was a facet of Boston. We knew each other to the last nervous centre, and feared each other's knowledge. We looked through each other like microscopes. There was absolutely nothing in us that we did not understand merely by looking in the eye. There was hardly a difference even in depth, for Harvard College and Unitarianism kept us all shallow. We knew nothing—no! but really nothing! of the world. One cannot exaggerate the profundity of ignorance of Story in becoming a sculptor, or Sumner in becoming a statesman, or Emerson in becoming a philosopher. Story and Sumner, Emerson and Alcott, Lowell and Longfellow, Hillard, Winthrop, Motley, Prescott, and all the rest, were the same mind,—and so, poor worm!—was I!

Type bourgeois-bostonien! A type quite as good as another, but more uniform. What you say of Story is at bottom exactly what you would say of Lowell, Motley, and Sumner, barring degrees of egotism. You cannot help smiling at them, but you smile at us all equally. God knows that we knew our want of knowledge! the self-distrust become introspection—nervous self-consciousness—irritable dislike of America, and antipathy to Boston. *Auch ich war in Arcadien geboren!*

So you have written not Story's life, but your own and mine, —pure autobiography,—the more keen for what is beneath, implied, intelligible only to me, and half a dozen other people still living; like Frank Boott: who knew our Boston, London and Rome in the fifties and sixties. You make me curl up, like a trodden-on worm. Improvised Europeans, we were, and—Lord God!—how thin! No, but it is too cruel! Long ago,—at least thirty years ago,—I discovered it, and have painfully held my tongue about it. You strip us, gently and kindly, like a surgeon, and I feel your knife in my ribs.

No one else will ever know it. You have been extremely tactful. The essential superficiality of Story and all the rest, you have made painfully clear to us, but not, I think, to the family or the public. After all the greatest men are weak. Morley's Gladstone is hardly thicker than your Story. Let us pray!

To ELIZABETH CAMERON

Washington, 10 January, 1904.

. . . I am not quick at catching on to the social tram, and this time the tram seemed to be very crowded and much in a hurry. My habitudes were deranged. Hay has not been out of his house since December 1, and is still too weak to walk round the square. At the same time he is regularly besieged and overrun by his diplomates and colleagues. At any other time the Panama business would absorb all our thoughts, but today the Jap-Russian affair dwarfs everything. I did not try to do anything but pay bills and clear my desk on Thursday, and run in for a cup of hot water next door at six o'clock, but Daisy wanted me to take her to the diplomatic reception in the evening, and I had to go. You cannot conceive how night-mared I was. An Indian from the plains would not have felt quite so ghostly. After an hour's battling with two thousand people down cellar, we were rescued by an usher and run up the back stairs. Received with war-whoops by the President and bidden to supper, we found ourselves penned into the next room with a hundred people who were perfect strangers to me and bowed and smiled and said: 'You don't remember me'; and ended by making me think that my social vogue was boundless. The Chinese Minister in marvelous dragons and jewels embraced me tenderly; Mrs. Whitelaw Reid in a harness of diamonds and rubies graciously allowed me to do homage; Mrs. Patterson, collared with solitaires, received me as a friend of the family; Mrs. Alger beamed on me; the new Mrs. Frank Emmons accepted me; Bammy Cowles expanded; Alice Hay was positively radiant with her young maternity; for an hour I was kept rattling with the court, until Miss Hagner told us to assemble in the blue room, and we formed a procession which marched up to supper in the gallery up-stairs.

I was already a good deal bewildered by this style of royalty, but I was completely staggered by what followed. Nanny had been kept at home by Cabot, and I was stuffed into her place at the imperial table, opposite Joe Chamberlain's daughter, whom I claimed acquaintance with. Root sat at the end of the table between us. Theodore next Miss Chamberlain with Schurman opposite, next me. Old Edward Everett Hale was at the other end. You can see me! Desperate at the outlook. I flung myself—*à la* Wayne—into the mad stream, trying to stem it, and Root tried to help me; but we were straws in Niagara. Never have I had an hour of worse social *malaise*. We were overwhelmed in a torrent of oratory, and at last I heard only the repetition of I—I—I—attached to indiscretions greater one than another until only the British female seemed to survive. How Root stands this sort of thing I do not know, for it is mortifying beyond even drunkenness. The worst of it is that it is mere cerebral excitement, of normal, or at least habitual, nature. It has not the excuse of champagne. The wild talk about everything—Panama, Russia, Germany, England, and whatever else suggested itself,—belonged not to the bar-room but to the asylum. What is curious is that the Russians are talking just as indiscreetly or more so. We are a boys' school run wild. . . .

I've soon learned that the town is hot and smoking with tales of the imperial court, and, curiously enough, our quiet, simple little Edie [Mrs. Roosevelt] of ten years ago has flowered into the chief object of attack. One does not know oneself. Tales of imperial etiquette are common as babies. Of course most of it is mere misunderstanding, but I see plainly that 'I' is serious. 'I' does not any longer like frivolous jests. Chaff is out of place.

What is one to do? Play Seneca to Theodonero? Open one's veins and invite Sister Anne and Rockhill to a last dinner? Socially it amounts to this. I have got to hide. Perhaps I may have to run. Yet the politics are so amusing that one wants to listen at the key-hole. I think this place is now the political centre of the world. Everybody is interested,—excited,—and all are anti-Russian, almost to a dangerous extent. I am the only—relative—Russian afloat, and only because I am half crazy with fear that Russia is sailing straight into another French revolution which may upset all Europe and us too. A serious disaster to Russia might smash the whole civilised world. Other people see only the madness; I see only the ruin. Russia is completely off her head.

Already I am crowded so deep with impressions that I could write a volume. . . .

To ELIZABETH CAMERON

Washington, 13 March, 1904.

The White House dinner was Wednesday, with no one outside our family circle except Moody, Secretary Navy, and Alice Roosevelt for half the dinner. The table is a little better this year, and Theodore has stopped talking cowboy and San Juan. Every idea centres now on the election, and he talks about that with all the fluency and *naïveté* of a school-boy. That he is still a bore as big as a buffalo I do not deny, but at least he is a different sort. As it chanced, there had been that afternoon, a sudden explosion of the pent-up fury of the House of Representatives against him. He was discussing it with Lodge and Moody, after dinner, without my taking part. His simpleness was astounding. One after another, all his friends in the House had been getting up on the floor in a frenzy of passion, and yelling 'liar' and 'scoundrel' at him all day, because he had done a little electioneering for himself at their expense. No such scene had ever taken place in Congress. All the wounded vanity of the Congressmen, two years in arrears, broke out, swept Speaker and leaders aside, and lashed itself into fits. The extravagance was all nervous. These Congressmen had seen themselves, as they thought, sacrificed to his selfishness and trampled on by his contempt, till they were mad for his blood. The fun was that he seemed to be quite unconscious of it. Apparently he had no suspicion of the hatred they feel for him. He looked like a sort of Nero or Commodus in his eye-glasses, incapable of conceiving that his followers will murder him. That he has not a friend except Cabot, who is really loyal to him, has been too clear to me ever since I returned, but I am interested in watching his state of mind, because it makes clearer some very interesting characters of history. He is really *déséquilibré* as the French say. In private life such things matter little, but on a throne they are dramatic. He will override Congress, no doubt, and crush the life out of it at the election, for the people like to see Congressmen licked; but he will do it without intending it, or understanding it. . . .

After a long month of delay, I am beginning to straighten out my Chartres snarl. The spring always sets the clock a-going. I suppose the world must do something, even if it's not sense. . . .

Monday. . . . Politics and affairs are now beginning really to squeeze us. We have got to take a big bump and get over the rough place. As the spring comes on, things look brighter, but not better. The stock-market is standing dead still. We are running into a big deficit for next year. Europe still obstinately refuses to face the Russian situation, and France pokes her nose into the sand to avoid seeing. Luckily for us, the Democrats as yet show no sort of unity, and we still hope to reelect Theodore without serious trouble. But he is quite mad, and anything may happen from day to day.

What always astonishes me most in governments is their incredible ignorance and imbecile helplessness.

If we here know so little, what can the poor Tsar know! And the Giant Gruffanuff Kuropatkin with his Eikons!

To CHARLES MILNES GASKELL

Washington, 20 December, 1904.

. . . Washington is now rather more amusing to me than other places, because I can laugh at all my friends who are running what they call a government. They are droll, like most men who run governments. We have arrived now at that age when we are allowed to laugh, because no one cares what we do as long as we don't ask for money. Your audacity in begging for a University takes away my breath. I am at a loss to learn what function a University now performs in the world. They are ornamental but expensive; and as you say, not one graduate in ten retains a shadow of liberal education. Of course we see it here more clearly than you. For this I could make my mourning with philosophy, seeing that it has always been so in my time, but the flamboyant self-esteem and moral platitude of the odd tenth man reconciles me to the premature demise of Thomas Aquinas and the late Duns Scotus.

Talking of Thomas Aquinas, I have just finished printing my *Miracles de la Vierge* [*Mont-Saint-Michel and Chartres*]. The book will run up to a pretty bulky size, but I print only a hundred copies, one of which will be for you. It is my declaration of principles as head of the Conservative Christian Anarchists; a party numbering one member. The Virgin and St. Thomas are my vehicles of anarchism. Nobody knows enough to see what they mean, so the Judges will probably not be able to burn me according to law. If there has ever been in the world a greater block-head than the school-master, it has been the judge. On the whole, I think the bishop has had an advantage over both, in so far as he had a sort of general idea what he represented.

This country is terribly interesting. It has no character but prodigious force,—at least twenty million horse-power constant; about as much as all the rest of the world together, by coal-output. We are running very fast indeed into the impossible, which you can measure on our coal and ore output. I cannot conceive what will happen. Logically we must strangulate and suffocate in just fifteen years,—at the point of 50-million tons annual steel output. Luckily I am out of it, and perhaps it has all been only a dream. I am not sure. If so, Russia has been an ugly one, and turns me green with horror.

All the same, our great managers of industry are dead scared. The rest is rubbish. I've no news.

To ELIZABETH CAMERON

Paris, 16 July, 1905.

Your letter of the 2d, at the moment of Hay's death, arrived yesterday. You were more shocked than I, and for the reason that I am so tiresome about preaching. I am a pessimist —dark and deep,—who always expects the worst, and is never surprised when it comes. Hay was by nature another, but never in his life had a misfortune or unhappiness till Del's death. Both of us knew, when we parted, that his life was ended, and that the mere day or month or year of actual death was a detail. We had been discussing it for at least two years. Naturally it surprised neither of us.

Pessimists are social bores. Optimists are intellectual idiots. If you want thorough work, always employ a pessimist. The optimist trusts to good luck; he gambles on his cards without calculating them. Luck in life is surely no more in favor of the player than it is at cards. In the long run, in life, one has got to lose. On the whole, Hay was a very great winner, even in his death. Between him and Clarence King, in that respect, the contrast was quite superstitious. Yet King had more *suite*, more chances of luck, more foresight, and vastly more initiative and energy. . . .

To CHARLES MILNES GASKELL

Washington, 23 April, 1906.

. . . Your old friends are of the heroic age. Sir John is Shakesperian. Here I am alone. Everyone is dead. Yesterday I was struck by seeing my own name in the columns of the *New York Times,* mentioned as *the late* H. A. *Tant mieux!* At least it is over, and *nil nisi.* Please read Horace Walpole again and note his ridiculous affectations of age—and everything else, for that matter. I pardon nobody for bad Gothic and Venetian taste.

Yet I once read Ruskin and admired! We even read Carlyle and followed! Lord, but we date!

My winter has been more mundane and yet more solitary than ever. Politically I am extinct. Domestic reform drivels. Reformers are always bores, as we knew in our youth, except when we meet our Gladstones who are worse. Theodore Roosevelt is amusing at least, and I find him exceedingly conservative, but he scares the timid wayfarer into fits. He talks of measures that ought to have been taken of course fifty years ago, and that all Europe adopted in our youth; and all our shop-keepers shudder. Talk of bourgeois, shop-keepers, middle-class and Philistines! Come here and study them! Nobody ever knew them till now!

To me, it is all one. I listen and assent to everybody. Why should I care? San Francisco burned down last week, and I have been searching the reports to learn whether the whole city contained one object that cannot be replaced better in six months. As yet I've heard of nothing. Only the Stanford University at Palo Alto was a very charming group of buildings, and I'm sorry it is hurt. Yet San Francisco on the whole was the most interesting city west of the Mississippi. I was fond of it, and my generation made it. It produced many of my best friends, and had more style than any town in the east.

What is the end of doubling up our steam and electric power every five years to infinity if we don't increase thought power? As I see it, the society of today shows no more thought power than in our youth, though it showed precious little then. To me, the whole lesson lies in this experiment. Can our society double up its mind-capacity? It must do it or die; and I see no reason why it may not widen its consciousness of complex conditions far enough to escape wreck; but it must hurry. Our power is always running ahead of our mind.

To WILLIAM JAMES

Washington, 9 December, 1907.

Of course you have a right to the volume [the *Education*] you want. In fact it was printed only for communication to you and a few others who were to help me—I fondly hoped—to file it into shape.

If I did not send it to you at once, as I did to Charles Eliot, it was because I feared your judgment more than his, but since, now, I must, let me explain.

Weary of my own imbecility, I tried to clean off a bit of the surface of my mind, in 1904, by printing a volume on the twelfth century, where I could hide, in the last hundred pages, a sort of anchor in history. I knew that not a hundred people in America would understand what I meant, and these were all taught in Jesuit schools, where I should be a hell-born scorpion. I need not publish when no one would read or understand.

Then I undertook,—always to clean my own mind,—a companion study of the twentieth century, where I could hide—in a stack of rubbish meant only to feed the foolish—a hundred more pages meant to complete the first hundred of 1904. No one would take the smallest interest in these. I knew they were safe. So was I.

Unless, indeed, you got hold of them! In that case, I was rather inclined to weep and wail in advance, for I knew your views better than my own.

With this I send the volume, which, as personal to me, is all in the last chapter. I meant to bid good-bye with graceful and sympathetic courtesy. The devil take it! I feel that Sargent squirms in the portrait. I am not there.

You, at least, and your brother Harry, have been our credit and pride. We can rest in that.

V

NUNC AGE

1908–1918

IF ALL the years since his wife's death had seemed to Adams an essentially supernumerary sort of existence, this was still truer of the decade that followed the completion of the *Education*. His circle of really intimate friends had been drastically reduced by the death of Clarence King, in 1901, and of John Hay, in 1905; and after Theodore Roosevelt's administration came to an end in 1909, Adams felt himself quite cut off from contact with the world of high politics. He was deeply saddened by the death in the same year of his young friend, the poet George Cabot Lodge, and later wrote a brief biography of Lodge, which was published in 1911. His intellectual activity by no means languished, in fact, and in 1910 he published his deliberately challenging "Letter to American Teachers of History," with its thesis that the Second Law of Thermodynamics has a historical as well as a physical application.

In 1912 his nerves were badly shaken by the sinking of the *Titanic,* on which he had planned to sail to Europe; he suffered a slight shock, and was ill for several months following. He continued, however, to make his annual stay in Paris until the actual outbreak of war in 1914, when he had to make his escape to England and then back to America for good. The last four years of his life were profoundly overcast by the events of the war, with their apparent confirmation of his darkest fears, but his letters continue with singularly little flagging of tone until virtually the end. He died at his home in Washington on March 27, 1918.

To HOMER SAINT-GAUDENS

1603 H Street, 24 Jan. 1908.

I will send you all I can find of your father's letters. They shall go to you by mail today.

I have only one favor to ask of you in return. Do not allow the world to tag my figure [the Adams Memorial] with a name! Every magazine writer wants to label it as some American patent medicine for popular consumption—*Grief, Despair, Pear's Soap,* or *Macy's Mens' Suits Made to Measure.* Your father meant it to ask a question, not to give an answer; and the man who answers will be damned to eternity like the men who answered the Sphinx.

Undoubtedly a beneficent Deity, whether he exists or not, will some day commit our entire American—and European—society to eternal Hell fire for *not* trying to answer your father's question; but this is no reason why we should undertake to act the part of Savior,—much the contrary.

To WILLIAM JAMES

Washington, 11 February, 1908.

You are as kind as possible, to write me a long letter. I am grateful, for I can find no man to play with. The American is a singularly unsocial animal. For social purposes,—as far as I have read the records of society,—he is the most complete failure ever known; and I am the champion failer of all.

As for the volume [*Education*], it interests me chiefly as a literary experiment, hitherto, as far as I know, never tried or never successful. Your brother Harry tries such experiments in literary art daily, and would know instantly what I mean; but I doubt whether a dozen people in America—except architects or decorators—would know or care.

I care little myself, and have put too many such *tours-de-force* into the fire, to bother about explanation. This will probably follow the others, for I have got it so far into shape that I can see the impossibility of success. It is the old story of an American drama. You can't get your contrasts and backgrounds.

So fully do I agree with you in having no use for time, that I expect soon to dispense with it altogether, and try the experiment of timeless space; but I am curious to know what our psychic friends think of it. Are they bored in space as much as I am in time? [Sir Oliver] Lodge is less clear on that point than I could wish.

Washington, 17 February, 1908.

As a wit and humorist I have always said that you were far away the superior to your brother Henry, and that you could have cut him quite out, if you had turned your fun that way. Your letter is proof of it. Did you ever read the Confessions of St. Augustine, or of Cardinal de Retz, or of Rousseau, or of Benvenuto Cellini, or even of my dear Gibbon? Of them all, I think St. Augustine alone has an idea of literary form,—a notion of writing a story with an end and object, not for the sake of the object, but the form, like a romance. I have worked ten years to satisfy myself that the thing cannot be done today. The world does not furnish the contrasts or the emotion. If you will read my *Chartres*,—the last chapter is the only thing I ever wrote that I almost think good,—you will see why I knew my *Education* to be rotten.

You do not reflect that I am seventy years old—yesterday,— and quite senile. It is time to be gone. I want to burn the *Education* first, but it does not press. Nobody cares. You do not even care to come on here to see real greatness, like the President.

Washington, 21 February, 1908.

If you really want the thing—which is to me exceedingly difficult to grasp in the circuit of my imagination,—I am proud and pleased. As I have measured the mass of our social movement, nothing can now deflect it, and it matters not a straw what anyone says or does. To me caring only for the future, and intensely bored by our present and immediate past, the whole interest falls on the next thirty years. At the end of that time I might begin to set a value on what has been said. At present I want only to watch.

The *Chartres* [*Mont-Saint-Michel*] I sent to the College Library. The three last chapters are alone worth reading, and of course are never read. I have no more copies. . . .

[Enclosure in Adams's writing.]

I forgot to say that when you have done with the volume— and have entered on the margin such damnatory comments as we lavish on our own works—I should be grateful for its return. They are only proof-sheets and I have so few copies that the people whose names are trifled with have become more numerous than the copies.

To THEODORE ROOSEVELT

Washington, 16 December, 1908.

If you were talking last night as President, I have nothing to say. Whatever the President says goes! The authorities used to say that Parliament had the power to do everything except make a man of a woman. Some day we will put that into the Constitution as an Executive Power—not requiring confirmation by the Senate. In regard to most of us elderly people, I admit that there is little or no difference between an old woman and an old man, even when Senator. Not for a moment would I challenge the fate of Pulitzer by affirming that there is—for I am with you on that as on other points.

But!!! After March 4, should you allude to my bronze figure [the Adams Memorial], will you try to do St. Gaudens the justice to remark that his expression was a little higher than sex can give. As he meant it, he wanted to exclude sex, and sink it in the idea of humanity. The figure is sexless.

Such is life! When you are 1,235,452,000,000 like me, you will repent too.

To BROOKS ADAMS

1603 H Street, 17 Feb. 1909.

The decay of my faculties about which you allow yourself such painful levity has now proceeded so far that I derive from it much humour, constant amusement, and some instruction. At the slightest strain or care or worry, I go to pieces and become a jelly. In that state I contemplate my fellow men with more pure joy than ever. They dance as though they were flies in the sun, and we are a joy to watch, even though I am old, ugly and idiotic. Yet this mental paralysis has practical drawbacks. One of these is my nauseous indigestion of American history, which now makes me physically sick, so that only by self-compulsion can I read its dreary details. This accounts for my slowness with your great work. You have toiled through a gigantic labor from which I shrank; you have accomplished an immense task which no one but yourself could have done; and which crushes me under its responsibilities and consequences; but I go all to pieces whenever I attempt to handle it, and roll on the ground in agonies of weakness. Your picture of our wonderful grandpapa is a psychologic nightmare to his degenerate and decadent grandson.

I make progress in the reading, but I reverse it in the criticism. Every effort sets me further back. The psychological or pathological curiosity of the study takes possession of me. The unhealthy atmosphere of the whole age, and its rampant meanness even in violence; the one-sided flabbiness of America, the want of self-respect, of education, of purpose; the intellectual feebleness, and the material greed,—I loathe it all.

If our dear grandpapa had been favored by God with a touch of humor in his long career! if he had indulged in a vice! if he had occasionally stopped preaching! but only when he goes for blood and slays some savage rival, does he provoke my filial regard.

I hated to gibbet him, but since his Diary has already done it, I suppose we can do no worse. The curse of a Diary is fatal. No man has ever taken his own life in that way without damnation.

The warning to me comes direct from Hell. It tells me never —never—to be didactic. Thank God, I have done little preaching in my life. I have tried to tell stories, and sometimes to found them on a carefully concealed foundation of idea; but I trust I have never tried expressly to improve my fellow-insects. Senile as I am, I still hope I may cling to that salvation. I would gladly amuse my world; but I refuse to improve or re-prove it. The only form of preaching that ever appeals to an old man is the familiar advice to repent, for the kingdom of heaven is at hand. This is for himself!

So, you may do what you like with the paper I sent you ["The Rule of Phase Applied to History"] which was, in my point of view, only a sort of jig-saw puzzle, put together in order to see whether the pieces could be made to fit. Too well I knew the inadequacy of the public mind, to let me imagine that any one could derive amusement from such trifles. The fools begin at once to discuss whether the theory was true. I cannot, even here, after months of search, find a physicist who can be trusted to tell me whether my technical terms are all wrong. The technologists cannot go beyond their laboratory materials. The American mind refuses even to amuse itself. It is a convention as flat as the surface of the ocean.

Perhaps my language is excessive, but you must make allow-ances for me. I am sorely beset. Yesterday I achieved my seventy-first birthday. At that age, mind and body and nervous energies enfeebled, I am obliged to look directly into four years of Ohio Fog. Four years of Bill Taft will kill me—thank God for that!— but four years of Bill Taft with Philander Knox on top of him, make a nightmare such as Sinbad never dreamed. . . .

To BARRETT WENDELL

1603 H Street, 12 March, 1909.

A letter, so kind as yours, calls for immediate acknowledgment. I am amused to find myself at last in a little atmosphere of criticism. This is partly Berenson's doing, who has acted as a sort of solvent on our widely separated salts. I had not expected such a result from his invasion, but I am glad of it, because we are smothered in this American vacuum, and gasp for intelligent attack. Poison is better than pure void. We shall have to get up a society for the administration of literary poisons. In fifty years of literary effort, I think I have never met with a published criticism that gave me the least help. Perhaps private comparison may do better.

I have just had a long discussion with Bay Lodge on our more-or-less common difficulties, and our less-than-more successful efforts to deal with them; and I am always discussing the same subject with my brother Brooks. We all roll on the ground and sprinkle dust on our heads in consciousness of our miserable state, but we can get no help. The disease has reached a point where we are obliged to compose our music for ourselves alone, and of course this sort of composition means that we go on repeating our faults. No echo whatever comes back. My favorite figure of the American author is that of a man who breeds a favorite dog, which he throws into the Mississippi River for the pleasure of making a splash. The river does not splash, but it drowns the dog.

My dispute, or rather my defense against self-criticism, is that our failures are really not due to ourselves alone. Society has a great share in it. When I read St. Augustine's *Confessions,* or Rousseau's, I feel certain that their faults, as literary artists, are worse than mine. We have all three undertaken to do what cannot be successfully done—mix narrative and didactic purpose and style. The charm of the effort is not in winning the game but in playing it. We all enjoy the failure. St. Augustine's narrative subsides at last into the dry sands of metaphysical theology. Rousseau's narrative fails wholly in didactic result; it subsides into still less artistic egoism. And I found that a narrative style was so incompatible with a didactic or scientific style, that I had to write a long supplementary chapter to explain in scientific terms what I could not put into narration without ruining the narrative. The game was singularly simple in that sense, but never played out successfully by any artist however great. Even allegory, as in Bunyan, remains only a relative success. The *Roman de la Rose* (the first part) is the best popular triumph ever won.

Yet I contend that the failure would be proportional (other things being equal) to the atmosphere, or setting. With St. Augustine's background, or Benvenuto's, or Saint-Simon's, the failure would be less perceptible than mine. Do what we please, the *tour-de-force* of writing drama with what is essentially undramatic, must always be unpleasantly evident. It is artistically violent in Bunyan, and only less so in William of Lorris because it is there disguised in verse; but both these great writers had the advantage of a dramatic *mise-en-scène* which I denied to myself. I feel sure that the want of action is not the difficulty. The *Roman de la Rose* has no action, and St. Augustine but little. The huge mass of military writers (except Froissart) who have nothing but action, have very rarely succeeded as artists. The modern novel may be full of action, or devoid of it; both schemes may succeed.

My conclusion is that we need far more art than ever to accomplish a much smaller artistic effect. That is to say, we are unduly handicapped. We are forced to write science because our purpose is scientific, and cannot be rendered by narrative. To us, who do not propose to instruct, but only to amuse, and whose own amusement is in the game rather than in the stakes, the highest scientific or didactic success is failure. To gain it, we must throw up our hand. My experiment of trying to find the exact point of equilibrium where the two motives would be held in contact was bound to be a failure, but was very amusing to carry out; and I still maintain that, if I could have had a dramatic setting like St. Augustine or Benvenuto or even Fanny Burney, I could have made it a success.

Of course, I make no question about pure narrative which is an art by itself, and does not concern me more than pure science.

At bottom, the problem is common to us all, which is my excuse for proposing it in the *Education* and in *Mont St. Michel*. The last three chapters of each make one didactic work in disguise.

To CHARLES MILNES GASKELL

Paris, Sunday, 6 [June], 1909.

Are you bold! To face calmly a touring-trip of a fortnight in these old haunts where everything suggests what we don't like, is next despair, so courageous is it. Why can we not invent a fresh variety of youth to look at! As for me, if my own feelings are to rule, I shall be here to welcome you, but my doctor says I've got some unknown nervous irritability which has worried me since arriving and, for some time, cut down my sleep; so that I am waiting for him to get done with his ridiculous experiments before sending me, as is always the end, to some ridiculous bath. He knows, and I know, and I know that he knows that the only successful bath for me is that of Odysseus, of the western stars until I die, but of course we must play our little parts to the end, as we were paid to do at the beginning *per* contract. . . .

Hats are quite abnormally hideous! That fact I gather from America at Laurent's; and that is all I gather. The streets are more dangerous than a battle-field. The shops contain nothing worth buying, except at £5,000 apiece. You can always give Mary a pearl necklace, and I will show you some nice ones at about £20,000.

In my desperate search for amusement, I have struck on your friend Lord Kelvin who began his career in 1849 by proving that the universe, including our own corner of it, was flattening steadily, and would in the end, flatten out to a dead level where nothing could live. Kelvin was a great man, and I am sorry I did not know enough mathematics to follow him instead of Darwin who led us all wrong. Our early Victorian epoch was vastly *naïf*! But I want Kelvin's writings, and I know I can't read a page of them. Is it not exasperating to see what one wants, and feel one's incapacity to seize it? . . .

To HENRY JAMES

Paris, 3 September, 1909.

Your letters, few as they are, have always the charm of saying something that carries one over the gaps; and when you describe Bay Lodge [who died on Aug. 21] as a great and abundant social luxury, you paint a portrait rather more lifelike than anything Sargent ever did. You paint even a group, for I believe we are all now social luxuries, and, as for myself, I am much flattered if regarded as bric-à-brac of a style,—*dixhuitième* by preference, rather than early Victorian. Nothing matters much! Only our proper labels! Please stick mine on, in your wonderfully perfect way, and I will sit quiet on the shelf, contented, among the rest.

As for what the newspapers report as the realities of life, I grow every day too detached to feel them, and as for the volume you mention—which I did, in fact, at one time, mean to recall in order to give it completion of form,—I do not care what is done with it, as long as I do nothing myself. Bay Lodge's experience last winter completed and finished my own. When his *Herakles* appeared absolutely unnoticed by the literary press, I regarded my thesis as demonstrated. Society no longer shows the intellectual life necessary to enable it to react against a stimulus. My brother Brooks insists on the figure of paralysis. I prefer the figure of diffusion, like that of a river falling into an ocean. Either way, it drowned Bay, and has left me still floating, with vast curiosity to see what vaster absence of curiosity can bring about in my Sargasso sea.

Mrs. Wharton in spite of her feminine energy and interest, is harder hit, I think, than I by the loss of Bay Lodge, but she has, besides, a heavy anxiety to face in the uncertainties of her husband's condition. We are altogether a dilapidated social show, *bric-à-brac* or old-clo' shop, and I find smiling a rather mandarin amusement. Mrs. Wharton has told you about it, no doubt, but she will not have cared to dwell on it. . . .

I speculate occasionally on your doings and interests, and those of your fellow Englishmen, if you have fellows still; and I have even gone so far as to ask such insects to return, from time to time, after penetrating the hive,—Mrs. Wharton, the Ralph Curtises, Berenson, and such,—what they have found in the way of wax or honey to store or consume, leaving small particles for me; but the sad heart of Ruth was nothing worth mentioning, compared with the small crop of gleanings that I have effected among that alien corn. As usual, I got more active

information from Berenson than from all the rest, and yet Berenson,—well! Berenson belongs to the primitives.

God be with you all the same! though I associate only with
aviators and talk of the North Pole with proper scepticism.

To HENRY CABOT LODGE

23 Avenue du Bois de Boulogne, 5 Sept., 1909.

You will have probably thought evil of me for not having
written to you when I wrote to Nanny and Bessy a week ago,
but I was literally afraid of doing harm. I have been surrounded
by such an avalanche of trouble among my friends, that the
mere contagion scared me, lest I should spread the disease.
John [Lodge's other son] will have told you how hard we were
trying to carry our anxieties here when your telegram a fortnight ago crushed us to utter helplessness. I was running from
invalid to invalid in Switzerland, greatly worried about them
all,—Bancel and Mabel, Mrs. Cameron and Martha, in equally
bad condition,—when your telegram to John, repeated to Mrs.
Cameron through Mrs. Wharton, made me turn back to Paris
at once, for fear of its effect on Sturgis Bigelow; and, true
enough, when I got back here a week ago, I found Sturgis
alarmingly worse. The excitement and strain had caused a very
dangerous relapse. We have had a week which can hardly be
called active anxiety, for we are passive and helpless, but I can
as yet see no light in any direction, and even if the light does at
last break, I see such a mass of ruin about my small fabric of
existence that I fear to talk about it, lest I should affect my
poor, struggling friends with my own depression. I tell you this,
although most of the load will fall on you, only to explain my
silence.

My own formula that I always expect the worst, and always
find it worse than I expected, comes into play now with awful

application. When life suddenly becomes a dream, and one seems to go on with it mechanically, without touching an actuality on any side, one can only drift till something touches us that we can again fasten on. At such moments, what troubles me most has been always the sense of unreality. I cannot believe that it is not all a dream. It is not in reason that I should be writing you now in almost the same terms that I wrote to John Hay so short a time ago, about the same calamity. Such things cannot happen over and over again to the same person in a real world. Probably you may not even yet have reached this point of losing your grasp of the actual, but Sturgis and I are far beyond it, and we work on each other, drowned in Sturgis's morphine to which he has had to resort as a diet.

You had better not repeat all this, even to Nanny, since, as you see, I say it only for yourself. You will have to pick yourself up, and go along, as Hay did, busying yourself with your work, and trying to keep your temper with the smaller vexations of your career. The worst of these blows is that they break our nervous systems and destroy our confidence in the future. You must probably accept this result, and calculate on it. Just so much of your vital energy will be gone, and you will have to do without it. You will still have enough left to answer your purposes,—which is more than I could ever say about myself.

Of Bay I cannot speak with the smallest calm, because the loss is so personal. That superb exuberance of youth which can find no outlet except its self-assertion, and no appeasement except in defiance of common-place, was the very last of my social foundations of hope. Nothing remains. I look around, over the whole field of human activity, and can see no one else to offer a ray of light.

It is awfully sad. I do not disguise it from you, but it can do no good to show it to others.

To MARGARET CHANLER

Paris, 9 September, 1909.

Thanks for your letter of August 25. Among the props of life which have fallen, or are falling, you are a column of support without match. My summer has been mostly an effort to keep pace with the ruin,—if one can keep pace with ruins, like other wrecks,—and I have no one left but you to serve me for a fixed star to measure my altitude. Bay is a crushing loss, but I am almost worse demoralised by the fear that his death will sweep Nanny and Bessie and Cabot and the whole family beyond my range of touch and feeling. No one can foresee what swath time's scythe will cut, when it starts in with a swing like that.

Well! being a poor bit of materialised *Energetik,* I have no resource but the old one, taught by one's brothers in childhood —to grin and bear it; nor is this refuge much ennobled by calling it stoicism. The defect in this old remedy is that it helps others not at all, and oneself only by a sort of moral suicide.

I try to busy myself with our favorite philosophy, but I rather agree with you and your friend Bergson that St. Thomas said all there was to say. On the whole I think I like to keep my milk and my flies separate. Bergson does not much amuse me. I like my Schopenhauer and I like my Kelvin—I like metaphysics and I like physics,—but I don't much care to reconcile them, though I enjoy making them fight. What I like most in the schoolmen is their rule of cutting infinite sequences short. They insist on stopping at the prime motor at once. Bergson and all the speculators who follow Kant, start with Space, and then merge that Space in Thought, and are bound to merge that Thought-space in Hyperthought-space and so on to infinity like our friend Keyser; but become scared and stop, without explaining the reason for stopping. They give me no sort of help. Time and Space are conditions of Thought, and so far good; but I can reckon an infinite hierarchy of them in mathematics, one just as good as the other,—concepts of concepts,—and why, in space, should I stop?

I have not seen Keyser's last paper; it will be an amusement for winter; but I have been amusing myself with a fable for instructors of history. I've a notion of printing a Letter to Professors. Pure malice! but History will die if not irritated. The only service I can do to my profession is to serve as a flea.

I like best Bergson's frank surrender to the superiority of Instinct over Intellect. You know how I have preached that principle, and how I have studied the facts of it. In fact I wrote once a whole volume—called my *Education*—which no one ever saw, and which you must some day look into,—borrow William James's copy, in hopes that he may have marginally noted his contempt for me,—in order to recall how Education may be shown to consist in following the intuitions of instinct. [Jacques] Loeb calls it *Tropism,* I believe; which means that a mother likes to nurse her own child.

No! on the whole, I won't make you go back to my destroyed volume; but will some day get you to read Fabre's dozen volumes of *Souvenirs Entomologiques;* the most fascinating and bewildering of anti-Darwinian philosophies.

I am glad that you mean to resume your duties in New York society. Except for women, society is now an infinite solution; a mere ocean of separate particles; and you can help it to one little centre. I own that the centre will do nothing; but it may play itself to be real.

To ALBERT STANBURROUGH COOK*

        22 Avenue du Bois de Boulogne, 10 Aug., 1910.

. . . All the early English or Norse or Danish poetry and prose is singularly rude and masculine. "Widsith" and "Beo-

* Reprinted from the *Yale Review,* copyright Yale University Press.

wulf," the "Battle of Maldon," the "Seafarer," the "Wanderer," are like rocks that the poet throws at you; and, for solid leaden pessimism, the close of the "Wanderer" (p. 55) fills even my lost soul with pure satisfaction; but I can't quite see your innocent boys in the lecture-room swallowing such rough fare. Our Norwegian ancestors were rude neighbors even then. Your students need to be all on the football team to enjoy them.

You can always raise the vigor of the student by setting his imagination at work; and this dark, despondent polar gloom can be made intensely appealing. I rather envy you in dealing with it. "Beowulf" always turned me green with horror at such a social entertainment—"joy of harp," indeed! "mirth of glee-wood!" They were gay companions in the hall.

To MABEL HOOPER LA FARGE

23 Avenue du Bois de Boulogne, 19 Sept. 1910.

I return you your father-in-law's letter. It is very sad and quite desperate. I see no way out. He must be cared for, and he cannot care for himself. Perhaps Teddy Wharton's case is worse, since he is younger; and I don't know but that Bob Chanler's case is the worst of all. The world is a very badly contrived structure, and, according to the doctors, it gets rapidly worse. The characteristic disease, they say, is the weakening of the will; and one mark of weakening will is inability to tell the truth or stick to a lie. Perhaps you noticed it in Teddy Wharton. I notice it in almost everybody except myself, which leads me to think that I must be far gone.

The doctors ought to let us die when nature tells us to do it. They kept him alive last spring only to turn him into a—what do you call it—paranoiac? And the world talks of progress! The world is a ass—but that you knew before!

I too am a ass to talk about it; but the subject will never let one alone. The proper human insect pays no attention to it, but goes on breeding. I suppose I am improper. I curl up under this sort of mental torture, and all the more because I feel it coming nearer every day. Damn!

So too, Sturgis! he is in Normandy, I don't know why or why not; but he had better go home, in my opinion. I would go home myself if I had a home to go to, but Washington contains hardly an acquaintance, and the next election is likely to sweep away even the politicians. I shall wait till Thanksgiving or Christmas to see what happens. Looly is hoping to get her apartment this week, but she can't get in to it for a century or two, and will drift.

Never mind! Hubert is married, and Lucy Stickney is engaged! I wonder how Joe would have liked it. We are pining to know who Mr. Mathewson is, and how he manages to live in Washington in winter, and at his ancestral estate in Connecticut in summer. Also what ma Stickney says! and Lisel! Also how Matilda Gay will like Miss Chapin downstairs. But what pleases me most is that old Levi P. Morton, who is hovering in or about the nineties, was in the Bernay R. R. accident the other day, and crawled out from the dead bodies through an upper window, got a cab nearby, drove two hours, caught another train, and got to Paris at eleven o'clock, while his daughters were turning over all the corpses on the field to find him. There's some style in that—when your daughters are handsome and named Edith Swansneck or something, and adore kings or dukes. The old man knew better than to be killed, and leave his daughters ten millions apiece. No Lear about him!

Send me up a copy of your rheumatic recipe. My rheumatics jump like fleas, never in the same place all night.

Love to imps.

To CHARLES FRANCIS ADAMS, JR.

Paris, 10 November, 1911.

Your volume of *Studies* arrived yesterday. The Life of Judge Hoar arrived a week ago, and the other papers still earlier. Many thanks! I believe I was fairly familiar with all the *Studies,* except so far as you have added to them recently.

The task of suitably putting our generation to bed and tucking them all nicely in, so as to rest in quiet for eternity, is one which much needs to be done by us, for I see no reason to suppose that our successors will concern themselves about it. As I watch the formation of the new society, I am more and more impressed with my own helplessness to deal with it, and its entire unconsciousness that I, or you, or George Washington ever existed. Therefore we had better do our own epitaphs, and do them quick.

Yet it is certainly a difficult job to make a sufficient picture of Judge Hoar, whose single dramatic moment was his dismissal from office by President Grant. I am glad to have that incident told so as to make it clear to me. I have always considered that Grant wrecked my own life, and the last hope or chance of lifting society back to a reasonably high plane. Grant's administration is to me the dividing line between what we hoped, and what we have got. Judge Hoar probably represents the exact point where the line broke.

On all the other matters I have less personal susceptibility. I care much more to find a kind word to say of anybody and anything, than to attain the truth. As I look back on our sixty years of conscious life, I have to search hard for a word of warm satisfaction. Again and again we pinned our hopes to some figure, but it always got drowned in the mud. The *Lives* of our contemporaries now fill our book-shelves, and not one of them offers a thought. Since the Civil War, I think we have produced not one figure that will be remembered a life-time. The most prominent is our beloved Theodore. What is more curious, I think the figures have not existed. The men have not been born.

If they had existed I should have attached myself to them, for I needed them bad. As life has turned out, I am dying alone, without a twig to fall from. I might as well be a solitary woodchuck on our old Quincy hills as winter comes on. We leave no followers, no school, no tradition. My correspondence and literary connection is fairly large, but it is as passive-minded and childlike in attitude as so much jelly-fish.

I am rather interested to see that Arthur Balfour has succumbed to the same conditions here. He can't force the coming generation. He expresses it rather well too. . . .

To ELIZABETH CAMERON

Washington, 16 April, 1912.

Saturday evening will be a date in history. In half an hour, just in a summer sea, were wrecked the *Titanic*; President Taft; the Republican Party, Boies Penrose, and I. We all foundered and disappeared. Old and sinful as I am, I turn green and sick when I think of it.

I do not know whether Taft or the *Titanic* is likely to be the furthest-reaching diaster. The foundering of the *Titanic* is serious, and strikes at confidence in our mechanical success; but the foundering of the Republican Party destroys confidence in our political system. We've nothing to fall back upon.

In a work which you never heard of, called the *Education of Henry Adams,* I figured on the values of society, and brought out my date of stoppage,—did I not,—at 1917. I feel today as though I were shaving it close. The confusion and consternation here are startling. If it were a question only of a Democratic administration, they were resigned to that, but no one now knows whether the people want representative government at all. They seem to want an Athenian democracy without representation. Last night the Lodges came to dinner; Jack White and a young Biddle came; Bessy brought Langdon Mitchell later. I listened to the talk. Mrs. Keep had already repeated to me the talk of Crane. Much was quoted from the talk elsewhere, among the parties. Through the chaos I seemed to be watching the *Titanic* foundering in a shoreless ocean.

By my blessed Virgin, it is awful! This *Titanic* blow shatters one's nerves. We can't grapple it. Taft, *Titanic*! *Titanic*, Taft! and Boies Penrose! and I! Where does this thing end!

And my apartment! I shall not get to Paris before May 10, which gives me six weeks to move. Can I do it! If not, what? Poor Mabel La Farge is struggling with the same conundrum with four boys on top.

I've shifted my passage to the *Olympic* on May 4. Of course, the *Olympic* has a bad record; but nerves are now so shaken that no ship seems safe, and if I am wrecked, I might as well go under.

Edith Eustis has just been in, naturally upset, but telling me of a dinner she had last night, where the admirals derided the possibility of such a disaster, and said it would upset the navy if true.

And Mexico down in the cellar!

Can't you imagine how happy I am! and your heart would glow over the gloom of my brother Brooks. We have all got a delightful shudder on us. We all squawk like guinea-hens! Isn't it gaudy! Telegraph at my expense if you see light.

To HENRY OSBORN TAYLOR

[*Washington*] *15 Feby. 1915.*

As you know, I am a poor and ignorant, besides being a se-nile, reptile, and in one respect also am morally bad, for I never loved or taught facts, if I could help it, having that antipathy to facts which only idiots and philosophers attain; but with these drawbacks perhaps you will allow me to thank you for your last volume. I have read it with grateful attention.

I cannot criticise. The field is not mine. I am concerned in it only as a spectator, and now a very blind one. I cannot correct or suggest, but I can do what may be equally useful,—I can tell you what effect your treatment has on me, and as I am probably an extreme case, you may infer its effect on opposite natures.

Perhaps I ought to say first, that once, at the most trying crisis of my life, and of his—our old teacher in wisdom, Gurney, said to me that of all moral supports in trial only one was nearly sufficient. That was the Stoic. I cannot say that I have found it so, except in theory, but I am talking theory. Putting myself in that position, I read your book.

You see at once what must follow—what did in fact follow. Of course all that goes before is futile except as failure; all that follows after is escape—flying the ring—by assuming an unprovable other world. Logically the religious solution is inadmissible—pure hypothesis. It discards reason. I do not object to it on that account: as a working energy I prefer instinct to reason; but as you put it, the Augustinian adjustment seems to be only the Stoic, with a supernatural or hypothetical supplement nailed to it by violence. The religionists preached it, and called it Faith.

Therefore to me the effect is of ending there. The moral adjustment, as a story, ended with Marcus Aurelius. There you lead us with kind and sympathetic hands; but there, over the door to the religious labyrinth, you, like Lord Kelvin, write the word Failure. Faith, not Reason, goes beyond.

What you intend, either as reason or faith, is another matter. I am giving only the effect on one mind. At the present moment, perhaps, the moral is somewhat pointed,—to me de-

cidedly peaked. If you are writing Failure over one door and
Lord Kelvin over another, and the Germans over the third and
last—that of energy without direction,—I think I had better
quit. I said so ten years ago, but I put it down to my personal
equation then, and I cannot believe that you mean it now. Are
we, then, to go back to Faith? If so, is it to be early Christian or
Stoic?

The early Christian I take to have been abandoned long ago
by the failure of Christ to reappear and judge the world. Whatever faith is to save us, it cannot be that. Is it, then, the Stoic?

I do not ask these questions for answers,—only to show you
what questions are roused by your book, in order that, if you
like, you may, in any case, insert some provision against misap-
prehension. Of course, had I been the author, I should perhaps
have been drawn into giving different values to the solutions,
and should very likely have labored damnably over the Bud-
dhists and the Stoics. Marcus Aurelius would have been my
type of highest human attainment. Even as it is, I would give a
new cent to have a really good book on the Stoics. If there is
one, lend it me. I need badly to find one man in history to admire. I am in near peril of turning Christian, and rolling in the
mud in an agony of human mortification. All these other fellows did it,—why not I?

To ELIZABETH CAMERON

Washington, 1 March, 1916.

Today the death of Harry James makes me feel the need of a
let-up; I must speak to some one, and here I have no one James-
ian to talk to, except Wendell Holmes, and I never see him, for
he is like me in avoiding contemporaries. Harry's death hits me
harder than any stroke since my brother Charles' death a year
ago. Not only was he a friend of mine for more than forty years,
but he also belonged to the circle of my wife's set long before I

knew him or her, and you know how I have clung to all that belonged to my wife. I have been living all day in the seventies.
Swallow, sister! sweet sister swallow! indeed and indeed, we
really were happy then.

To CHARLES MILNES GASKELL

Washington, 19 February, 1918.

Your letter of January 26th arrived here on the morning of
the 16th of February and was marvellously well shot, because
the 16th was precisely my birthday and of all birthdays the
most momentous. I was eighty years old that morning. I recollect telling you some ten years ago that I thought the man had
made a success in life who had attained his 70th year, because
he had distanced most of his fellow beings in one of the great
objects of life, if nothing else. But I am inclined to say now that
the man who has attained 80 years has achieved the most stu-
pendous failure possible, because he has, at least in my case,
seemed to have got to the bottom of everything, and has left no
experience that has not failed. I find this reflection very con-
solatory, in the midst of all our public anxieties. In the first
place I have buried all my contemporaries except you, and have
nothing more to ask from them; and when you come to think of
it, this is a very admirable result. I can't be hurt on that side
any more. In the second place, it is quite clear that whatever
the next generation is going to do, or to suffer, it will be something that does not concern me. The various horizons which you
and I have passed through since the '40's are now as remote as
though we had existed in the time of Marcus Aurelius, and, in
fact, I rather think that we should have been more at home
among the Stoics, than we could ever hope to be in the legislative bodies of the future. I derive a sort of stale satisfaction
from having the wisdom of our philosophic President, Mr.
Woodrow Wilson, read to me, but I certainly do *prefer* that of

Marcus Aurelius and I am quite sure that if I were fool enough to live ten years longer, I should find myself in an atmosphere stranger still. I don't know whether you ever read, and I certainly would not advise you to read, the last three chapters of my *Education,* which I sent to you a dozen years ago. But if you had been unfortunate enough to read and remember them, you might realize the enormity of time that has passed and is passing since those chapters were written. Already I can see ahead quite far enough to satisfy my wildest desires and even the temptation of seeing *more,* does not tempt me to go on. That you and I should be left within that time to beg our bread, as it were after the manner of Belisarius, might be humorous but somewhat too cloying.

I rather prefer the extraordinary fate of my friend Spring Rice, whose doctor has just sat half an hour with me, quite enraged because he could find no reason whatever for Spring Rice's sudden death, and was evidently more than half inclined to suspect that a German had killed him, although there was no German, and no possible motive, capable of accounting for the act. So we go on! and I am, for the first time in fifty years surrounded by talk of war and weapons, which I cannot escape and which have less meaning to me now, than they had then, although your British aëroplanes are sailing up and down under my windows at all hours, as though I were myself a master of Aëroplane Horse in a new universe of winged bipeds. It is only twenty years since my friend, Professor Langley, at my table, talked about all these things as dreams of the future, and we're already wishing to heaven that they had remained dreams of the past. I am in a new society and a new world which is more wild and madder by far than the old one, and yet I seem to myself to be a part of it, and even almost to take share in it. I speculate on what is to happen as actively as I did at your table fifty years ago, and the only difference is that I terribly miss your father's conversation and his dry champagne. I no longer indulge in champagne or anything else, but I still look on at the British Secretaries of Legation enjoying their Pommery brut, even though we ordinary people in Washington are no longer permitted to have it. The world is improved! We kill each other by the hundred thousand, without remorse, but we are denied our dry champagne. I suppose that George Canning would have approved the new dispensation.

I wish you were still wise enough to help me to put together the various legs of these conundrums, or tell me the bond between my Lord Reading and his somewhat primitive associations on the one side, and his associates in the British Cabinet and Mr. Woodrow Wilson on the other, for I am getting to be wholly at a loss to comprehend what these alliances mean, or where we are to look next for our support and comfort. Sometimes I think that we are to be told to seek our ally at Potsdam against the tempests of Eastern Europe, and their after-outbreaks in the West; but I think I shall have to live at least nine months more to settle these doubts, and really I question whether a man of ordinary intelligence, even though 80 years old, can possibly put himself to such trouble. It is not worth it, especially because I have not, like you, the interest of children to attach me to the Synagogue. Really I have nothing whatever here to remind you that we had common friends fifty years ago. I can send you no news of anybody you ever saw or heard of. I doubt a little whether you have anybody whom I ever knew, to talk about. Spring Rice's last letter to me was rather full of John Morley and his reminiscences, such as they were; but Morley came after my time and belongs to a circle with which I was never in concert. I feel at times a little curiosity to know something about George Trevelyan and his eccentric son [G. M. Trevelyan], but I do not believe I should enjoy the information. You may remember my old friend, Ralph Palmer, who is still alive and very deaf; but I hear of him through Mrs. Cameron who has been in England for the last three months, trying to save her daughter from all sorts of fatal oriental diseases, acquired from a long residence in Egypt. She is at their house at Stepleton in Dorsetshire, struggling with the want of food and fuel, and with the charms of a semi-arctic winter. We have had all these social advantages here too, but luckily without the diseases.

I hope that you too have got through the winter tolerably, for at least you ought to have had coal enough. I hope the family is still all right and I wish you would give them my best regards. Perhaps our next letters will grow more cheerful with the improvement of the world.

INDEX

INDEX